Advanced praise for
The Architects of Dignity

"Pham demonstrates how poorly we've understood shame under colonialism. Neither a sign of internalized inferiority nor a wound of assimilation, he shows us something stranger and truer in Vietnam: shame could be a deliberate instrument of self-assertion, the manifestation of a people's wish to surpass their colonial condition. An astounding book."

—**Kevin Duong**, University of Virginia

"Kevin Pham smashes two-dimensional Anglophone pictures of 'Vietnam' as simply a war, skilfully bringing to life the vast richness and originality of twentieth-century Vietnamese political ideas and the diverse thinkers who sought to motivate national independence through a sense of collective dignity."

—**Douglas Thompson**, University of South Carolina

"A profoundly original study of an underserved group of thinkers, this book elegantly recovers the granular nuance of its protagonists' arguments and situates them in the wider ideological constellation of anticolonial politics. This is comparative political theory at its finest."

—**Inder Marwah**, McMaster University

Studies in Comparative Political Theory

Series editor: Diego A. von Vacano, Texas A&M University

Consulting editors: Andrew March, Harvard University, and Loubna El Amine, Northwestern University

Human Rights between Universality and Islamic Legitimacy
Mahmoud Bassiouni

Democracy after Virtue: Toward Pragmatic Confucian Democracy
Sungmoon Kim

Tantric State: A Buddhist Approach to Democracy and Development in Bhutan
William J. Long

Misplaced Ideas?: Political-Intellectual History in Latin America
Elías J. Palti

The Architects of Dignity

Vietnamese Visions of Decolonization

KEVIN D. PHAM

OXFORD
UNIVERSITY PRESS

Oxford University Press is a department of the University of Oxford.
It furthers the University's objective of excellence in research, scholarship,
and education by publishing worldwide. Oxford is a registered trade mark of
Oxford University Press in the UK and in certain other countries.

Published in the United States of America by Oxford University Press
198 Madison Avenue, New York, NY 10016, United States of America.

© Oxford University Press 2024

All rights reserved. No part of this publication may be reproduced, stored in
a retrieval system, or transmitted, in any form or by any means, without the prior
permission in writing of Oxford University Press, or as expressly permitted
by law, by license or under terms agreed with the appropriate reprographics
rights organization. Inquiries concerning reproduction outside the scope of the
above should be sent to the Rights Department, Oxford University Press, at the
address above.

You must not circulate this work in any other form
and you must impose this same condition on any acquirer

Library of Congress Cataloging-in-Publication Data
Names: Pham, Kevin D., author.
Title: The architects of dignity : Vietnamese visions of decolonization / Kevin D. Pham.
Other titles: Vietnamese visions of decolonization
Description: New York, NY : Oxford University Press, [2024] |
Series: Studies in comparative political theory | Includes bibliographical references and index.
Identifiers: LCCN 2024022852 (print) | LCCN 2024022853 (ebook) |
ISBN 9780197770269 (hb) | ISBN 9780197770276 (pb) | ISBN 9780197770290 (eb)
Subjects: LCSH: Intellectuals—Vietnam—History—20th century. | Decolonization—Vietnam. |
National characteristics, Vietnamese. | Dignity—Vietnam. |
Vietnam—Politics and government—20th century.
Classification: LCC DS556.9 .P4684 2024 (print) | LCC DS556.9 (ebook) |
DDC 325.597—dc23/eng/20240705
LC record available at https://lccn.loc.gov/2024022852
LC ebook record available at https://lccn.loc.gov/2024022853

DOI: 10.1093/9780197770306.001.0001

Paperback printed by Marquis Book Printing, Canada
Hardback printed by Bridgeport National Bindery, Inc., United States of America

Cho bố mẹ

Contents

Acknowledgments ... ix

Introduction ... 1

1. The Engines of National Shame and Indignation ... 15

PART I THE COLONIAL CONDITION

2. Phan Bội Châu's Nationalist Groundwork ... 31
3. Phan Chu Trinh's Democratic Confucianism ... 53

PART II WHAT SHALL WE DO WITH TRADITION?

4. Nguyễn An Ninh's Tagorean Call ... 81
5. Phạm Quỳnh's Cultural Resistance ... 102

PART III REVOLUTION AND ITS DISCONTENTS

6. Hồ Chí Minh's Rehumanizing Blueprint ... 131
7. Nguyễn Mạnh Tường's Montaignean Solace ... 159

Conclusion ... 182

Notes ... 195
Index ... 215

Acknowledgments

After attaining my undergraduate degree, I lived in Vietnam for eight months to learn about the country that my parents left as refugees. My interest in Vietnamese history and ideas grew as I walked through streets named after the country's heroes and as I met with young people whose families were on the "other side" of the war. It seemed inevitable that, upon my return, I would fuse my interest in Vietnam with my love of political theory.

It was Daniel Brunstetter who showed me how exciting political theory could be as I sat in his classes the year before I went to Vietnam. In addition to offering comments on drafts of this book, he has offered invaluable advice as a mentor and support as a friend for many years. At the University of California, Riverside, where I did my PhD, I owe gratitude to Chris Laursen, who showed me how to think freely, as a skeptic, and to write clearly; to John Medearis, who taught me how to carefully frame arguments; and to Farah Godrej, who introduced me to the field of Comparative Political Theory, gave incisive suggestions on these chapters, and provided me with crucial academic advice that always proved right.

This project developed through discussions and feedback from many other people. Thanks to Christina Schwenkel, Georgia Warnke, David Biggs, Mariam Lam, Bronwyn Leebaw, Stefan Kehlenbach, Chi Pham, John Emery, Matthew Bowker, Niklas Plaetzer, Aylon Cohen, Ruth Abbey, Leonard Feldman, George Dutton, Mauro José Caraccioli, Whitney Mannies, Nathan Pippenger, and Shuk Ying Chan. Special thanks to Daniel Wehrenfennig, whose "Olive Tree Initiative" and "Center for International Experiential Learning" gave me opportunities to travel the world to learn directly from human beings about how they respond to political crises and conflict, and whose ethos of perspective-taking informs this book. I am grateful to have found a welcoming and helpful community in the world of Vietnamese studies. Thanks to Martina Nguyen, Vinh Pham, Keith Taylor, Olga Dror, Duy Lap Nguyen, Trinh Luu, Wynn Gadkar-Wilcox, Alvin Bui, David Marr, Sophie Quinn-Judge, Adrienne Minh-Chau Le, Kevin Li, Peter Zinoman, Hue Tam Ho Tai, Tuan Hoang, Sean Fear, and Alex-Thai D. Vo. Special gratitude goes to Yen Vu, my co-host of Nam Phong Dialogues, for making this journey through Vietnamese intellectual history much more meaningful and joyful than it would have been without her, and for introducing me to Nguyễn Mạnh Tường, one of the six figures studied in this book. I also thank Stacey Liou for our weekly Zoom writing sessions where we nurture our projects both alone and together. I thank the U.C. Riverside Graduate Research Mentorship Program for generously funding a year of archival research in Paris where I worked on much of this book. In Paris, I was fortunate to have an intellectual community with Astrid Von Busekist, Annabelle Lever, Agatha Slupek, Đoàn Cầm Thi, David Kretz, Noémie Beslon, Joseph Ciaudo, Albert Wu, Michelle Kuo, Steve Sawyer, Jacob Hamburger, and the late Pierre Brocheux who kindly read my chapters and invited me for coffee in his apartment in the winter of 2017. During my time at Gettysburg College, my colleagues—Caroline Hartzell, Bruce Larson, Lindsay Reid, Scott Boddery, Roy Dawes, Yasemin Akbaba, Ashley Woo, Doug Page, and Valerie Andrews—made the charming Gettysburg an even more pleasant place to work on this book. I am thrilled to have found a new intellectual home at the University of Amsterdam with Eric Schliesser, who read and commented on parts of this project, and other theorists, such as Enzo Rossi, Johan Olsthoorn, Lillian Cicerchia, Marcel Maussen, James Pearson, Adrian Kreutz, and Paul Raekstad.

This book greatly benefitted from a First Book Manuscript Workshop hosted by the Association for Political Theory in 2021. There, I was fortunate to have Kevin Duong, Angélica Bernal, Quỳnh Phạm, and Doug Thompson serve as discussants. They offered lively conversation and extremely valuable, in-depth feedback. Ben McKean, Inder Marwah, and Keally McBride also generously read the entire manuscript and offered wonderful advice. Many thanks to Angela Chnapko, my editor at Oxford University Press, who showed interest in this project from the start, and to Lacey Harvey, the project editor, for expertly guiding the manuscript through. Both have made the entire process of publishing a book enjoyable. I thank Loubna El Amine, Andrew March, and Diego von Vacano for their support and for including my book in the Studies in Comparative Political Theory book series. Very special thanks to Simon Luo and Tuong Vu, who eventually revealed to me that they were my anonymous reviewers. Both gave perceptive, detailed reports that improved this book a great deal. Parts of the book were previously published in different forms. Chapter 2 was published as "Phan Chu Trinh's Democratic Confucianism" (*The Review of Politics* 81, no. 4 (2019), pp. 597–620). And Chapter 3 appeared as "Nguyễn An Ninh's Anti-Colonial

Thought: A New Account of National Shame" (*Polity* 52, no. 4 (2020), pp. 521–550). In sum, this book is the result of the collective labor and care of many people who spent their precious time reading my work, listening to my presentations, and offering comments and discussion.

I thank Mohamed Shehk and Kaeli Hall for more than two decades of endless, late-night debates about how the world works, how it should, and how it shouldn't, which have developed much of my political thinking. I thank them for what Montaigne called "the most fruitful and natural exercise of our mind," a thing "sweeter than any other action of our life": *conversation*.

This book would not have been possible without the love, support, humor, perspicacity, and friendship of Bérénice. I learned French to speak with her and her family, and that made it coincidentally possible for me to read the writings of Vietnamese figures in this book who wrote in French.

This book is dedicated to my parents. Both left Vietnam by boat (my father in 1975 and my mother in 1980), not knowing where they would end up. They had dreams to pursue the arts and teaching, but those dreams were put on hold indefinitely due to a language barrier in a new country and the need to work various jobs to support themselves and their siblings and send money back to family in Vietnam. Their sacrifices made it possible for my brother and me to pursue our passions (which turned out to be in the arts and teaching). They were always supportive of us. At one point, they did try to talk us into being medical doctors, but they eventually cheered my brother on as he finished his tattoo apprenticeship and as I finished my PhD in political theory. They'd ask Alan: "When will you finish your apprenticeship so you can give me my first tattoo?" And they'd ask me: "When is your book finally coming out?" Here it is, *bố, mẹ*.

Introduction

On a winter evening in 1919, in an apartment at 6 villa des Gobelins in the thirteenth arrondissement of Paris, the well-known Vietnamese nationalist Phan Chu Trinh got into a heated argument with his mentee, an unknown man young enough to be Trinh's son. The young man was impatient. French colonizers, he argued, had been humiliating the Vietnamese for over six decades, and it was time to take direct, violent action. But Trinh urged prudence:

> You want twenty millions of our compatriots to do something when our hands are empty of weapons to oppose the terrifying weapons of the Europeans. Why would we commit suicide in vain? . . . . It would be better for us to ask calmly, but with determination and patience, for the rights that human dignity [*phẩm cách con người*] allows us to claim.[1]

The young man responded:

> Our people have been waiting for changes for sixty years and the [French colonial] government has done little to satisfy them. If anyone raises their voice to express to the authorities their suffering and to plead for remedies for their suffering, they are answered with prison, exile, and death. If you keep relying on the government to improve current conditions, you will have to wait forever.[2]

He got angrier:

> Why don't our twenty million compatriots do anything to force the government to treat us as human beings? We are humans and we must live as humans. Anyone who does not want to treat us as his fellow man is our enemy. . . . If others don't want to live with us as fellow humans, then it is useless to live humiliating lives and be insulted on this earth. You're older

and more experienced than I, but our compatriots have been demanding reforms for sixty years and have received what? Very little![3]

The world would come to know this young man as Hô Chí Minh. Famous in the West for being the face of Vietnamese Communism, Hô Chí Minh is not often thought of as a creative political theorist. And Phan Chu Trinh is virtually unknown in the West. But valuable "political theory" can be unpacked in their words that evening. They appear to have expressed something that many would consider universal: the desire for recognition. Human beings want to be recognized by others as fellow humans, as having a certain worthiness. The Ancient Greeks called this *thymos:* the part of the soul that craves recognition of dignity.[4] If humans are denied this recognition, they will feel insulted. This feeling can be painful and intense, and, as history teaches us, it might be channeled through political and violent action.

Among other Vietnamese colleagues present that evening was an undercover police agent who recorded this dialogue. The agent was instructed by French authorities to follow the young Hô around because earlier that summer, Hô had aroused their suspicion when he delivered a formal-looking petition to delegates at the Paris Peace Conference in Versailles. The petition contained requests for the recognition of basic liberal rights for the Vietnamese while they were under French colonial rule. It did not ask for independence. Hô signed it on behalf of the *Groupe des Patriotes Annamites* (of which he and his mentor, Phan Chu Trinh, were part) and, later, felt that the requests went unrecognized. As we know, he went on to become a leading figure of the Vietnamese Communists through the August revolution in 1945, through war with the French in the First Indochina War (1945–1954), and through war with the Americans and South Vietnamese in the Second Indochina War (1955–1975). The latter conflict—known to Americans as "The Vietnam War," to Vietnamese Communists as "The Resistance War Against America to Save the Country," and to some Vietnamese anti-Communists as the "War against Northern Vietnamese Communist Invasion"—took the lives of over two million Vietnamese and over 58,000 Americans, and produced hundreds of thousands of Vietnamese, Laotian, Hmong, and Cambodian refugees. Hô Chí Minh seemed to have vindicated Hegel's claim that history can be understood as the story of the struggle for recognition.

Another political theory to be unpacked from that evening is connected to the idea of recognition: a theory of dignity. It is ultimately our dignity that we want others to recognize. Hô and Trinh appear to have expressed a familiar view of this idea: dignity is something inherent in individual humans, it is a justification for rights, and it requires social recognition. Trinh thought the Vietnamese should ask the French "for the *rights* that human dignity permit us to claim." Hô countered by arguing that the Vietnamese should force the French to give *recognition* to the dignity of the Vietnamese.

This view of dignity is conventional and familiar for us in the West today, expressed in formal declarations by the United Nations at its founding after the Second World War. The introduction to the 1945 founding Charter of the UN speaks of its "faith in fundamental human rights, in the dignity and worth of the human person, in the equal rights of men and women and of nations large and small." Similarly, the first article in the UN's 1948 Universal Declaration of Human Rights begins: "All human beings are born free and equal in dignity and rights." Although dignity and rights are placed side by side, they are more than related concepts. Dignity is the *foundation* for rights. One has rights because one has intrinsic dignity.[5]

But notice that these statements are powerful because they are declared by the United Nations. The statements themselves perform an act of recognition of all people's dignity, satisfying that important desire—or vital need—for human beings.[6] Recognition from an important entity like the United Nations is especially meaningful to oppressed and colonized peoples who have not been recognized as equal human beings by powerful groups that dominate them. Yet, on that evening in 1919, there was not yet a United Nations to recognize Vietnamese dignity, and Hô and Trinh knew this. What then?

These men were beginning to realize the limitations of this conventional view of dignity. Knowing that dignity is inherent in individuals does not ease their pain of witnessing the denial of their people's dignity. How long must they wait, and how many times would they have to "demand" that French colonizers recognize their people's dignity and, thus, their rights? If the French will never, then what? And what if there is no entity more powerful than the French to punish the French or force them to recognize Vietnamese dignity? What is to be done, then? The obvious answers are resistance and revolution. But these require *power* which, as Hannah Arendt put it, "corresponds to the human ability not just to act but to act in concert. Power is never the property of an individual; it belongs to a group and remains in existence only as long as the group keeps together."[7] Far less obvious was how the Vietnamese could generate power, and what forms resistance and revolution should take.

This book traces an intergenerational debate among six influential and controversial Vietnamese political thinkers of the French colonial period: Phan Bội Châu (1867–1940), Phan Chu Trinh (1872–1926), Nguyễn An Ninh (1900–1943), Phạm Quỳnh (1892–1945), Hồ Chí Minh (1890–1969), and Nguyễn Mạnh Tường (1909–1997). Each had different ideas about how the Vietnamese should respond to French colonial subjugation. Most of them were interlocutors. Their ideas were sometimes harmonious, sometimes fiercely opposed. Despite their differences, this book shows that a common thread emerges from their writings. They came to see dignity (1) as ultimately a property of nations instead of individuals, (2) as rooted in the duties a nation's people embrace instead of in the qualities of persons, and (3) as something to be asserted by the nation instead of being dependent on recognition by colonizers. This perspective departs from Western conventional wisdom about dignity because it offers an alternative to the liberal (natural rights) or Hegelian (recognition) frame. The tendency of scholars to think of oppressed peoples' movements in terms of struggles for "recognition" or "demands" for "rights" obscures how some oppressed people abandoned these frameworks to assert their self-respect and dignity in other ways.[8] For these thinkers, Vietnamese dignity ultimately requires the national duty of self-assertion. Returning to Vietnam in 1924, Trinh will exhort his fellow Vietnamese: "You should take part in tackling our national affairs; without doing so, we will not be able to raise our heads."[9] Hồ Chí Minh, after three decades abroad, will return to Vietnam in 1941 and tell his compatriots: "Saving the country is our common cause. Everyone who is Vietnamese must shoulder responsibility. Those with money will contribute money. Those with strength will contribute strength. Those with talents will contribute talents."[10]

For Trinh, Hồ, and the others, fighting the French and expelling them from Vietnam would not be enough. Vietnamese society, culture, and people—the entire polity—had to be remade anew in ways that would affirm and sustain for the Vietnamese a sense of personal and national self-worth. One challenge for these thinkers, then, was to find something that could motivate their compatriots to engage in these acts of resistance, revolution, and national remaking. It was not enough to appeal to colonial exploitation, immiseration, and humiliation to rally the people. Colonial cruelty may have been enough to spark a sense of indignation in the Vietnamese people, but it was not enough to move them to devote themselves to doing the daily, hard work of changing themselves—their habits, values, and social relations—for the purpose of nation-building and revolution. Something else was needed. These six thinkers turned to the power of shame.

Rather than demand that their colonizers recognize Vietnamese dignity, a more effective approach, they believed, was to *shame* their fellow Vietnamese into asserting their national self-worth and self-respect. In addition to bringing attention to colonial cruelties to invoke powerful feelings of indignation in their compatriots, they also sought to instill in their countrymen a sense of national shame toward their own people's perceived moral, intellectual, cultural, and political failures. For them, shame could be a kind of emotional engine to goad their people into productive action. These thinkers engaged in what we might call, for lack of a better term, "victim blaming." Phan Bội Châu wrote to his countrymen: "Those whom I blame most deeply are my people themselves."[11] Phan Chu Trinh lamented: "it is a shame that our people ... cannot look after their basic personal needs and prepare for their old age, let alone think of society or humanity. How could we not respect the Europeans if they are so superior to us?"[12] Nguyễn An Ninh declared to a crowd of Vietnamese in Saigon that, compared to India, Japan, and Europe, Vietnam "is still only a child who does not even have the idea or strength to strive towards a better destiny, towards true deliverance." Phạm Quỳnh scolded the youth, stating that they were lacking in "personal power, strength, temper of character, that vigor of spirit and that moral virility which, more than intelligence and knowledge, would make them 'men' in the full sense of the word."[13] Hồ Chí Minh wrote in a letter: "Instead of blaming others, I think it is more reasonable to blame ourselves. We must ask ourselves, 'For what reasons have the French been able to oppress us? Why are our people so stupid? Why hasn't our revolution succeeded?'"[14] And after the French were finally expelled from the north of Vietnam in 1954, Nguyễn Mạnh Tường expressed a different kind of shame, directed not at the Vietnamese people but at revolutionary leaders for having "alienated their individuality and even their personality, replacing it with a double of themselves whose reactions are remote controlled from the outside."[15]

They understood that the most reliable recourse they had was to engage in fierce self-criticism, self-blame, and self-shame. It was futile to blame the French for denying Vietnamese dignity. And there was no higher authority available—not God, the United Nations, not some stronger country—to blame for not punishing the French. The most productive thing to do was to turn inward toward themselves and their fellow compatriots to call for a program of national "self-help." Central to this approach was shaming their people into action. This would not be a suppressed or unacknowledged shame, but a shame that was confronted, intensified, and then consciously responded to in ways meant to transcend it and transmute it into dignity. Shame would play this powerful role in the first three decades of the twentieth century. But even as the mood in Vietnam became more optimistic and confident from the late 1930s onward, there would always remain the practice of turning inward to self-criticize and self-shame, to chide their own countrymen for not being as virtuous as they knew they could be, to push themselves to rise to the occasion.

Shame is a painful feeling of being judged negatively by others. It is a feeling of humiliation, provoking the desire to hide, an unpleasant emotion that these Vietnamese would want to get away from so that they could feel pride, which, by contrast, is the pleasant sensation of wanting to stand up confidently and appear to the world in all one's glory. The most well-known articulation of this meaning of shame as self-consciousness was made by French existentialist philosopher Jean-Paul Sartre. In his 1943 book, *Being and Nothingness,* Sartre asks us to imagine that we are standing in a corridor and want to sneakily peer through a keyhole or press our ear to the wall to look at or hear what is happening in a room. We know that we are not supposed to be doing this, but we go ahead anyway. We are not conscious of our own ego because we are absorbed in what we are doing as we strain to get a better look or listen. But suddenly, we hear footsteps in the corridor. Someone is looking at us. We become conscious of ourselves as the object of someone else's gaze. Sartre argues that self-consciousness arises from this feeling of shame, of realizing that you are being looked at and judged by others, no longer just a subject who looks upon the world, but also an object for other subjects who are looking at you. "Shame is shame of *oneself*; it is the *recognition* that I really *am* this object that is looked at and judged by the Other."[16] This feeling of being looked at and negatively judged is what these Vietnamese figures believe the Vietnamese *should* be collectively experiencing. For them, national shame is the embarrassment and dishonor of being Vietnamese under foreign domination, of lacking an indigenous intellectual tradition, and of moral and political failures. They are acutely aware of how they appear to each other and to the world.

In contrast to thinkers from China and India who were also debating how to respond to Western domination in the nineteenth and twentieth centuries, many of these Vietnamese thinkers struggled to identify a national cultural heritage to be proud of or take guidance from. For them,

Vietnam was a periphery ruled by the Chinese for a thousand years (111 BC to AD 938). From Chinese colonialism, Vietnamese society had become thoroughly "Confucianized." All six of these figures spoke about the difficulty of identifying cultural aspects that were uniquely Vietnamese, distinct from those of the Chinese. But rather than despair, they channeled feelings of shame about their own country's perceived shortcomings into their nation-building projects. They will show us that shame is not always a wound inflicted by powerful colonizers onto their subjects. Sometimes, shame is the result of revolutionary self-criticism, an expression of an oppressed group's desire to rise to the occasion to be, borrowing the words of W. E. B. Du Bois, "a co-worker in the kingdom of culture."

Therefore, this book shows how these six Vietnamese thinkers offer an alternative perspective to the conventional Western view that shame is primarily destructive. As we will see in the next chapter, one widespread assumption animating much of "postcolonial theory" is that any time a colonized person expresses shame toward themselves, they must be experiencing "internalized inferiority," "false consciousness," or "colonial mentality." However, the Vietnamese thinkers in this book were ashamed on their own terms, used shame productively, and were anticolonial at the same time.

Another aim of this book, as mentioned, is to explain dignity from another perspective. Surprisingly, scholars of the concept of dignity seem to have overlooked how colonized peoples have conceptualized dignity for their own emancipatory projects. To my knowledge, the three best books dedicated to exploring the concept of dignity are George Kateb's *Human Dignity*, Michael Rosen's *Dignity: Its History and Meaning*, and, more recently, Colin Bird's *Human Dignity and Political Criticism*. These books engage a great number of theorists of dignity throughout history but make virtually no mention of what "non-Western" colonized people had to say about the concept. This is an odd omission because colonized peoples have theorized dignity a great deal, given their colonizers' systematic denial of it. Whereas powerful, dominating peoples can assume their dignity and take it for granted, colonized peoples evoke the word "dignity" often and have provided many insights into the idea. They may not usually produce what looks like traditional "political theory" to scholars in the West (e.g., written, systematic treatises). But their expressions—in speeches, pamphlets, books, memoirs, songs, plays, stories, poems, and oral histories—display productive theoretical interpretations of their situation under domination, interpretations that enable them to respond to such domination and to create their own dignity.

This book takes such expressions seriously, engaging these thinkers as "think partners" to think about this precious concept of dignity.

Americans often think of Vietnam as the site of a war, but Vietnam has been a crossroads of empires—as well as a colonizing empire in itself—and therefore it has been a site of rich cross-cultural intellectual engagement. Its thinkers drew on diverse, foreign intellectual traditions, and their writings display creative, culturally hybrid political thinking. Yet, scholars in the academic field of political theory in political science departments in North American and Eurocentric universities have overlooked Vietnam while beginning to explore the political thought of the leading figures in decolonization movements in India, the Islamic world, Africa, Latin America, and elsewhere.[17] This book is intended especially for those scholars and readers who are interested in political theory but have little knowledge of Vietnam.

This book is also directed to those in the academic field of Vietnam Studies, which has grown tremendously in the past few decades. Working in Western universities, pioneering historians of Vietnam and emerging generations of scholars have produced illuminating works on Vietnamese history beyond the Vietnam War.[18] The names of the six figures in this study often appear in these historians' works, which usually describe the roles these six figures have played in the epic story of Vietnamese modernization and revolution. But rarely do these historians take these thinkers seriously *as thinkers to think with*. Little sustained attention has been given either to their writings or to their theories regarding perceived problems under colonial rule. And we rarely get a sense of how their insights might discipline or change our own thinking about our political life. To be fair, this is a job for a political theorist, not a historian. In this book, these Vietnamese voices are given center stage and are often quoted at length. I make sense of their aspirations and seek to understand how they understood themselves and their world. This book frames their ideas as providing "new," overlooked, provocative perspectives on timely topics in political theory such as shame, dignity, and more.

As human beings whose ideas and identities develop in response to changing social and political environments, the six figures as examined in this book negate the overused habit of slotting colonized peoples into binaries (e.g., resisters or accommodationists) and rigid typecasts (e.g., conservative, radical, Communist, liberal) who play mere roles in the drama of anticolonial struggle. This makes them important figures in how we think about people subjected to colonialism and engaged in indigenous movements struggling for dignity and rights.

There are many other fascinating Vietnamese intellectuals worthy of study, but these six are clearly the most important, being the most well known in Vietnam and key figures for anyone who wants to understand modern Vietnamese history.[19] Four of them—Phan Bội Châu, Phan Chu Trinh, Nguyễn An Ninh, and Hồ Chí Minh—are Vietnamese national heroes to this day, officially praised by the Vietnamese Communist Party. Countless streets and schools are named after them. The other two—Phạm Quỳnh and Nguyễn Mạnh Tường—were once influential but, because of their politics, they were either silenced or ignored for decades. Yet, these two men are making a dramatic comeback in contemporary Vietnam, as we will see. Vietnamese commentators have analyzed the political ideas of these six thinkers for Vietnamese audiences,[20] but this book brings their ideas to light for contemporary debates and audiences in the West who specialize in political and postcolonial theory.

All of these thinkers traveled abroad, East and West, to learn from foreigners. This makes them "theorists" in the old sense of the term. Many of the ancient Greek city-states, Susan McWilliams reminds us, commissioned a *theoros*—a theorist—whose job it was to visit foreign city-states or religious oracles. The *theoros* was supposed to look at the *particulars* of different cultures and places, but with an eye toward the *universal,* so that they saw beyond the particular and toward the sacred and profound, toward general patterns that appear to stretch across all of humanity. And then, the *theoros* was expected to return to his home city and report on what he had seen. Thus, the purpose of travel was to enhance political practice at home.[21] Crossing political borders, the theorist had to think seriously about the differences among political entities and, crucially, about how to translate what he had seen and learned to his own people upon his return. As we will see, Phan Chu Trinh, upon his return from fourteen years in France, tried to explain to his fellow Vietnamese in Saigon what "liberalism" (*tư tưởng tự do*) was, and told them about statues and monuments he saw in Paris that represented liberty. Hồ Chí Minh returned to Vietnam after three decades, and on September 2, 1945, he stood before a crowd of tens of thousands of Vietnamese in Ba Đình Square and declared the independence of the Democratic Republic of Vietnam. He did so by translating—from English and French to Vietnamese—passages from the 1776 American Declaration of Independence and the 1791 Declaration of the French Revolution on the Rights of Man and the Citizen. The *theoros* had to think about how to effectively communicate what he had learned to those in his own community.

This was a tricky task, for bringing back new, foreign ideas can evoke suspicion, even hostility, among those who are more comfortable with the old and familiar. Furthermore, the traveling *theoros* occupied a special intellectual position of being close to both centers of power and at the margins of society. These Vietnamese thinkers traveled to powerful centers (Japan and France) and at the same time knew the periphery (Vietnam) well. With a multifocal lens onto diverse forms of political life, they were better positioned than those who were only in the center or in the margins to develop creative insights that could be of practical use in enhancing politics in their own community.[22] To use Farah Godrej's description of the activities of a cosmopolitan political theorist, these Vietnamese thinkers engaged in "self-dislocation." They left their home—literally and conceptually—to immerse themselves in an alien world, followed by "self-relocation" in which they returned home and called into question their people's prevailing presumptions.[23]

Upon their return to Vietnam, they reconstructed Vietnam's Confucian foundations by creatively adapting ideas from Japanese, Chinese, Indian, French, American, and German thinkers. Comparing and contrasting European and Asian ideas, they imaginatively synthesized and sometimes creatively (mis)interpreted foreign ideas and traditions to apply them to the demands of the moment. They did not seek intellectual "purity" for their projects of constructing national dignity. Instead, they arranged, designed, and assembled the resources of Western and non-Western political thought in unexpected ways to motivate their people to build their culture anew.[24]

In short, in the early twentieth century they were espousing what we theorists in the West would today call "comparative political theory." Specifically, they were doing *engaged* comparative political theory.[25] It was "engaged" because they were theorizing in an effort to find the right ideas *for them*. Unlike scholars in the West who have the luxury of just studying ideas, these thinkers were forced by circumstance to do it as a political practice to generate new conceptions of Vietnam, the Vietnamese people, and their place in the world. And they did it for public use in high-stakes decolonization politics. It was "comparative" because they were moving between what they saw as distinct moral traditions between "East" and "West." To be sure, no system of thought is ever cleanly self-contained. Hybridity and cross-cultural borrowing characterize most, if not all, intellectual traditions. Yet, *they* perceived foreign nations to have distinctive moral doctrines and traditions and compared them. One benefit of seeing these thinkers as "engaged comparative political theorists" is that they may be models for us—citizens in the West—and inspire us to devise engaged comparative political theory of our own. Given the challenges we face in our globalizing world—including inequality, climate change, and polarization, we, too, should be looking to different cultures to find the right ideas for us. That they did engage in comparative political theory should not be surprising. Many non-Western thinkers who struggled against "Western" domination throughout the twentieth century also mixed ideas from East and West to make sense of and respond to their predicaments.

Ultimately, the Vietnamese case brings our attention to desires that were common to colonized and oppressed peoples around the globe: the desire for dignity and pride, and the desire to harness indignation and shame in productive ways. The Vietnamese thinkers in this book may not always use these words when speaking or writing in Vietnamese ("dignity": *phẩm cách con người,* "indignation": *phẫn nộ;* "shame": *xấu hổ,* "pride": *kiêu hãnh;* "duty": *nghĩa vụ*) or in French (*la dignité, l'indignation, la honte, la fierté, le devoir*). However, their speeches and writings are very much animated by these feelings and concepts.

Structure of the Book

In Chapter 1, I discuss prevailing assumptions in political and postcolonial theory about two related sets of concepts: national shame and pride, and national indignation and dignity. In this way, in the following chapters we will more clearly see how these Vietnamese thinkers challenge and enhance our understandings of these concepts. The book is then divided into three parts, with two chapters in each part. Each chapter focuses on one thinker and includes, early in the chapter, a very brief biography.

Part I, The Colonial Condition, engages two of Vietnam's indisputably most famous nationalists of the early twentieth century—Phan Bội Châu and Phan Chu Trinh. By examining their work and their relationship to each other, these chapters explicate their political thought and, in doing so, show how they intellectually navigate between the legacies of Chinese colonialism and the realities of French colonialism.

This part begins with Chapter 2, which surveys early Vietnamese reactions to French colonialism through the eyes of Phan Bội Châu (1867–1940), Vietnam's first modern nationalist. Through his writings, we see him construct a Vietnamese nation. His goal was to convince his compatriots that they were citizens of a country rather than mere subjects of a ruler, thus shifting Vietnamese political thought from royalism to notions of popular sovereignty. His writings about French cruelty purposely seek to induce indignation in his readers, enabling them to channel these feelings into the national consciousness and political action. He also seeks to induce pleasure and joy by presenting utopian descriptions of what Vietnam *could be* in the future if the Vietnamese put in the necessary hard work. In this way he strives to motivate his readers to fulfill their national duty of improving their nation. Along with Phan Chu Trinh, Phan Bội Châu inspired the creation of the Tonkin Free School in 1907, one of the first serious attempts in Vietnam to expose young Vietnamese to ideas from the West. The school's curriculum, influenced by the prevailing Social Darwinist assumptions of the day, promotes what I call the Vietnamese Enlightenment, namely, a turn to reason and to new ideas from the West, and the development of literacy and the national language. Phan Bội Châu's fledgling resistance against the West would provide a nationalist framework that the rest of these thinkers would work from and develop in new directions.

Chapter 3 engages Vietnam's first democrat, Phan Chu Trinh (1872–1926). Five years younger than Phan Bội Châu, Trinh placed greater emphasis on the power of ideas. The Vietnamese people were ignorant of true Confucianism, Trinh argued, an ignorance that was caused by a history of tyrannical monarchs who had distorted Confucianism to justify their autocracy. The lack of genuine Confucian morality in Vietnam was *the* reason why the Vietnamese were sick and vulnerable to foreign conquest. The solution, Trinh argued, was for the Vietnamese to revive Confucianism so that Vietnam could gain the necessary strength it needed to gain independence. And the proper "medicine" that could do this was the adoption of European liberalism and the form of government that he thought came from liberalism: democracy. Trinh conducted comparative political theory to construct a dignified cosmopolitan national identity. He shamed the Vietnamese for having inferior ethics compared to Europeans, and he used this shame to motivate them to adopt liberal democracy to enhance Confucianism. His claim is puzzling, considering that contemporary political theorists agree that liberalism and Confucianism are opposed to each other. Trinh, it turns out, ignored liberalism's individualism while celebrating other aspects of liberalism and Western civilization. His interpretation of Western ideas, though naive, was creative, offering an important lesson: that is, it may be useful to view foreign ideas as foreign, to interpret them generously, and to import the creative distortion to revive our own cherished, yet faltering, traditions.

Part II of the book, What Shall We Do with Tradition?, explores how a younger generation of Vietnamese sought to answer that question. Whereas Phan Bội Châu and Phan Chu Trinh were writing in Chinese, possessed little knowledge of the French language, and had limited knowledge of Western philosophy, this younger generation was educated in French schools in Vietnam and France and were comfortable with Western ideas. The two intellectual giants of this generation, Nguyễn An Ninh and Phạm Quỳnh, built on the work of Châu and Trinh. Writing in the 1920s before Marxism–Leninism became a predominant ideology in Vietnam, these thinkers advanced different, sometimes opposing, visions of how the Vietnamese ought to merge or balance Confucian and Western moral and political thought in their effort to construct a new, modern Vietnamese identity.

Part II begins with Chapter 4, which focuses on a leading anticolonialist in the 1920s, Nguyễn An Ninh (1900–1943). Ninh argued that the Vietnamese should not revive Confucianism but should instead abandon it entirely to create the Vietnamese identity anew. The Vietnamese have only badly and pathetically parroted what they believed to be Confucianism, he thought, thus failing to nurture their national dignity through genuine, original efforts to be creative. Ninh drew on Rabindranath Tagore and other foreign thinkers to shame his fellow Vietnamese and to harness this shame to create a national identity from scratch.

Chapter 5 provides a new interpretation of the infamous Phạm Quỳnh (1892–1945). Historians and nationalists often typecast Quỳnh as an "archcollaborator" with the French colonial regime, but closer attention to his writings reveals that he used his colonial privilege as editor of a French-commissioned journal, *Nam Phong* (The Southern Wind), to resist colonial discourse. His writings sought to conserve, develop, and assert Vietnam's national language and culture. For Quỳnh, Confucianism embodied Eastern wisdom, which he thought the Vietnamese should embrace to resist the domination of the Western ideal of power, while also adapting the "best" ideas from the West. This synthesis of East and West, he believed, could provide a basis for Vietnamese national dignity. Ultimately, Quỳnh is best understood not as a collaborator or a resistor, a villain or a hero, but as an architect of a modern Vietnamese national identity.

Part III, Revolution and Its Discontents, explores how Hồ Chí Minh and Nguyễn Mạnh Tường thought Vietnamese Communists sought to cultivate a dignifying revolutionary ethos, but, after achieving national dignity by expelling colonizers, faced new national indignities and shame: conformity, dogmatism, and authoritarianism.

Part III begins with Chapter 6, which depicts Hồ Chí Minh (1890–1969) as a theorist of humanization, namely, as a critic of dehumanization and an architect of rehumanization. Whereas Trinh saw Vietnamese national shame as coming from within Vietnam, Hồ viewed its source as European capitalism. As a critic of dehumanization, he explained that the racial dehumanization faced by the Vietnamese was a consequence of capitalism and colonialism. And as an architect of rehumanization, Hồ envisioned how the Vietnamese could restore their dignity. Namely, party cadres had to cultivate their revolutionary moral virtue, he stated, thereby making them trustworthy in the eyes of "the people" they were to serve and enabling them to effectively guide "the people" toward the goals of independence and Communist revolution. I call this vision *paternalistic democracy*.

Chapter 7 shows how Nguyễn Mạnh Tường (1909–1997), the first Vietnamese to receive two doctorates from France, also sought to create a "new Vietnamese man" for a postcolonial Vietnam. But Tường had a very different vision of national dignity than Hồ. In the mid-1950s, Tường was excommunicated from the party for criticizing revolutionaries for becoming dogmatic and authoritarian. Tường turned to the sixteenth-century French essayist Michel de Montaigne for solace, seeking to develop a distinctly Montaignean understanding of dignity based on the individual (rather than the nation), as well as on skepticism and love of diversity. For Tường, national dignity required defending and celebrating the individual right to freedom of thought.

The book concludes with Chapter 8 and a discussion of the fates of these six thinkers, connecting them to anticolonial and revolutionary thinkers from around the globe, including Frantz Fanon, Malcolm X, and Marcus Garvey. Ultimately, we must realize that the Vietnamese case is not so unique: Many oppressed peoples have sought to channel their indignation and shame in creative ways to nourish feelings of self-respect, worthiness, and self-confidence.

1
The Engines of National Shame and Indignation

Nationalism remains. Some have even argued that nationalism—the idea that humans form distinct tribes based on common language, culture, and history—is the most powerful force in the world.[1] So much has been written on nationalism, national identity, the formation of national consciousness, and the like. What is remarkable is that despite how vast this academic literature is, there is a consistent and typical way that scholars talk about national identity and its related concepts such as national pride, national shame, and national responsibility. As we will see, this is because much of this literature takes it for granted that it is assuming the perspective of powerful, dominating (usually Western) nations. They make at least three assumptions related to national shame that would not be shared by thinkers from less powerful, dominated nations like Vietnam.

National Shame

First, scholars typically assume that national identity comes from pride.[2] "Nationalism" is certainly synonymous with national pride, but even if we distinguish national identity from nationalism, much of the literature still assumes that national identity requires national pride and that national pride is the cohesive force for national identity. Farid Abdel-Nour argues that the "national bond is a bond of pride that allows modern individuals to be something in the world, to have a certain standing in it."[3] Our modern understanding of the nation, Liah Greenfield points out, can be traced to early sixteenth-century England, when being a member of a nation started to mean that one "partake[s] in its superior, elite quality . . . [that renders all other] . . . lines of status and class . . . superficial."[4] She writes: "Nationality makes people feel good. . . . National identity is fundamentally a matter of dignity. It gives people reasons to be proud."[5] Anthony Smith notes that although national identity poses the danger of exacerbating conflicts by dividing humanity into nations, it is at the same time "a source of pride for downtrodden peoples."[6] Farid Abdel-Nour goes so far as to suggest that if we do not feel a sense of national pride when we view the achievements of our compatriots, then we might not have national identity.[7]

Contrary to these assumptions, the Vietnamese figures in this study will show that shame, rather than pride, can be the basis for national identity. This is because shame can spur action that leads to the formation of national identity. In other words, individuals may be motivated to move their country in a desirable direction when national shame outweighs pride. To be sure, Vietnamese nationalists did draw on national pride to create a sense of national identity, such as evoking the Trưng Sisters who resisted the Chinese in the first century and other national heroes who resisted foreign invasion. But far more prevalent in their exhortations is shame and pointing out the shortcomings of their own people. This kind of national shame is different from the kind of national shame that is typically discussed, which brings us to the second assumption in literature on national shame.

Scholars usually assume that national shame comes from bad actions toward weaker (outside or internal) groups. National shame for Germans usually means the shame they feel toward what Germans did to Jews during the Nazi Holocaust. For Americans, national shame usually means the shame of the enslavement of Africans or the genocide of Native Americans.[8] This sort of national shame has been understood as an emotion that threatens to unravel national identity. Yet, the Vietnamese thinkers who are the focus of this book shed light on a different kind of national shame, one that arises not from bad acts toward others or even from being humiliated by others, but from a sense of moral, intellectual, and political inadequacy.

Third, because the kind of national shame this literature refers to is the shame of doing bad things to others, mainstream discussions of national shame usually include discussions of "national responsibility," which is assumed to mean the responsibility that nations have to right the wrongs of their bad actions or to help those they harmed.[9] Under the heading of "collective responsibility," a vast literature addresses the question of whether groups or nations of people are collectively responsible for the harms they perpetrate against others.[10] Domestically, there are debates about what kind of responsibility nations have for their past injustices, such as concerning reparations for the enslavement of Black people in the United States.[11] Internationally, national responsibility is evoked in discussions of global justice. Some, like

Thomas Pogge, insist that wealthy nations have a responsibility to share their wealth with those of the global south.[12] But others insist that each nation has a right to devote its "national responsibility" to its own members first. David Miller, a proponent of "national responsibility," attempts to solve the conflict between these opposing intuitions by preserving respect for national self-determination and constructing minimal principles for global justice. For him, national responsibility should be thought of not as a demand for the uniform treatment of individuals across national boundaries, but rather as upholding the universal protection of human rights.[13] In all these cases, the responsible nation is assumed to be a powerful one that has either harmed a weaker group or has power to help weaker others. However, these Vietnamese thinkers will exhort their compatriots to take on a different kind of national responsibility, one focused on renewing national identity.

Again, one reason why existing political theory has conceptualized national identity, shame, pride, and responsibility in these ways is that scholars have taken it for granted that they are talking about *their* nations, meaning powerful, dominating, and colonizing nations. This should not be too surprising as most of these scholars are citizens of powerful Western nations, and so it is natural that they would adopt the perspective of their country or countries like their own. However, from the perspective of the Vietnamese and other weaker, historically dominated and colonized nations, these concepts can mean something very different. The six Vietnamese thinkers we will engage show us that national identity can come from shame (rather than pride), that national shame derives from perceived inadequacies (rather than bad actions toward others), and that national responsibility means the duty to create national identity anew (rather than righting the wrongs of bad actions against others).

We would naturally turn to the academic field of "postcolonial theory" to make sense of the perspective of the colonized. After all, postcolonial and "decolonial" theory, though not a single, homogeneous ideology, has the purported aim of giving attention to the ideas and subjectivities of colonized peoples. This is a laudable aim considering that more than three-quarters of people living in the world today have had their lives shaped by colonialism. Yet, such discourses have often focused more on the destructive aspects of the colonial relationship for the self-understanding of the colonized, therefore overlooking how colonized natives have engaged in internal conversations about their own shortcomings. As Antonio Vázquez-Arroyo has aptly put it in his critiques of postcolonial literature, "violent conquests constitutive of colonial situations inaugurate predicaments of power beset with forms of historical and political agency that complicate the dyad colonizer/colonized and call for political explanation as opposed to moralization."[14] Taking the perspective of the colonized would help us gain "a historically accurate understanding of colonialism and the different—because asymmetrical—but real modalities of political agency constituting rulers and ruled."[15] Attention to how these Vietnamese thinkers use shame to spur the construction of a new national identity is illuminating because it challenges, while also enhances, postcolonial and decolonial thought. There are at least three blind spots in these literatures that preclude explorations of the kind of national shame that our six Vietnamese thinkers express.

First, there is simply a paucity of explorations of how colonized peoples have expressed a sense of their own cultural, intellectual, moral, and political shortcomings. We don't hear much about it. Existing studies of the political thought of colonized peoples have shown the complex ways colonized people demonstrate creative agency, but even these studies do not give much, or any, attention to self-expressions of shame.[16] In literature about colonialism in general, the focus tends to be on how colonizers view the colonized as inferior, leaving blurred in the background the ways in which colonized peoples *saw themselves* as inferior. In the two most widely cited introductory texts to postcolonialism that survey the field of postcolonial literature, one finds much evidence for a tradition of Europeans viewing non-Europeans as intellectually, culturally, morally, politically, and biologically inferior, thus justifying the Europeans' conquest, colonization of their lands, and exploitation of their labor.[17] Yet we rarely see how colonized people expressed their own sense of shortcomings.

Second, if any attention is given to colonized peoples' expressions of shame arising from a sense of inferiority, such expressions are usually interpreted in a dismissive way. They are viewed primarily as psychological consequences of colonialism rather than taken seriously on colonized peoples' own terms. Colonized peoples' self-proclaimed inferiority is diagnosed as internalized inferiority reflecting a "colonial mentality." It is "false consciousness" in which they have internalized their colonial masters' beliefs in their own inferiority. Internalized oppression is used to describe "a condition in which the oppressed individuals and groups come to believe that they are inferior to those in power."[18] Scholars view "internalized oppression" as a "salient consequence of systematic and sustained oppression." Implicit in claims like these is that groups cannot really come to believe that they are inferior on their own or for their own purposes. Rather, it is implied; feelings of inferiority are always solely the product of sustained oppression. While foreign conquest may initiate feelings of shame among the conquered, we should pay attention to how conquered peoples attempt to explain how they became conquered. And these explanations may center on their own shortcomings. Rather than dismiss these claims as "false consciousness," we should take them seriously, despite what we might think are the real reasons for their being conquered. The tendency to attribute self-expressions of shame to "false consciousness" is not surprising considering that, according to Robert Young, Marxism (the chief promulgator of the term *false consciousness*) "remains paramount as the fundamental framework of postcolonial thinking."[19]

I do not deny the existence of at least some variants of internalized oppression and false consciousness. Scholars have shown how colonialism can distort colonized peoples' sense of self-worth and even beauty standards in significant ways.[20] I am also not suggesting that most postcolonial and decolonial scholarship holds that self-shame on the part of the colonized can *only* be a sign of internalized inferiority and false consciousness. Nor am I saying that fields as complex as postcolonialism and decolonialism give us only two options for the colonized person: false consciousness (apology for colonialism) versus agency (rejection of colonial values). There is a complex recognition in this literature of how agency and oppressed consciousness work together, especially in the work of postcolonial literature after the 1980s which moved their concern beyond "epistemic violence" (the notion that colonialism silences indigenous knowledge while privileging Western modes of knowledge production) and toward the agency of the colonized.[21] What I am saying is that the use of terms such as *internalized inferiority* discourages us from exploring and taking seriously instances of self-critique that may not turn out to be internalized inferiority. In short, most postcolonial and decolonial discourses—following Karl Marx, Edward Said, Frantz Fanon, and Jean Paul Sartre—deter us from seeing how self-professions of inferiority on the part of the colonized may actually be part of their anticolonial struggle.

When I say that we should try to understand these Vietnamese thinkers' expressions of national shame on their own terms, I do not mean to suggest that shame has nothing to do with colonization or empire. Indeed, any response on the part of the colonized to the colonial situation is mutually constituted by colonizer and colonized, and this interdependence should not be ignored. When we read the writings of people who are colonized, we should read between the lines to consider the colonial world they are responding to. Similarly, when we read the writings of people from colonizing countries, we should read between the lines to consider the colonized peoples who play a role, even though they might receive no mention. This is what Edward Said meant when he exhorted us to read texts "contrapuntally," namely, that we should read with an eye toward perspectives that the text omits or excludes but are relevant because those perspectives belong to people who play a hidden role in the story. For Said, a "contrapuntal reading must take account of both processes, that of imperialism and that of resistance to it, which can be done by extending our reading of the texts to include what was once forcibly excluded."[22] For instance, we should take into account the fact that the Bertram family in Jane Austen's novel *Mansfield Park* (1814) was so wealthy because of the British colony of Antigua, although Antigua is "referred to only in passing."[23] For Said, a contrapuntal reading would bring Antigua to the fore in our minds and allow us to see the bigger picture, to read the novel not as something ahistorical or concerned solely with private, domestic issues, but to read the forgotten Other back into the text.

Such a reading is admirable. However, thinking through the lens of these Vietnamese thinkers, Edward Said is not contrapuntal enough. If we want to take a more deeply contrapuntal approach to history, it is not enough to reveal the interdependence of colonizer and colonized within the texts of European writers only. Contrary to what Said implies in his book *Orientalism*, there *is* a way to engage the texts of non-Europeans without being problematically "orientalist."[24] Whereas Said privileges the texts of those from powerful/colonizing nations, I privilege the perspective of the colonized. For Said, culture is a crucial factor in Europeans' desire to found and maintain imperial regimes, and this is what makes his contrapuntal readings of European texts useful: such readings challenge these imperialistic cultures. Yet the Vietnamese thinkers that we will engage show a different use of culture. For them, a lack of culture or a lack of asserting one's culture can cause national vulnerability to foreign subjugation, and, conversely, a robust culture can enable their nation to stand up to and resist imperial regimes. And the way to push the Vietnamese to create a robust culture is by shaming them into action.

Third, and lastly, in assuming that colonialism destroys "original" indigenous traditions (moral, intellectual, cultural, and political), postcolonial theorists overlook the fact that some colonized people themselves were unsure about the existence of their own "indigenous" traditions. Postcolonial theorists simply assume that colonized, "non-Western" people have "their own" traditions. This is the premise underlying what Robert Young describes as the main assumption that postcolonial theory operates on, namely, the belief that "the intellectual and cultural traditions developed outside the west constitute a body of knowledge that can be deployed to great effect against the political and cultural hegemony of the west."[25] While indigenous traditions have certainly developed outside the West, little attention has been given to how some non-Western thinkers, particularly in "peripheral" nations like Vietnam, have questioned the existence of their own indigenous intellectual traditions.

In *Black Skin, White Masks,* Frantz Fanon famously defines all colonized peoples as those "in whom an inferiority complex has taken root, whose local cultural originality has been committed to the grave."[26] But these six Vietnamese thinkers would say that Vietnam had little "local cultural originality" to begin with. All knew that "their people" were ruled by the Chinese for a thousand years and admitted that Confucius was Chinese, not Vietnamese, and, despite this, he had been Vietnam's moral leader. They were ashamed of lacking their own great thinkers, but this shame led not to depressing self-hatred but to self-renewal.

Like Fanon, Ngũgĩ Wa Thiong'o asserts that colonialism destroys indigenous cultural achievements through a "cultural bomb":

> The effect of a cultural bomb is to annihilate a people's belief in their names, in their languages, in their environment, in their heritage of struggle, in their unity, in their capacities and ultimately in themselves. It makes them see their past as one wasteland of nonachievement and it makes them want to distance themselves from that wasteland. It makes them want to identify with that which is furthest removed from themselves; for instance, with other peoples' languages rather than their own.[27]

This may have been true for some colonized peoples, but not for the characters in this study. Most of them *did* see Vietnam's past as a wasteland of nonachievement. But this was not the "effect of a cultural bomb" dropped by French colonialists. It was their own conclusion, independent of what colonialists may have said about the Vietnamese. And recognition of Vietnamese nonachievement does not make them want to distance themselves from their "Vietnamese-ness." Rather, such recognition inspires them to re-create their nation anew through engagement with a variety of traditions, non-Western and Western.

Jean-Paul Sartre argues that if colonized Black people consume the French culture and education imposed upon them, they will be alienated from their authentic roots. The solution to alienation, Sartre argues, is to "breach the walls of the culture prison" of the whites and to "return to Africa."[28] This would allow them to "die to the white world in order to be reborn to the black soul."[29] Sartre assumes that there is an "authenticity" and indigenous "soul" that Blacks can recover or return to. These assertions are well intended but problematic, Marie Paule Ha rightly argues, because they share the same assumption with racist arguments that essentialize groups.[30] The reality is that there may be no "authentic soul" to begin with and that if a colonized person acknowledges this reality, they are not necessarily apologetic for colonialism or expressing a "false consciousness."

If colonized peoples say that they are culturally, morally, or politically inferior to their colonizers, postcolonial theorists usually interpret this admission as mere parroting of their colonial masters who said that their subjects were inferior, rather than an expression of colonized peoples thinking on their own terms. Ania Loomba remarks that countless colonial intellectuals "parroted the lines of their masters" and that at least some Indian students willingly adopted "the role of Macaulay's English-educated Indian who acts as a surrogate Englishman."[31] Thomas Babington Macaulay, the architect of English education in India, infamously proclaimed the inferiority of Indian culture compared to English culture: "It is, I believe, no exaggeration to say that all the historical information which has been collected in the Sanskrit language is less valuable than what may be found in the paltry abridgments used at preparatory schools in England."[32] Leela Gandhi argues that what Macaulay is doing here is "canon formation." Macaulay establishes English literature as "the normative embodiment of beauty, truth, and morality," and this, in turn, "enforces the marginality and inferiority of colonized cultures and their books."[33] Yet some of our thinkers, such as the anticolonialist Nguyễn An Ninh, essentially say the same thing as Macaulay. Ninh argues that European literature *is* worth more than Vietnamese literature, but he does not make this assertion to uphold European nations' works as "normative embodiments of beauty and truth." Rather, Ninh views the great works of other cultures as things to admire and learn from, and he believes that if the Vietnamese fulfill their national responsibility, they too can create great works. Rather than internalizing what colonizers want them to believe, these Vietnamese thinkers are an example of being self-critical while also rejecting colonial attempts to establish normative "truths." Ania Loomba argues, as many scholars do, that colonialist production of knowledge included a "clash with and a marginalization of the knowledge and belief systems of those who were conquered."[34] Yet such claims rarely also consider that some colonized peoples actually wanted to marginalize their existing native knowledge and belief systems to re-create their culture anew.

A dismissal of Vietnamese thinkers' judgments of their own culture risks being a dismissal of their ability or agency to judge. Indeed, some postcolonial theorists, such as Gayatri Spivak, have been wary of too easy a recovery of the "agency" of colonized peoples.[35] Edward Said's *Orientalism,* Megan Vaughan argues, suggests that "the historical experiences of colonial peoples themselves have no independent existence outside the texts of Orientalism."[36] Thus, Said appears to have unwittingly denied "the possibility of any alternative description of 'the Orient', any alternative forms of knowledge and by extension, any agency on the part of the colonized."[37]

To be sure, studies of colonialism are rich with attention to the agency of colonized peoples to not only violently resist colonialism, but also to their agency to hybridize ideas and resist colonial discourse.[38] One influential example of the latter is Homi Bhabha's concept of "mimicry." Mimicry refers to a kind of exaggerated copying on the part of the colonized of the language, culture, manner, and ideas of their colonizers.[39] This copying usually occurs after colonizers attempt to create a loyal indigenous class that speaks and thinks in the colonizers' language. If the colonizer feels that the English or French-speaking indigenous class begins to resemble the colonizer too much, the colonizer may experience an unsettling anxiety. This anxiety, Bhabha thinks, opens a space for the colonized to resist colonial discourse. Mimicry, therefore, threatens to undermine the colonizers' apparently stable, original identity: "The menace of mimicry is its double vision which in disclosing the ambivalence of colonial discourse also disrupts its authority."[40] Related to mimicry is Bhabha's notion of "hybridity," which also challenges colonial discourse. Hybridity refers to how postcolonial identity is always a mix and a new creation, and to the impurity of cultures in the first place, as there is never pure or "authentic" cultural identity to begin with, despite familiar forms of "official" culture. Hybridity is significant because it challenges the tendency of colonizers to set up distinctions between pure cultures.[41]

Long before Bhabha introduced the concept of hybridity, Vietnamese thinkers like the ones presented in this study exhorted their compatriots to borrow freely from as many cultural traditions as possible. They were aware that cultures are always already mixed and impure, so originality or purity is never their goal. Rather, they think the Vietnamese should aim to be sincere and genuine in their creative efforts to construct a new culture as they learn from other cultures. To Bhabha's point, these thinkers' use of French ideas and language to subvert the French colonial project certainly provoked anxiety within French colonizers. However, while Bhabha's concepts of mimicry and hybridity might be useful to understand how these thinkers disrupt *colonizers'* self-perceptions, these concepts take on different purposes once we consider these Vietnamese thinkers' perspective. Whereas Bhabha is concerned with how mimicry and hybridity challenge colonizers and their colonial projects, these Vietnamese thinkers exhort colonized Vietnamese to avoid mimicking colonizers and instead to work on sincere creations that generate hybridity to transmute their shame into national dignity. At stake for Bhabha is challenging colonial discourse. At stake for these Vietnamese thinkers is creating Vietnamese identity anew.

National Indignation

For these six thinkers, national shame is not the only emotional engine they use to drive projects that construct national dignity. Another is indignation. Whereas shame initially makes one want to hide, indignation initially makes one want to respond with rage. Indignation, argues Nick Bromell, is a flash of emotion that one feels when one's dignity is denied or misrecognized. It is evidence that *something* within us was violated. Therefore, indignation is the surest proof that dignity is intrinsic and in need of social recognition.[42] The Vietnamese account of dignity advanced in this study—that dignity is for the nation and requires assertion rather than being dependent on recognition by colonizers—is a response to the failure or refusal of colonizers to recognize the dignity of the colonized.

Indignation is most often a socially shared rather than an individualized experience. One can feel indignation when one sees someone else's dignity being denied. In the summer of 2020, millions of people in the United States and around the world saw video footage of Derek Chauvin, a white police officer, press his knee onto George Floyd's neck for nine minutes, killing Floyd, an unarmed Black man who was in handcuffs. Many who saw this video felt indignation and were compelled to take to the streets, inaugurating the largest nationwide protests since the civil rights movement. Dignity lies dormant, so to speak, to be awakened when we feel that someone else has failed to recognize us or others as morally equal human beings.

The social aspect of indignation can be especially pronounced when one sees, hears, or reads of a member of one's own ascriptive group being abused by a member of a more powerful group. This is particularly the case for minorities, colonized, and racialized peoples. A Vietnamese man who sees a Frenchman abuse another Vietnamese person feels that *he himself* is being abused by the Frenchman. For the Vietnamese figures in this study, indignation (and therefore the concomitant goal of dignity) over mistreatment by French colonizers is always a collective, rather than an individualized, experience. Vietnamese writings from the first three decades of the twentieth century are replete with expressions of indignation, not usually over what the writer experienced personally, but over stories they have heard or read about cruel, dehumanizing French treatment of their fellow Vietnamese, or the exploitation and destruction of their land. For them, a "we," not an "I," was being humiliated.

One way Vietnamese writers attempted to induce feelings of collective indignation among their fellow Vietnamese was to create sacred objects to be profaned. As we will see in the following chapters, these Vietnamese thinkers wrote, and therefore constructed, histories of Vietnam to portray their country as something sacred, a gift bequeathed to them by their ancestors. They emphasized that this sacred object was now being desecrated by French colonizers or by corrupt or inert Vietnamese who allowed colonial desecration to persist.

We have detailed accounts of what French colonization of the Vietnamese landscape looked like.[43] What is particularly relevant for us are the ways the Vietnamese experienced that colonization as a violation of national dignity. Derived from the Latin word *colonus* meaning "farmer," colonialism describes how a foreign group not only dominates a native group, but directly reshapes the natives' land. Vietnamese writings describe how French-constructed roads (which used Vietnamese corvee [i.e., forced, unpaid] labor) were built without consideration of locals' geomantic beliefs, ancestral burial sites, and sacred spots revered by communities, therefore desecrating these sacred areas.[44] These writings, whether sincere or strategic, generated collective indignation by constructing something holy to be profaned. This method is not unique to Vietnam but is common throughout the history of revolutions. We can better understand the Terror of the French Revolution, Sophie Wahnich argues, by paying attention to how popular feelings circulate in the "dynamic of emotional economy."[45] When Jean Paul Marat, the French revolutionary leader and advocate for human rights, was assassinated, Parisians were filled with dread because he had represented something sacred. "By embodying the Declaration of the Rights of Man and of the Citizen, this was a sacred body, and its assassination a severe profanation."[46] The task of political leaders at Marat's funeral ceremony, then, was to sublimate those feelings into demands for vengeance, terror, and enthusiasm for revolution.

Vietnamese newspapers frequently recounted daily indignities in which Vietnamese were belittled, neglected, or abused. A popular saying was, "Automobiles belong to the French and the mandarins [government officials in the civil service], while bullock carts are for the Vietnamese."[47] Stories recounted car accidents that left Vietnamese pedestrians dead and the French driver driving away.[48] In the cities, such as Saigon or Hanoi, the sections of town where French or other Europeans lived were dignified with tall trees and excellently maintained pavement, but local Vietnamese were not welcome to linger.[49] A Vietnamese man was drinking coffee on a terrace when two Frenchmen passed by on the sidewalk. One of them stopped and knocked the cigarette out of the Vietnamese man's mouth, yelling "Impolite! Insolent! Why don't you salute Frenchmen?" Frenchmen would slap the faces of natives for no known reason. A French commissar of police slapped a Vietnamese man who later turned out to be the son of a high mandarin in the royal Court of Annam. When the commissar had to apologize to the family, he offered the excuse that he mistook the Vietnamese for a *nhà quê* (a peasant).[50] Future revolutionaries like Hồ Chí Minh will explain such indignities as consequences of colonialism, telling his compatriots that the "conqueror is very concerned to ensure submission and respect from the conquered. The Annamese in the towns and countryside are required to take off their hats in front of Europeans."[51] In the chapters to come, we will present more examples of how our thinkers evoke colonial indignities and use them for nation-building.

Contemporary scholarly discussions of the idea of dignity and indignation typically ignore *national* dignity and *national* indignation or dismiss them as irrelevant or passé. Such discussions prefer to focus on dignity for individual humans. But indignation is almost always felt as an assault or violation of one's sense of belonging to a particular group, be it a nation, gender, class, or race. And the victimizer is usually seen as belonging to a more powerful group. A victim of insult would probably feel less indignant if he assumed the victimizer was merely a malevolent individual. Indignation is usually a feeling that "*they* are doing this to *us*."

There are reasons for the contemporary focus on individual, not group, dignity. In 2001, the UN Secretary General Kofi Annan declared: "In the twenty first century, I believe the mission of the United Nations will be defined by a new, more profound, awareness of the sanctity and dignity of every human life. . . . The sovereignty of states must no longer be used as a shield for gross violations of human rights."[52] In other words, national dignity had become synonymous with sovereignty, and demands for sovereignty were only relevant during the age of anticolonial struggle. But now, the argument goes, since nations already have sovereignty, the protection of *individual* dignity through human rights is more urgent. Yet, it would be a mistake even in the third decade of the twenty-first century to dismiss national dignity as outdated.

We have not moved toward a world in which nations matter less to human beings, but we have experienced the opposite. Nations and nationalisms are reasserting themselves and do not seem to be going away. As right-wing populism asserts itself around the globe, liberal political theorists are attempting to salvage nationalism by promoting a kind of nationalism that liberals would find dignifying, namely, "enlightened patriotism" and "liberal nationalism" to counter illiberal forms of nationalism.[53]

When "national dignity" does appear, the term is treated with suspicion or contempt. Michael Rosen urges us to resist the notion of national dignity, arguing that it comes "frighteningly close" to those "laws against lèse-majesté that tyrants have traditionally used to defend themselves."[54] Decades after formal decolonization, Rosen might have a point. Yet, few would argue that postcolonial states—most states in the world—today are really "equal" just because they have sovereignty like more powerful states do. National dignity is still on the minds of those in postcolonial states as much as it was during the colonial era when colonized peoples used the term *national dignity* quite often. "*Dignité nationale*" and "collective dignity" routinely show up in the writings of Frantz Fanon and Amilcar Cabral, two famous theorists of anticolonial struggle who understood that for racially oppressed peoples, indignation is never "individually" experienced. For them as for the Vietnamese thinkers in this study, dignity for the individual could only be achieved through affirming national dignity.

Indignation can ignite one's impulse to react violently. In response to (national) indignation, some Vietnamese during the colonial era responded with violence, terrorism, and riots. Some killed French recruiters who roamed the countryside seeking new laborers,[55] and some assassinated or attempted to assassinate French officials. Yet, these acts often resulted in severe colonial repression. As Nick Bromell put it when discussing Black Americans during slavery and the Jim Crow era, "prompt and direct expression of anger would have been dangerous, even fatal, while total repression of it would have been self-denying and self-destructive."[56] Once the victim is aware of possible destructive or counterproductive consequences of unorganized or isolated violence, the victim is forced to channel their emotions elsewhere. Often, that meant inwardly, into the self. Anger at denials of dignity, Bromell writes, "often *had* to take this inward turn into reflection." Indignation sets "the mind on fire," provoking an "analysis of the causes and conditions that have sparked it." One is compelled to think about their indignation, to reflect on it, to make sense of it, and to think about how to productively respond to it. Their challenge was "to try to guide their anger toward productive political and social ends." Examples of inward canalization of indignation are the speeches of Martin Luther King Jr., Malcolm X, and Marcus Garvey addressed to Black people, exhorting them to self-strengthen, to imagine the world anew, and to work toward creating that world.

PART I
THE COLONIAL CONDITION

2
Phan Bội Châu's Nationalist Groundwork

When Phan Bội Châu (1867–1940) was nine years old, scholar-gentry in his home region of Nghệ An called for an armed uprising against the French. "On hearing this," Châu recalled, "I assembled the children at my school; using bamboo tubes for guns and lychee pits for bullets, we ourselves played at *Bình Tây* (Put Down the French)."[1] Passionate and patriotic at a young age, Phan Bội Châu would become *the* pioneer of Vietnamese anticolonial nationalism and Vietnam's best-known patriot in the early twentieth century. He would lay the moral, political, and intellectual foundation upon which the rest of the thinkers featured in this book would develop and take in new directions.

Châu was an ardent anticolonialist, a Confucian, a monarchist-turned-republican—and a self-admitted failure. Through some attention to his personal journey and his writings, we gain the best introduction to the most fledgling phase of Vietnamese anticolonial resistance. He was determined to do *something*, though he was often at a loss for what exactly he should do. Through him, the Vietnamese people would take their first steps toward learning about the Western world so that they could stand up to it. Ultimately, Châu's story is one of frustration and defeat. Yet, he planted the seeds for Vietnamese assertion of national dignity, and he laid the groundwork for what it might mean to channel shame and indignation, which the other five national figures discussed in this book would nurture.[2] Setting the tone for the others, he turned inward to his own people, shaming them for failing to stand up for themselves: "Those whom I blame most deeply are my people themselves; my deepest love is for my people, and my deepest blame is for my people."[3] He called the Vietnamese "barbaric," even, for not standing up for themselves. "Barbarism" is not, as some Vietnamese think, "using leaves as clothes to cover the body or catching snakes and centipedes as food." Rather, "those who are dependent are barbaric. Weak people without self-reliance are barbaric."[4]

A Brief Biography: Phan Bội Châu

Born in 1867 in Nghệ An, Phan Bội Châu studied Confucian texts under the guidance of his father, a Confucian scholar. From 1885 to 1900, he studied for the mandarinate examinations, and, after six attempts, he passed a regional exam in 1900 but failed the highest level exam in 1903. Around the turn of the century, Châu began absorbing the ideas of European thinkers through Chinese translations.

From 1900 to 1905, Châu traveled around Vietnam to seek support—particularly from the gentry and bureaucracy—to organize a resistance movement against the French. Inspired by the Japanese military victory over Russia in 1905, Châu went to Japan that year to learn from its reforms and to seek military assistance. He also coordinated a movement called the Đông Du (Go East) to send Vietnamese students to study in Japan. There, he met with the Chinese reformer Liang Qichao who advised Châu to write about Vietnam's situation under colonial rule. He also met with Phan Chu Trinh and together they visited schools in Japan, schools that would inspire the creation of the Đông Kinh Nghĩa Thục (Tonkin Free School) in Hanoi in 1907. Around 1908, however, Japan agreed with France to disband the Đông Du movement.

Expelled from Japan because the country was no longer open to the Vietnamese, Châu went to South China to contact Chinese revolutionaries. There, he purchased weapons with money sent from Vietnam and tried to find a way to smuggle them into Vietnam, but to no avail. He donated the weapons to Sun Yat Sen's revolutionary party. With the success of the Chinese republican revolution in 1911, Châu tried to create an Asian alliance against European powers.

From 1912 to 1925, Châu's base of operations was China. In 1914, he was arrested and imprisoned by a Chinese ruler who suspected Châu of liaising with the ruler's enemies. He gained his freedom in 1917, and from then until 1925, he tried to reach out to foreigners beyond China and Japan, such as the Germans. Briefly, Châu even considered working with the progressive French Governor-General Albert Sarraut, but soon returned to his former anti-French stance.

After the First World War, Châu played an increasingly passive role in the nationalist movement. In 1925, he was again arrested in China; this time he was brought to Hanoi and placed under house arrest in Huế, marking the end of his years of anticolonial resistance. He died in 1940.[5]

French Conquest

With Napoleon Bonaparte's defeat in 1815, the five major European powers—Britain, France, Prussia, Russia, and Austria—agreed to maintain a balance of power in Europe. Constrained by treaties and unable to flex their muscles at home, European nations ramped up their efforts in Asia to attain the "three G's" that had motivated European adventures abroad: *glory*, in the form of national prestige; *gold*, in the form of economic opportunity and exploitation of new resources and human labor; and *God*, in the form of missionary work which served to justify colonialism. By the 1850s, Britain had gained control over India, Burma, Singapore, and Malaya, and had also exerted its power in China. The Netherlands controlled Java. By then, the Philippines had already been part of the Spanish empire for almost three centuries. If France was to maintain its glory, many French officials believed, it, too, had to assert itself in Asia.

Like other European leaders during the nineteenth century, French leaders believed they could gain prestige for France by extending their nation's empire into Asia to be part of the growing European presence there. Napoleon Bonaparte's nephew, Napoleon III, became the first president of the French Second Republic in 1848 and believed colonies would provide France with markets, human labor, and natural resources such as cotton, silk, sugar, rice, coffee, and rubber. To trade with the Far East, France would need bases to fuel and repair their ships. Not wanting to depend on British goodwill for access to China via Singapore and Hong Kong, French officials argued that Saigon could be France's "Hong Kong."[6]

One way that French officials sought to gain approval from the public and from the Catholic Church for France's colonial projects was to ensure the security of French missionaries.[7] In 1857 the French had the perfect pretext for entering Vietnam by force. That year, the Vietnamese emperor Tự Đức executed two European missionaries. Although European Catholic missionaries had been showing up on Vietnam's shores to convert the Vietnamese people to Catholicism since the sixteenth century, and although Christianity was already largely integrated into Vietnamese society by the mid-nineteenth century, Vietnamese rulers were aware at that time of the rapid growth of the European presence in Asia. They were increasingly anxious about foreigners teaching their subjects new ideas and thus undermining their rule. Vietnamese officials, motivated more by fear of European imperialism than by Christianity, published new anti-Christian edicts, thus beginning a new wave of persecution of Catholics and missionaries. In response to that year's executions, France, along with Spain, sent a fleet to punish the Vietnamese. Led by Francis Garnier (1839–1873), both nations attacked Đà Nẵng and occupied the port town.

The punitive expedition became a colonial one, and French conquest of what would become known as Indochina (today's Vietnam, Laos, and Cambodia) proceeded in two stages. By the time Phan Bội Châu was born in 1867, the first stage was complete with the creation of the French colony of Cochinchina in the south of Vietnam. The second stage ended in 1885 with the creation of Annam in the center and Tonkin in the north, both of which were technically under the authority of the Vietnamese imperial court but under French "protection." By the late 1880s, French subjugation of Vietnam was complete, with Vietnam divided into three sections. By the end of the nineteenth century, all countries in the Southeast Asian region—except for Siam, which is today called Thailand—were under European colonial rule.

When Châu assembled his peers with bamboo guns and lychee bullets, the year was 1876, with France's second stage of conquest underway. As Châu grew up, he, like typically ambitious Vietnamese young men, went on to study Chinese Confucian classics in preparation for the civil service exams. Although he passed a regional exam with honors in 1900, he had no interest in an official career in government. More urgent for him was liberating Vietnam from colonial rule.

In 1901, Châu's father died, and for Châu, this presented an opportunity. "The heavy charge of my family fell away, and my shoulders were lightened; thus I began to set about my revolutionary plans."[8] His plans were simple and straightforward. Surmising that a mass violent uprising was necessary, Châu planned to travel throughout Vietnam to contact remnants of the failed *Cần Vương* movement and other patriots and to mobilize them for another military uprising. Then, he would send Vietnamese abroad to get weapons. The aim of these plans, Châu writes, "was exclusively to restore Vietnam and to establish an independent government. Apart from this, there was as yet no other idea."

Cần Vương

Sixteen years earlier, in 1885, the *Cần Vương* ("Save the King") movement began when the young emperor Hàm Nghi urged scholar-leaders around the country to mobilize their areas for war against the French. Many did, and it became the first organized, large-scale, anti-French armed resistance campaign in Vietnam. It was to be a conservative revolution, aimed merely at reinstating the emperor to power and restoring the country's independence. At the time, visions of new ways of doing politics like democracy were simply not on their minds. Yet, the movement set in motion new ideas about the proper relationship between citizen and country. We might attribute the emergence of such new ideas to the leader of the *Cần Vương* movement, Phan Đình Phùng (1847–1896), a man Phan Bội Châu deeply revered.

The French tried to arrest Phan Đình Phùng by using his brother as bait. If Phan Đình Phùng collaborated, the French offered, he would be given a high office; if not, they would kill his brother. Phung responded by saying he was no longer concerned with his immediate family, but considered the whole country to be his family:

> Now I have but one tomb, a very large one, that must be defended: the land of Vietnam. I have only one brother, very important, who is in danger: more than twenty million countrymen. If I worried about my own tombs, who would worry about defending the tombs of the rest of the country? If I saved my own brother, who would save all the other brothers of our country?[9]

Phùng died of dysentery in 1896, after which the *Cần Vương* movement disintegrated,[10] but his remarks on saving all the brothers of his country gave birth to a new idea. Although the movement was a royalist one, not a nationalist one, and did not have an agenda to modernize Vietnam, Phung's remarks are one of the first expressions of popular sovereignty and Vietnamese protonationalism. His suggestion that one ought to love their country more than their family or king was significant, even radical, considering Vietnam's Confucian traditions which emphasized filial piety and loyalty to one's king rather than any conception of loyalty to one's nation.

By 1904, Phan Bội Châu was still convinced that organized violence could spark a more effective, general uprising to expel the French. Yet, he was also increasingly critical of the Vietnamese imperial court and mandarins whom he saw as both incompetent and immoral. He thus began to recognize the shortcomings of monarchism and to find more attractive the modern notion of popular sovereignty and republicanism. Eventually, he realized that "modernizing" Vietnam was just as urgent as violently overthrowing the French.

Throughout his travels in the country, Châu gathered young Vietnamese into what became known as the Vietnam Modernization Society (*Việt Nam Duy tân Hội*).[11] Focused on socioeconomic reforms, the organization was more progressive than the *Cần Vương* royalist movement. They prioritized education. So, as part of Châu's plan to send Vietnamese abroad for help, the organization urged the Vietnamese people to study in Japan.

Japan's Shining Example

By the time Japanese Meiji leaders took power in 1868, the Japanese had already been learning about European science and ideas from material provided by Dutch traders.[12] Anxious about encroaching Europeans, Meiji leaders called on the Japanese to engage in "Western studies" to help the country modernize. It worked. Japan soon became a modern nation state with military and economic power on a par with the West. Inspired by the Japanese example, Chinese reformers like Liang Qichao, Kang Youwei, and Sun Yat Sen traveled to Japan, hoping the Meiji would provide Chinese students with the modern knowledge and military science needed to build a new China.

Japan's 1905 military victory over the Russians in the Russo-Japanese War further affirmed for many Asians and "nonwhites" that Japan's example ought to be followed. Rabindranath Tagore and the young Jawaharlal Nehru in India, Mustafa Kemal (later known as Atatürk) in Turkey, Sun Yat Sen in China, W.E.B. Du Bois in the United States, and others reacted with joyful optimism. Gandhi, in white-ruled South Africa at the time, wrote: "When everyone in Japan, rich or poor, came to believe in self-respect, the country became free. She could give Russia a slap in the face.... In the same way, we must, too, need to feel the spirit of self-respect."[13] Vietnamese thinkers took part in this excitement. Finally, there was evidence, it seemed, that white men were not invincible and that East Asians could stand up to them.[14] The "most important reason" Japan was able to defeat Russia, Phan Bội Châu wrote, was that "the Japanese were patient, and were able to endure hardship and withstand suffering."[15] For Châu, this would become a prominent theme in his thinking: one must endure the bitterness of present hardships of patriotic duty—to self-educate, modernize, organize, and mobilize—to taste the sweetness of the future.

In 1905, Phan Bội Châu went to Japan himself to ask the Japanese to supply weapons to the Vietnamese, but to no avail. There, he met with Liang Qichao, the Chinese reformer who was also in Japan at the time to learn about modernization. At the time, Châu writes, Liang "was writing I-ta-li san-chieh chuan (Biographies of the Three Heroes of Italy)." After Liang showed it to Châu, Châu "became a great admirer of Mazzini, as in the account of him there were these words: 'Education and insurrection should go hand in hand,' which filled me with enthusiasm."[16] Now convinced that violent resistance must be accompanied by a change in mindset, Châu became receptive to Liang's advice that Châu ought not to rely on the Japanese for military aid, but that Châu should reform Vietnamese minds before violently resisting colonizers. "Your country," Liang argued, "should not be concerned about not having a day of independence, but should be concerned about not having an independence-minded people."[17] To this end, Liang argued, Châu should focus on writing texts addressed to the Vietnamese people, to awaken them to the idea that they belonged to a country and that their country was being violated. "In that moment," Châu recalls, "the horizons of my consciousness and vision suddenly broadened. I became painfully aware that up to that time my ideas and my actions had all been thoughtless and imprudent. Thereupon I began to write the book *Việt Nam vong quốc sử* (The History of the Loss of Vietnam)."[18]

The book criticized Vietnamese emperors for failing to reform the country. It celebrated *Cần Vương* heroes and described the evils of French colonialism. Châu had his texts, written in classical Chinese, recopied and translated to *quốc ngữ* (Romanized Vietnamese), which were then circulated clandestinely and read out loud to villagers. Châu would continue to follow through on Liang's advice, writing more essays that would later become foundational nationalist texts.

Châu's writings sought to show ordinary Vietnamese that it was *them*, not the king, who embodied Vietnam. It was *they* who were being humiliated by foreigners. As the most well-known political actor at the time, Châu, through his writings, virtually singlehandedly shifted Vietnamese political thought from the idea that the mystical body of the emperor represented Vietnam to the idea that the people represented Vietnam. Recognizing that power is the human ability to act in concert, Châu exhorted his compatriots to realize that if the French method of conquest was to divide, then the solution for the Vietnamese was to unite around the idea of Vietnamese peoplehood: "Unanimity can protect the country. Failure to agree with each other will lead to the destruction of the country. If you don't agree with your people, you will eventually be enslaved by others."[19] For Châu, solidarity was a necessary condition for national dignity, while division was the cause of the indignity of vulnerability to foreign conquest: "Divided strength is weakness. A divided heart is a broken heart. If we are isolated and they are united, then they will always win, and we will always fail. A handful of chopsticks is difficult to break, but it is easy to break one piece at a time. That's obvious."[20]

Others, like Phan Chu Trinh, would develop the notion of Vietnamese peoplehood more fully. For the first six decades (1860s–1920s) of French colonialism, the Vietnamese term *dân* broadened beyond its original meaning, transforming it from "children of the ruler," to "persons of a common ethnic identity," and finally to "citizens of a modern state."[21]

In one open letter to the Vietnamese people in 1907, titled "The New Vietnam," Phan Bội Châu felt it necessary to begin by simply describing the physical aspects of the country to give his readers a sense that it was theirs and something to be revered: "The area of our country is 250,000 square miles; isn't that spacious? Our country's population has more than fifty million people; isn't that a lot? The land is fertile. Our mountains and rivers are beautiful. Compared with the strongest countries in the other five continents, our land is not inferior. So why should we submit to the 'protection' of France?"[22] Then, he reminded his readers that their people had shamefully submitted for a millennium to another colonizer, the Chinese: "Our slave mentality is deep rooted. Our habit of dependence is heavy." In this way he was creating a sacred object (the country) and showing how this object was being profaned by French colonialism and a Vietnamese "slave mentality" was inherited from the era of Chinese colonialism.

A Brief Detour: Colonizers from the North

From 111 B.C. to A.D. 938, Chinese rulers, seeing themselves as rulers of a universal empire and desiring easier access to Indian Ocean markets, conquered and incorporated the people living to the south of them into their empire. Chinese officials referred to these people using the term *Yue* ("Việt"), meaning something like "those people over there, from beyond." To this, they often added Nan ("Nam"), meaning "south,"[23] giving us the terms Yue Nan ("Việt Nam") or Nan Yue ("Nam Việt"). Therefore "Vietnam" literally means something like "those people over there, to the south of us." The term is Chinese-centric.

This peculiar predicament evokes a "double-consciousness" reminiscent of what W. E. B. Du Bois argued Black Americans experienced due to their marginalization in American society. Those with double-consciousness, Du Bois stated, were "gifted with second sight," able to see the world from more perspectives than those from the dominant group. For the Vietnamese, the condition of being on a periphery of perceived civilizational "centers"—specifically the "centers" of India and China (and that is why Vietnam was part of "Indochina")—and later a colony of a Western power lent these Vietnamese thinkers multitudes of sight. This position—geographical, civilizational, and political—enabled them to see the world from various Eastern and Western perspectives. The Chinese, like the French, may have taken their universalistic pretensions for granted, but many Vietnamese were self-conscious of their status as being on the periphery and, later, the periphery of the periphery (if we consider Europe a "center" and China a "periphery"). By virtue of being on the margins, these thinkers had no choice but to be think of themselves in cosmopolitan terms. Sources of national identity simply had to come from foreign traditions. By the third decade of the twentieth century, they would become intensely nationalistic and see no irony or paradox in their cosmopolitan nationalism.[24]

It would not be until around 1945 that the term *Việt Nam* would be commonly used to refer to the country. Yet, the double-consciousness that the term evokes colored Vietnamese self-understanding of what it meant to be Vietnamese in the early twentieth century. From a millennium of Chinese rule, the Vietnamese adopted Chinese culture, social practices, and political institutions, notably the Chinese civil service exams which selected individuals for bureaucratic service based on their knowledge of Confucian classic texts. Vietnamese social relations, rituals, and attitudes were thoroughly "Confucianized," and much of that remains to this day. As we will see, thorough Sinicization of Vietnamese life would make it difficult for the Vietnamese in the early twentieth century to identify any cultural heritage that they could proudly proclaim as uniquely "Vietnamese." While all cultures are hybrid creations, not all peoples have been able to assert with the same ease of pride that "their people" possess "their own" culture.

To be sure, a basis for a separate Vietnamese national *identity*, if not culture, could be found in the pantheon of heroes who resisted foreign invasion: the Trưng Sisters who resisted the Chinese in the first century (39–43

B.C.), Trần Hưng Đạo who defeated invaders from the Mongol Empire in the thirteenth century, the emperor Lê Lợi and his strategist Nguyễn Trãi who defeated the invading Chinese Ming dynasty in the fifteenth century, and so on. These figures are national heroes to this day, honored as saints, even gods, and worshipped in temples and shrines.[25] The trope of resistance against foreign aggression would become central to the Vietnamese national identity. Indeed, *anyone's* national identity, "while discursively constructed, gains real significance," Ranjoo Seodu Herr reminds us, "when a hostile and powerful Other threatens one's national integrity through conquest, subjugation, domination, oppression, exploitation, or marginalization."[26]

Another source of national pride was that, after gaining independence from Chinese colonizers, the Vietnamese became proud colonizers themselves, expanding their own empire. From the tenth to eighteenth century, the new state of Đại Việt ("Greater Viet," named by those who beat back Chinese enemies) expanded southward, conquering those—notably the Cham peoples—in their path. These Vietnamese imperialists used Chinese military science and Chinese imperial and bureaucratic models to manage the conquered territories and people. Ironically, these Vietnamese saw themselves as part of a civilized East Asian Confucian world with a duty to fulfill a civilizing mission of "barbarians."[27]

Phan Bội Châu refers to these conquests with pride, asserting that without the heroic efforts of the Vietnamese people, Vietnam would be "no more than the lair of the people of Linyi, Ailao, and Chenla [Champa, Laos, and Cambodia]."[28] Yet, it is thanks to these people that the Vietnamese possess a country: "Our ancestors bequeathed this land to us, their descendants, and we, the descendants, inherited this land from them. This country is our family fortune, and our treasured heirloom." Shamefully, however, "our people also have abandoned it. Consequently, our people must also take it back."[29] He connected contemporary Vietnamese to their ancestors, evoking in the former a sense of indebtedness and national responsibility. As we read Châu, we see in real time his construction of the Vietnamese nation as something that belonged to "the Vietnamese." For the Vietnamese to begin cultivating their own dignity, they needed a genealogy of a dignified past. And Châu gave it to them: "A few centuries ago, we were able to destroy the Yuan [Mongol] army and pacify the Wu [Ming] bandits, defeat the Qing armies and extend this great land.... Thinking about our race, we are most definitely not a kind of ignorant, squirming, weak animal."[30]

In contrast to their heroic ancestors who fought off Chinese invaders, Châu argued, the Vietnamese were now cowards who accepted subjugation under the French. The French

> treat our fathers like buffaloes and horses; they suck the blood and fat from our people.... Our country is our country. Our people are our people. The lives of a thousand Vietnamese are not equal to a single French dog.... Behold, those people with blue eyes and pink beards. They are not our fathers nor our brothers. They are not our teachers. How can they squat here, shitting and pissing on our heads? Are you men not ashamed, humiliated, or resentful enough to kill these invaders?[31]

With impassioned prose, Châu set in motion a genre of writing in Vietnam that sought to evoke indignation from ordinary Vietnamese.

Indignation

And there were many colonial indignities to write about. France controlled production of rice in Vietnam to be exported to Chinese markets, and tea and coffee to be exported to European markets. The French set up large rubber plantations where Vietnamese were forced to meet the rising demand for rubber, particularly in the United States where Henry Ford was perfecting the assembly line to mass produce cars. On these plantations, Vietnamese workers were exploited for .3 to .4 piastres per adult per day,[32] forced to work around twelve hours if daylight lasted, and, despite the heat, allowed fifteen minutes of rest at midday. Severe beatings by French owners, French supervisors, or Vietnamese foremen were regularly reported, and these beatings sometimes led to death.[33] Workers sang songs at these plantations, one of which went, "How healthy and beautiful are the rubber trees! Under each of them, a corpse of a worker is buried."[34] Trần Tử Bình, a Vietnamese who worked on the Phú Riềng rubber plantation in the 1920s, described it as "hell on earth" in his memoir *The Red Earth*. The most common forms of punishment, Bình writes,

> were to make the person drop his pants, then beat him on the buttocks, or beat his feet until the soles were in ribbons. After a beating, the worker would be locked up in a dark room, legs shackled, and left without food

for two or three days. Some people were forgotten there until they died of thirst.[35]

Workers suffered appalling and humiliating treatment while their overseers enjoyed spacious and luxurious living quarters. Workers were crushed by trees, suffered malaria and dysentery, and "endured an extremely austere diet."[36]

To increase the efficiency of resource extraction and production, the French appropriated land from peasants and concentrated it into the hands of a few, creating a new class of Vietnamese landlords. By the turn of the twentieth century, peasants who had once lived off the land now worked for a wage or paid rent. The Vietnamese, many of them now dispossessed, increased their consumption of opium and rice alcohol, which the French monopolized and profited from, too.

Meanwhile, a class of Vietnamese who supported the French colonial regime enjoyed concentrations of wealth and flaunted new Western clothes and lifestyles.[37] Colonial authorities governed mainly through these native collaborators who collected taxes, acted as police agents, and were public works engineers.[38] Yet, natives in the countryside and cities still experienced indignities from the French.

Frenchmen inflicted quotidian physical violence on natives, something Truong Buu Lam attributes to the lower-class status of most Frenchmen who came to the colonies, arguing that they were more predisposed than their upper-class counterparts to use their fists, feet, or weapons for resolving frustration.[39] During Phan Bội Châu's travels to Hong Kong, a colony of the British Empire, he remarked how different it seemed from French-occupied Vietnam.

> On the streets [of Hong Kong], we never saw anyone be stopped by soldiers to interrogate their identity. There was no one who went out at night without a light and was brought back by an armed soldier. There are no brutal and insolent patrollers arresting innocent people in the middle of the road, no scenes of native people being bullied by Europeans and having to hide on the side of the road.[40]

In addition to colonial cruelty, symbols of colonial rule humiliated the Vietnamese. In a poem titled "Patriotism" that Châu wrote in 1910, he laments the French flag being flown in Vietnam:

> Now I sing a song of patriotism.
> What can I love more than my country?
> Dignified on all four sides of the mountains and rivers...
> For forty years the country has been lost, its power gone...
> The tricolor flag of Indochina,
> To look at it is humiliating, and to speak of it is painful!
> The country is humiliated, but the people are hurt first.[41]

In *The History of the Loss of Vietnam,* Châu described the "French policy of governing Vietnam" as fourfold: "instilling misery" (*làm cho khốn khổ*), "instilling ignorance" (*làm cho ngu dốt*), "instilling weakness" (*làm cho hèn yếu*), and "instilling blindness" (*làm cho đui mù*) in the Vietnamese people.[42] He proceeded to list colonial cruelties such as French soldiers killing Vietnamese who refused to submit, stripping their bodies naked, hanging them on the city gates, throwing them into fire, and imposing many different kinds of unjust taxes. Before doing so, however, he felt the need to say to his readers: "What I am about to present next is something I have seen with my own eyes and heard with my own ears and is absolutely not a fabrication or exaggeration with intention of defaming the French."

As mentioned, writings on colonial violence and humiliation functioned to evoke a sense of collective indignation in the Vietnamese reader, in the hopes that it would be harnessed as a nation-building tool. These descriptions of colonial violence also served to level previous hierarchies among the Vietnamese (e.g., emperor, mandarin, subjects, peasants). Such distinctions meant little now that *all* the Vietnamese were being humiliated. These indignities cohered the nation, and descriptions of them functioned to implore all Vietnamese to realize that no matter their social status, "the Vietnamese" as a whole were under assault.

But Châu did not seek to induce *only* indignation in his readers. In his essay "The New Vietnam," Châu evoked positive, pleasurable emotions for productive ends, too. He asked his readers to imagine a future Vietnam, one so technologically modern and militarily powerful that France would ask *it* for protection.[43] This "new Vietnam" would be so economically advanced that Vietnamese goods would be synonymous with quality and would be sought after all over the globe. To achieve this new Vietnam, they must invite professors from Japan, Europe, and the United States to educate the Vietnamese, but once the modernization phase was complete, he wrote, "our country's talents will surpass theirs, so there will no longer be any need to invite foreigners to teach." By then, "we will become their teachers." In this new Vietnam, all Vietnamese citizens would love to travel and learn about new ideas. Imagine, he exhorted his readers, a new Vietnam with railroads thousands of miles long and buildings "ten thousand meters high." When the Vietnamese are in buildings that high, he said, they will be able to see "the stars, the moon, and the sea outside the window" as if they were "in the palm of your hand." This future will be "infinitely sweet" but to taste it, they must endure the bitterness of struggle today. "We vow to taste that bitterness, knowing that there will be endless joy in the future. Today's hardship is the basis for that joy." Here, Châu exhorted readers to take upon themselves national responsibility. They were certainly capable, he thought, of enduring it because their ancestors were themselves great conquerors and nation-builders.[44] Châu's use of emotions—indignation (at their subjugation), pleasure (in imagining a better future), and pride (in their past conquests)—was harnessed to construct national dignity.

The Two Phans

Phan Bội Châu may have been a well-respected pioneer of Vietnamese nationalism, but he also had his critics, the most well known of whom was another celebrated nationalist and friend: Phan Chu Trinh. The two met for the first time in 1904. In 1906, they traveled together to Japan where they visited schools in Tokyo and admired the country's political and economic conditions.[45] Trinh, moved by the experience, remarked to Châu:

> The level of their people is so high, and the level of our people is so low! How could we not become slaves? That some students now can enter Japanese schools has been your great achievement. . . . Please stay on in Tokyo to take a quiet rest and devote yourself to writing, not to making appeals for combat against the French. You should only call for "popular rights and popular enlightenment." Once popular rights have been achieved, then we can think about other things.[46]

Indeed, while in Japan, Châu played a significant role in getting over three hundred Vietnamese from all three regions to study in Tokyo. Partially funded by wealthy landowners who also sent their own children to Japan, the "Go East" movement provided an opportunity for Vietnamese to engage in

Japanese, Western, and Chinese ideas while abroad, and to debate with each other how to build a new Vietnam. "Every day," when he and Trinh

> talked about the affairs of our country, [Trinh] singled out for bitter reproach the wicked conduct of the monarchs, the enemies of the people. He ground his teeth when talking about the ruler of the day, who was bringing calamity to the country and disaster to the people; as much as to say that if the system of monarchical autocracy were not abolished, simply restoring the country's independence would bring no happiness.[47]

Trinh wanted to overthrow the monarchy and promote popular rights. Only then, he thought, could the Vietnamese be ready for independence. Châu disagreed, arguing that "first the foreign enemy should be driven out, and after our nation's independence was restored we could talk about other things. My plan was to make use of the monarchy, which [Trinh] opposed absolutely."[48] Trinh argued that he was able to refute Châu's belief in violence "several times, so [Châu] did not like to be in my company."[49] Trinh applauded the fact that Châu was "a person of unparalleled will, power, energy, patience, and audacity," but lamented that:

> once [Châu] believes in something, he adheres to it and never abandons it. Even thunder cannot change his mind.... Regrettably, besides having shallow knowledge, he is ignorant of world trends and is fond of using intrigues, fooling himself and the people.... Being thoroughly conservative, he adamantly refuses to read New Books.[50]

Despite their differences, the two men's efforts would inspire a movement in Vietnam to read "new books."

The Vietnamese Enlightenment and the Tonkin Free School

Although they did not themselves create it, Phan Bội Châu and Phan Chu Trinh inspired the founding of the Tonkin Free School (Đông Kinh Nghĩa Thục) in northern Vietnam in 1907. Modeled on non-fee-paying private schools in Japan that the Vietnamese saw when they were there, the Tonkin Free School aimed to modernize the Vietnamese people by exposing them to new ideas from the West through Chinese translations of Japanese translations, and by promoting the national identity. Hundreds enrolled. Trinh was the school's most popular speaker.[51] Students sang songs about colonial exploitation and read texts praising Cần Vương resistors.[52] It was a site of nascent nationalism. At the school, David Marr writes, "a functionary in the local bureau of cartography made a big map of Vietnam of white cloth, which he used at the school to describe the S shape of the country.... People are said to have come from other neighborhoods just to view that map—probably the first time that they had seen their country rendered schematically.[53]

The school's unofficial manifesto was an essay titled "A New Method to Study Civilization," written by anonymous authors.[54] This significant work captured the intellectual mood of the early twentieth century, expressing the Social Darwinist assumptions of the time. Vietnam was conquered because it was weak and France was strong, it argued. The manifesto blamed conservative elites for weakening Vietnam, thereby preventing it from progress and making it vulnerable to foreign conquest. They called for the Vietnamese to dignify themselves through their own efforts by breaking free from constraining traditions. It emphasized rationality as a means to progress. In short, the manifesto called for a Vietnamese Enlightenment.

The anonymous authors distinguished between what they called "uncivilized," "semi-civilized," and "civilized" peoples, arguing that many Vietnamese were uncivilized and that they should aim for "civilization," a "beautiful word, idea." "Civilized people," they argued, are openminded, capable, and quick while the less civilized are narrowminded, incapable, and slow. To become civilized, they should promote competition—among themselves and with other nations. And competition requires, and rewards, openmindedness. Their logic was simple: competition requires thinking and the use of reason; more competition generates more thinking; and more thinking requires a mind that is open to new ideas because new ideas provide more conceptual tools with which to think. Europe's road to modernity sounds similar. "The plurality of small states in Europe," Alan Macfarlane argues, "almost incessantly at war and when not at war, in fierce cultural and social competition, was the ideal context for rapid productive and ideological evolution."[55] Competition and therefore enlightenment, these Vietnamese authors argued, would rectify the shame of Vietnam's lack of creative thinkers: "Do we have anyone ... a person in the caliber of a Watt or Edison?" Enlightenment would also help rid Vietnam of the influence of conservative elites who had been "covering up new ideas" and were therefore promoting a "slave mentality." This would be an uphill battle, the authors noted, considering that the Vietnamese were still narrowminded, stuck in tradition, and engaged in irrational practices like geomancy and magic.

The authors of the manifesto criticized Vietnamese civilization for being "static" while favorably presenting the West as "dynamic." Western readers following Edward Said may balk at this essentialist trope about the "East" and "West," which Western imperialists have historically used to justify European colonial conquest,[56] but these Vietnamese used the trope to push their compatriots to self-strengthen by opening their minds to new ideas. Vietnam was static, they argued, because the Vietnamese studied only Chinese books, whereas Europeans studied diverse subjects that suited their talents. The Vietnamese valued obedience and silence, whereas Europeans asserted their opinions and debated to make decisions. The Vietnamese had no concept of their nation, whereas Europeans valued their nation as a kind of "family." The Vietnamese were timid about traveling, whereas Europeans loved to travel. The Vietnamese ought to develop their country's economy and industries by rewarding those who invented new products or learned new methods of production. Vietnam ought to have intellectual property rights like the Europeans did. And the Vietnamese should publish newspapers to "open peoples' minds with new ideas." In all these respects, the authors argued, the Vietnamese had to emulate Europeans if they were to strengthen Vietnam for independence, and they could do it because "our yellow people have nothing less than the white men."

We see a budding liberalism in the authors' argument that Vietnamese teachers should "not constrain students' ideas." Encouraging freedom of thought was especially necessary, they argued, because the old examination system had atrophied their minds by merely testing their memorization capability of a limited set of Chinese texts. These authors and others at the Tonkin Free School mocked the old degree system. When some students talked about studying old texts to prepare for the civil service exams, a man who had earned his *cử nhân* (an equivalent of a bachelor's degree) replied, "you still want that useless *cử nhân*? Here, give me a penny, and you can have mine!"[57]

The Tonkin Free School regarded modernization not merely as an intellectual exercise but as something to physically embody as well. Texts from the school emphasized the importance of good hygiene and exercise.[58] The school urged young Vietnamese men to cut their hair short, which symbolized modernity. Seeing a young man who cut his hair, Phan Chu Trinh praised him, "Nice cut indeed! Nice look indeed!"[59]

There was even a song about haircutting as a kind of self-strengthening anthem:

> Left hand holds comb,
> Right hand holds scissors.
> Clip! Clip!
> Straight, straight, be careful!
> Get rid of cowardliness,
> Get rid of foolishness,
> To be wise, to be strong.
> You are living with Mr. French![60]

Some conservative scholar-gentry were skeptical or resistant against this new fashion of cutting hair, arguing that it turned people into "*dân trọc*" ("bare heads"), a pun also meaning "impure, corrupt people." For them, cutting one's hair was unfilial. However, in a reinterpretive move that cast modernization as supportive of, rather than a departure from, tradition, reformers at the school retorted that hair-cutting actually expressed filial piety more than not cutting hair because it kept away lice, infection, and illness.[61]

As mentioned, Social Darwinism, adopted from Chinese reformers, was the prevailing theory at the time and so it was promulgated at the school. This is unsurprising considering that Herbert Spencer—who coined the term *Social Darwinism* by applying Darwin's idea of natural selection to society and politics—was "the single most famous European intellectual in the closing decades of the nineteenth century."[62] It became self-evident to many Vietnamese that their country was conquered because it was weak—morally, intellectually, economically, socially, and politically—and France was strong. There were racial overtones to this mind-set as well, reflecting late-nineteenth-century and early-twentieth-century European trends of classifying human beings into modern racial categories and developing racial theories in physical anthropology. At the Tonkin Free School, songs and poems expressed this racism. Here is one poem from the school:

> The Races are clearly divided
> According to the Continents.
> The Yellow and the White

> Are strong and wise.
> The Black, the Red and the Blue
> Are stupid and silly.
> All of life is a struggle.
> The wise race will survive,
> The stupid will perish."[63]

Young Vietnamese refused to accept that their race was naturally inferior to the white race and on a par with other nonwhite races, and so they wrote poems that shamed compatriots into self-improvement:

> Why is the roof of [the Western] universe the broad lands and skies,
> While we cower and confine ourselves to a cranny in our house?
> Why can they jump straight, leap far,
> While we shrink back and cling to each other?
> Why do they rule the world,
> While we bow our heads as slaves?
> Take up a mirror, look at yourself,
> Where on that face is there something to brag about?
> Taking steps outward, we fear what others think,
> We intend to try, but where's the ability?
> Our spirit is as cold as ash,
> Our body has the form of a shriveled tree.
> We have eyes, but they seem to be blind.
> Who will bring the lamp to light the path?
> Our ears might as well not be there.
> Who will bring the bell and ring it noisily?[64]

By the 1930s, Social Darwinism would largely be supplanted by Marxism–Leninism, which provided a very different explanation for why Vietnam was conquered, as we will see in the chapter on Hồ Chí Minh (Chapter 6). Yet, Social Darwinist thinking, particularly its emphasis on self-strengthening, would never disappear entirely but would take on new forms and be infused into the Communist revolutionary program. The Vietnamese students at the Tonkin Free School admired their conquerors in addition to resenting them and wondered why they were conquered. The school was a space where they could engage these issues openly.

One major effort advanced by the school was to advocate and develop the new writing system: *quốc ngữ* (literally "national language script"). For centuries, the Vietnamese had been speaking Chinese and Vietnamese and writing in classical Chinese and *chữ nôm* (Chinese characters that expressed Vietnamese words). However, Portuguese missionaries in the sixteenth century introduced *quốc ngữ*, a Romanized, alphabetic Vietnamese script. The script was further developed in the seventeenth century by the French Jesuit Alexandre de Rhodes who produced the *Dictionarium Annamiticum Lusitanum et Latinum*, a Vietnamese–Portuguese–Latin dictionary, printed in Rome in 1651, using his spelling system. The writing system went largely dormant until French colonizers came to Vietnam in the mid- to late nineteenth century. At the Tonkin Free School, intellectuals believed that increasing literacy through *quốc ngữ* was central to the modernization and Vietnamese Enlightenment project. Roman characters were easier to learn than Chinese characters, they believed, and cheaper to print than *chữ nôm*. A text at the Tonkin Free School argued: "*Quốc ngữ* is the saving spirit in our country, we must take it out among our people. Books from other countries, books from China, each word, each meaning must be translated clearly."[65]

The French colonial regime also promoted *quốc ngữ*, with some French officials seeing Chinese script as antithetical to "progress."[66] Vietnamese nationalists, reformers, conservatives, and anticolonial activists of the early twentieth century, like Phan Chu Trinh, Nguyễn An Ninh, Phạm Quỳnh, Hồ Chí Minh, and many others would also exhort the Vietnamese to abandon the Chinese *nôm* script and adopt Latin script for their own anticolonial and nation-building projects. Phan Chu Trinh argued that "Vietnam cannot be saved without getting rid of Chinese characters."[67] Phạm Quỳnh, the subject of Chapter 5, more explicitly placed language and the development of *quốc ngữ* on his nation-building agenda, but he also pushed the Vietnamese to learn languages beyond their own: "Today, our country must study *quốc ngữ* and French letters, but neither must Chinese writing be abandoned."[68] Perhaps the most systematic argument for why *quốc ngữ* was essential to Vietnam's spiritual, material, and political strength was laid out when an intellectual named Phan Văn Trường delivered a speech in 1925 titled "Educational efforts among the Annamite people" to the Cochinchina Society for the Promotion of Study. In this speech, he argued that education, language, and writing systems were all interdependent, and if all three were done properly, Vietnam would have a much better chance to strengthen itself to be free from French rule.[69]

Colonial Reform?

Just a year after the Tonkin Free School opened, it was shut down by French colonial authorities. In early 1908, a revolt broke out against demands for forced, unpaid labor, and the French discovered a plot to poison French troops. In response, the French sentenced thirteen Vietnamese plotters to death and many more to prison terms. They saw the school as part of a larger anticolonial plot, and so they arrested most of the school's leadership, brought them to trial, and sent them to the prison island of Poulo Condor (Côn Đảo).[70] Phan Chu Trinh was sent there where he remained until 1911 when the French sent him to France.

After Phan Bội Châu was evicted from Japan in early 1909, he went to South China to build relationships with Chinese revolutionaries. And when the Chinese republican revolution broke out in 1911, Châu finally converted to republicanism.[71] In the following years, he was arrested, at the request of the French governor-general Albert Sarraut, and spent three years in prison from 1914 to 1917. Upon Châu's release, he wrote an essay titled "A Letter of Opinion on Franco-Vietnamese Harmony," which called for friendlier relations between the French and Vietnamese. His change in tone was probably a result of feeling discouraged by his old plans for violent revolt and of the fact that Sarraut was a progressive who promised liberal reforms. Sarraut tried to make a deal with Châu: publicly renounce his revolutionary intentions and he would receive a high post at court. Châu refused when he eventually realized that Sarraut had no real intention of following through on his reforms. In the postwar period, Châu faded from the nationalist movement spotlight. In 1920, he displayed interest in socialism after reading a book in Japanese about Soviet Russia, and he even thought of sending Vietnamese students to Moscow to study. But he never followed through.[72]

In 1925, Phan Bội Châu was arrested by the French and put on trial on charges of incitement to murder and supplying a weapon that was used to kill a Vietnamese governor and two French majors.[73] At his trial, he gave his last famous speech in which he summarized his life's patriotic efforts. If he and the Vietnamese

> had a few hundred thousand sailors, a few tens of thousands of soldiers, armed with many guns, warships and airplanes, then I would submit my declaration of war and righteously resist the colonial government. But I am merely a student. My pockets are empty of money. I have no

weapons. I cannot engage in armed resistance. Thus I have only sought to use culture—which is to say that I tried to mobilize the people to demand political reforms. . . . My work is merely to use my tongue and my pen, and my goal is political reform; the movement I lead is simple and righteous. If I have done wrong, my only sins are the following: 1. Even though no one else opposed the colonial government, I alone resisted, because I wanted the country to be independent; 2. The country formerly had an absolute monarchy, but I wanted it to become a republic; 3. The colonial state banned people from travelling overseas for study, but I fled and recruited students to go to foreign countries to study; 4. I tried to mobilize and awaken the people of the country of the south, to demand that the government institute political reforms to complete its mandate to bring enlightenment [to the country].[74]

Contrary to Phan Chu Trinh's characterization of Phan Bội Châu as stubborn, here we see Châu's willingness to change and adapt. He had tried to resist colonialism with violence, then with culture, first with royalist ideology, then with republicanism. The speech evoked a public outcry of sympathy for him. Aware that Châu was a hero to young Vietnamese, the French avoided making a martyr out of him by sending him to Huế to live in solitude rather than imprisonment. To this day, Trinh is often considered the "reformist" counterpart to the "revolutionary" Phan Bội Châu, but this binary is misleading. It may be true that Phan Bội Châu was less interested in ideas than Phan Chu Trinh and more interested in using violence, but the labels obscure the fact that Châu very much wanted the Vietnamese to reform themselves through education. The labels also obscure how very revolutionary Trinh's ideas were for the Vietnamese at the time.

3
Phan Chu Trinh's Democratic Confucianism

With the entire view of Vietnam in Google maps, type in "Phan Chu Trinh" and you will see schools named after him speckled throughout the country. Zoom in a little closer to any part of the country or any city, search his name again, and watch as countless more "Phan Chu Trinh" schools and streets emerge. With his name immortalized in public spaces throughout the north, center, and south, Phan Chu Trinh (1872–1926) clearly remains an important figure and a source of national pride to this day. A patriot, pioneering nationalist, and Vietnam's first proponent of democracy, he proffered the first sustained argument in Vietnam of how Western and Vietnamese ideas ought to be synthesized to construct a nation to be proud of.

On a November evening in 1925, months before his death, Phan Chu Trinh delivered a speech to compatriots in Saigon in which he exhorted them to "break the tyrannical chain and bring in liberal ideas from Europe as a medicine for our people."[1] The Vietnamese were sick, Trinh believed, owing to the abandonment of Confucianism caused by tyrannical monarchs and corrupt mandarins. This explained Vietnam's vulnerability to French conquest and colonization. For Trinh, Confucianism needed to be revived if Vietnam was ever to gain the necessary dignity and strength for independence.

The Vietnamese shamefully lacked, and sorely needed, a sense of Confucian morality, he argued. Strangely, he maintained that the proper "medicine" that could help the Vietnamese fill this gap was to adopt European liberalism, *tư tưởng tự do* (literally, "thoughts of freedom"), along with the form of government he thought was based in liberalism: democracy.

This claim is puzzling when we consider that contemporary political theorists, at least in the West, typically agree that liberalism and Confucianism are opposed. Liberals often associate Confucianism with rigid social hierarchy, strict gender roles, and a conservative emphasis on correct behavior.[2] Some scholars have tried to counter this negative stereotype by showing that Confucianism and liberalism can at least learn from each other,[3] but they would still agree with the claim that any "attempt to construe Confucianism as a liberal philosophy is an illusion."[4]

There are indeed significant differences between the two philosophies. The Western liberal tradition, though diverse, generally views society as emerging from independent, rational, self-interested, rights-bearing individuals who consent to a social contract. In contrast, the Confucian tradition views society not as a contract but as a large family in which rulers and leaders ought to care for their subjects like parents ought to care for their children. Unlike the liberal tradition, the Confucian tradition places no emphasis on the division between public and private spheres, and it has no concept of individual rights. As Chenyang Li states, "For Confucius the concept of individual rights has no place in morality. Morality is a matter of fulfilling one's proper role in society, as a son, a brother, a father, and, further, as a ruler or subject under the ruler."[5] If liberalism and Confucianism are so opposed, then how is Trinh able to argue not only that the two are not only *not* opposed, but also that adopting liberalism will allow the Vietnamese to achieve national dignity by becoming better Confucians?

Perhaps less puzzling is Trinh's assumption that democracy is derived from liberalism. Indeed, for those in the liberal West, "democracy" typically means "liberal democracy." However, some political theorists have argued that illiberal ideas such as Confucianism are also compatible with democracy, and that if East Asians are to democratize, Confucianism rather than liberalism will best buttress their democracy. For example, Daniel Bell argues that the usual justifications for democracy in the West, such as that "democracy is the best form of government for autonomous individuals," will "not capture the hearts and minds of East Asians still impregnated with Confucian values and habits."[6] For East Asians, a more effective argument for democracy would be that democratic governments "protect and facilitate communitarian ways of life." Liberal-democratic institutions, Sungmoon Kim argues, "are not socially relevant in East Asian societies."[7] Democracy in such societies would be most politically effective and culturally relevant only "if it were rooted in and operates on the 'Confucian habits and mores' with which East Asians are still deeply saturated, sometimes without their awareness—in other words, if democracy were a Confucian democracy."[8]

Thus, we see virtually unanimous agreement on three claims in scholarly literature that explores the relationship between Confucianism, liberalism, and democracy: democracy does not belong exclusively to Western liberalism; Confucianism and liberal democracy are opposed; and Confucianism buttresses democracy for East Asians better than liberalism. Yet, little to no attention has been given to Vietnam in these scholarly discussions, which have hitherto focused on contexts in China, Taiwan, South Korea, and Singapore.

This chapter introduces Phan Chu Trinh to these discussions. For Trinh, Confucianism was synonymous with national dignity, and he shamed the Vietnamese for failing to understand and practice genuine Confucianism. And one way he shamed them was to show them that Europeans—with their democracy and liberalism—were better Confucians than the Vietnamese. He made a peculiar set of claims that democracy was part of liberalism, that both democracy and liberalism were properly Western, and, if they were adopted by the Vietnamese, democracy and liberalism would not only revive long-lost Confucianism in Vietnam but also allow Confucianism to find its fullest expression. Unlike the contemporary scholars mentioned above, Trinh was unaware, or intentionally downplayed the idea, that a widely held interpretation of liberalism "takes the individual as the ultimate and irreducible unit of society and explains the latter in terms of it,"[9] while lauding other aspects of liberalism and Western civilization. This misreading may not be surprising, as he was among the first Vietnamese to seriously engage Western ideas. At the end of his life, he said that "about Western things, I am highly ignorant."[10] Yet his perceptions of the West and reworking of its ideas for his own ends provide fruitful terrain not only for political theorists but also for those of us who are curious about ideas from foreign countries and cultures. Ultimately, Phan Chu Trinh shows us that we should not always fear cultural appropriation or creative misunderstandings of other traditions of political thought.[11] Misunderstandings themselves may be invigorating and instructive. They can even inspire members of a nation to assert their national dignity.

We will see how Phan Chu Trinh "engaged comparative political theory" by comparing different traditions to find the best ideas for the Vietnamese. He thought Confucianism was the goal because a lack of genuine Confucianism created Vietnam's vulnerability to foreign domination. To strengthen Vietnam, Confucian morality—which had been eroded by a history of monarchic and autocratic rule in Vietnam—must be restored. The "medicine" that would revive Confucianism, he maintained, was European ethics and liberal democracy. He was able to make this argument because he misinterpreted liberalism, centering it on popular rights rather than on individual rights, and he argued that the importation of Western-style liberalism and democracy would improve familial, social, and national ethics in Vietnam, thus remedying the "autocratic disease of Vietnam." Confucius emphasized that rulers ought to be virtuous, so Trinh had no problem with monarchy in principle, but Confucius was silent on what form of government the people should adopt if the monarch is oppressive. In Trinh's view, democracy picks up where Confucianism leaves off.

A Brief Biography: Phan Chu Trinh

Phan Chu Trinh was born in 1872 in Quảng Nam Province. When he was fifteen, his father was killed, allegedly by members of the anticolonial Cần Vương movement who suspected Trinh's father was working against them. As a child, Trinh trained in martial arts and later the literary arts under the guidance of Confucian scholars. Among his favorite Chinese classics were the *Analects* and *The Mencius*. In 1900 and 1901, Trinh received degrees for passing mandarinate exams, and, in 1903, he went to Huế to serve as secretary in the Ministry of Rites. Around this time, he, like Phan Bội Châu, read about European thinkers through Chinese translations. According to one account, Trinh "was so fascinated by them that he would even neglect eating and sleeping."[12] Trinh retired from his secretarial position in 1904, believing, as he put it, that one "cannot just sit in a corner and talk about things in the outside world, especially in the present state of affairs, when the winds of change are blowing in all directions," so one must "go and look to see what is happening."[13]

Trinh arrived in Japan in 1906 where he met Phan Bội Châu. Both were inspired by the Japanese reforms they saw. Soon after returning to Vietnam, Trinh wrote a letter to Governor-General Paul Beau in 1907, scolding the colonial regime for giving too much freedom to corrupt Vietnamese mandarins and demanding changes in colonial policy. Trinh also inspired the creation of the Tonkin Free School in Hanoi which opened that year. Believing the Vietnamese should engage in commercial entrepreneurship to modernize Vietnam, he created a company to process cinnamon trees. In 1907 he lived in Quảng Nam, but he would go to Hanoi to give speeches on the progress of the Tonkin Free School.

As mentioned, the school was shut down in 1908 by colonial authorities. Phan Chu Trinh, Phan Bội Châu, and others were accused of anticolonial activity and were arrested. Trinh was transported to Huế and then sentenced to life imprisonment on Côn Đảo Island. However, with the intervention of a Frenchman named Ernest Babut, Trinh's sentence was reduced. After some time of imprisonment on the island, Trinh was released in 1910, again with the help of Babut. In 1911, Trinh went to Paris where he stayed for fourteen years, made a living retouching photographs, and stayed in touch with other Vietnamese expatriates, such as Hồ Chí Minh. While there, Trinh also wrote works decrying Vietnam's feudal system and translated into Vietnamese Liang Qichao's Chinese translation of the Japanese political novel *Kajin no kigu* (*Strange Encounters with Beautiful Women*), a story of a Japanese man who learns about Western ideas of rights and revolution through chance encounters with Western women. In 1914, Trinh was briefly jailed in Paris on suspicion that he sought Germany's help in fighting France. As mentioned in the Introduction, in 1919, Trinh, Hồ Chí Minh, and a Vietnamese lawyer named Phan Văn Trường put together the *Revendications du Peuple Annamite,* a list of demands for liberal rights (not independence), and submitted them to delegates of the Paris Peace Conference. Trinh returned to Vietnam in 1925 and delivered two significant speeches in November—"Morality and Ethics in the Orient and in the Occident" and "Monarchy and Democracy." He died a few months later, in 1926.[14]

Democratic Confucianism

Phan Chu Trinh's theory for achieving national dignity is best described as what I call "democratic Confucianism," a term rarely seen in literature on the controversial relationship between Confucianism and democracy. By "democratic Confucianism," I mean the proposal that democratic ideas and institutions should be used to achieve the goal of Confucianism, which is viewed as ultimately more important than democracy. For proponents of "democratic Confucianism," democracy is not an ideal or good to be realized globally, but rather a means to a more important end. To the Western reader, "democratic Confucianism" would sound odd, since "Confucianism" would likely not be their goal.

Some contemporary scholars trained in the West do appear to promote democratic Confucianism, even though they may not use the term. Daniel Bell, in his later work, argues that the political ideal in China is a system that upholds Confucian ideals. Therefore, for China, he proposes a political meritocracy with democratic lower levels of government and meritocratic upper levels where members are selected by competitive examination. Bell calls this the "China model" or a "vertical democratic meritocracy," in which the Confucian ideal of "meritocracy" is the noun and "democracy" is the adjective.[15] Another proponent of "democratic Confucianism" is Joseph Chan, for whom the main problem facing contemporary Confucian societies is the gap between the Confucian ideal and political reality.[16] There is nothing wrong with the ideal, he argues; the puzzle is how to achieve it. Chan shows that democratic institutions, based on Confucian conceptions of the good rather than liberal conceptions of the right, can be used to achieve Confucian ideals. Stephen Angle's notion of "Progressive Confucianism" also promotes a kind of democratic Confucianism, as it is based in part on the aim of realizing "fundamental human virtues that Confucians have valued since ancient times."[17] To realize these virtues, Angle argues for a separation of morality and politics that also emphasizes the ability of democratic institutions to help people achieve such moral virtues.

Despite these approaches, far more prevalent in the literature is the reversed term: "Confucian democracy," used by theorists to describe how Confucian ideas might be used in order to achieve democracy (which is considered more important than Confucianism). Confucian democracy is more palatable to Westerners who ultimately cherish democracy and want to see if a foreign idea like Confucianism can help reinvigorate it.

Confucian Democracy

Exemplary of Confucian democracy is Brooke Ackerly's essay "Is Liberalism the Only Way toward Democracy? Confucianism and Democracy."[18] Ackerly answers the question in the negative. For her, liberalism—specifically, its core value of respect for the "autonomous rights-bearing individual"—is often presumed to be the ideology that supports democracy. She shows that this need not be the case and aims to rectify the fact that so far, the "unexamined characterization of Confucianism as hierarchical and static prematurely closes off its consideration as a source of insight for theories about democracy." Confucianism, which downplays individualism and instead can emphasize healthy "nonexploitative hierarchy," also has democratic potential. A Confucian democracy, according to Ackerly, would be a democratic form of government guided by three democratic-friendly ideas that she finds in Confucian texts or within debates internal to the Confucian tradition: (1) the expectation that all people are capable of *ren*—"the overarching virtue of being a perfected human being"—and are therefore potentially virtuous contributors to political life, (2) an expectation that institutions function to develop virtue, and (3) "a practice of social and political criticism that, when guided by *ren* and the cultivation of human nature, is democratic." Ackerly aspires to examine ways toward the destination and goal of democracy that do not rely on the liberal way. Similarly, Sor-hoon Tan declares in her book *Confucian Democracy* that "We shall look for a Confucian route to democracy."[19]

Mutual Enhancement

In between "democratic Confucianism" and "Confucian democracy" is what I would call "mutual enhancement," an ideal in which Confucianism strengthens democracy and vice versa. For scholars who promote this ideal, there is a dialectical interaction between Confucianism and democracy in which they enhance each other. This makes it difficult to tell if the scholar privileges one over the other. For example, Sungmoon Kim is motivated by the conviction that democracy is needed in East Asia and that East Asians should not try to surpass liberal democracy but should instead "attempt to Confucianize partially liberal and democratic regimes that currently exist."[20] In this view, Confucianism is supplemental rather than instrumental to democracy. Although Sor-hoon Tan promotes what she calls "Confucian democracy," a closer reading shows that she favors a dialectical relation between Confucianism and democracy. She argues that the ideas of the pragmatist philosopher John Dewey can help make democracy more Confucian and Confucianism more democratic. Pragmatists have much in common with Confucians, she argues, because both have relational conceptions of selfhood and want to temper liberal talk of individual liberty by acknowledging that individuals require community to flourish. Here, Deweyan pragmatism is a practice that mutually enhances Confucianism and democracy. Similarly, the philosopher Shaun O'Dwyer argues that, in contemporary East Asia, democratic reform of community life, such as the enhancement of participation and deliberation within associations, coupled with instituting civil freedoms, will "help preserve the continuity of Confucian moral traditions cherished in a number of East Asian societies."[21] Also promoting mutual enhancement are David Hall and Roger Ames who argue that a promising task at hand for political theorists and Confucians "is to try to demonstrate to the more traditional of the Confucians that Dewey's philosophy holds the greatest promise for achieving a Confucian democracy in which central Confucian values are retained still largely intact."[22] The goal for these scholars is democratic practice that embodies Confucian values.

The point of drawing these (often fuzzy) distinctions between ways of relating Confucianism to democracy is to show where Phan Chu Trinh would be positioned in these debates. It is also to remind us that scholars' personal commitments matter. Those who have been more immersed in a democratic tradition would be more inclined to promote Confucian democracy. Conversely, East Asians immersed in a Confucian tradition may want to introduce democracy to their Confucian societies to enhance Confucianism, and, for Trinh, Vietnam without Confucian morality would be a country without dignity. It is intuitive that someone would privilege elements of their native identity and use foreign ideas as instruments to preserve or enhance those elements, a task that may seem especially urgent if one feels that their native identity is losing stability and thinks that some foreign idea can be used to stabilize it. Most of the contemporary scholars mentioned above have been well immersed in both Western and Chinese philosophical traditions, but overlooked in their discussions are views of individuals further back in history when the encounter between East and West was fresher. Trinh's writings provide a window into Vietnamese Confucian society as it was just beginning to learn about what the West called democracy.

Phan Chu Trinh identified as a Confucian scholar, spent most of his life studying Confucian classics, and eventually received the highest mandarin degree. At age thirty-nine, he went to France, and, upon his return to Vietnam fourteen years later in 1925, he attempted to introduce and advocate to his fellow Vietnamese the "democracy" that he had learned while abroad.

Unlike his predecessors who had studied Confucian thought exclusively, Trinh had the advantage of being well trained in Confucianism and well aware of the modernizing world outside of Vietnam, more so than Phan Bội Châu. Unlike other Vietnamese, Trinh was able to speak at length about the American Revolution.[23] Inspired by Japan's Meiji restoration and military defeat of the Russians in 1905, Trinh went to Japan with Phan Bội Châu to learn about Japan's modernization process. And like Châu, Trinh was also exposed to Liang Qichao's reformist writings. But unlike Châu, Trinh was less of a critic of French colonialism and a harsher critic of Vietnamese rulers, whom he saw as oppressive and responsible for Vietnam's vulnerability to foreign conquest. In 1922, Trinh accused the Vietnamese emperor

Khải Định of seven offenses, including recklessly promoting autocratic monarchy, doling out unfair rewards and punishments, and extravagance. This letter, together with his letter to Paul Beau in 1907 that criticized the French for allowing corrupt Vietnamese mandarins to freely exercise power, can be read as Trinh's justifications for revolution, not merely replacing one leadership with another, but a radical change in the minds and habits of the Vietnamese people.

He left behind a large body of writing,[24] but I will pay special attention to two speeches that he gave upon his return from France, shortly before his death: "Morality and Ethics in the Orient and the Occident" and "Monarchy and Democracy." They are notable for their "comparative political theorizing" and were delivered in the same week in November 1925 to a Vietnamese audience at the Vietnam Society House in Saigon.

The Goal: Confucianism

Why is Confucianism the fullest expression of national dignity for Trinh? To answer this question, we must begin with why he thought Vietnam was conquered by the French: "our country was weak; therefore, it fell into the hands of the French."[25] Such weakness, he argued, was a result of Vietnam's lack of a solid moral foundation upon which everything else depends. From time immemorial, "regardless of the country, regardless of the race," a nation had to "rely on morality as its foundation. For a nation that has fallen down, in order to rise up and avoid being trampled over by others, it is all the more necessary to have a moral foundation even firmer than that of wealthier and stronger nations." Where does this morality come from? For Trinh, morality is "the fine values and superior qualities that [a nation's] ancestors, over thousands of years, have left, so that they will earn respect from other nations."[26]

Trinh clarified the idea that a moral foundation has two components: morality, which never changes, and ethics, which can, does, and ought to change. Morality, and, above all, Confucian morality, is universally applicable. In contrast, ethics are the expression in lived practice of this true morality and do vary from place to place and from time to time.

For Trinh, morality was simply a list of qualities or virtues that any human being, anywhere and at any time, ought to have to be good. "To be a human being, one is expected to have *nhân* (humaneness), *nghĩa* (righteousness), *lễ* (propriety), *trí* (wisdom), *tín* (trustworthiness), *cần* (diligence), and *kiệm* (frugality)." A person with these qualities "behaves according to the way of human beings" (*đạo làm người*). These ideals never change, and they apply everywhere and always, regardless of culture. Morality "remains the same, old or new, Oriental or Occidental," and everyone "must preserve it in order to be a complete person." Even though "political systems might be different— be it democratic, monarchic, or communist—the truth of morality cannot be ignored" and can never be changed.[27] Trinh viewed Confucius and his students, such as Mencius, as Vietnam's ancestors who gave the Vietnamese this moral foundation. The morality that Confucius taught was true, eternal, and universal, he thought, not because Confucius taught it but because it was true, eternal, and universal. Any other nation's truly wise ancestors could recognize and teach this morality, just as Confucius did. Thus, when Trinh refers to Confucian morality, he means true, universal morality. The characteristics of this morality "have been crystallized over an extended period of time; like jade, they will not wear off when polished, and like tempered iron, they will not break into pieces when struck."[28]

Whereas morality refers to the qualities that a human being ought to have, ethics is how an individual ought to behave toward others. Unlike morality, ethics (*luân lý*) is variable and could, "depending on the time and the place," change.[29] It is like "a robe that can be changed according to the size of the person." In contrast, "morality is like rice, water, and nutrition—all are needed for everyone, one cannot change one's morality even if one wishes to, and if it is changeable, it is false morality." Through ethics, one exercises one's morality and one's morality is cultivated through ethics. Referring to the famous Five Relationships of Confucianism, Trinh said that Asians had five spheres of ethical relationships. Relations were between (1) ruler and subject, (2) father and son, (3) husband and wife, (4) older brother and younger brother, and (5) friend and friend.[30] Social, economic, and political power came from fulfilling these ethical duties. Vietnam was weak, Trinh thought, because it lacked the proper Confucian moral foundation, and as a result Vietnamese people were unable to fulfill their proper ethical duties in those five spheres.[31]

For Trinh, as for other Confucian-minded thinkers such as Phạm Quỳnh and Hồ Chi Minh, there existed an essential continuum between individual morality and public morality. For Trinh, morality (of the individual) and ethics (between individuals) were inextricably linked. This is evident in the famous "Confucian formula" which Trinh cited as key to his political theory and his prescription for the Vietnamese.[32] Morality (humaneness, righteousness, propriety, wisdom, trustworthiness, diligence, and frugality) is a set of goals that make up the self-cultivation component of the famous Confucian formula found in the book of Great Learning. This formula positions eight verb–noun compounds in cause-and-effect sequence: (1) investigate things, (2) deepen knowledge, (3) make thoughts sincere, (4) rectify the heart-mind, (5) cultivate the self, (6) regulate the family, (7) govern the state, and (8) pacify the world.[33] The first four take place within the individual self, so the entire formula can be simply restated as "cultivate the self, regulate one's family, govern one's country, and pacify the world [*thiên hạ*]."[34] While morality takes place within the self, three of the five Asian ethics (father-son, husband–wife, brothers) take place within the family. The "govern the state" component would be satisfied by proper ethics between ruler and subject. Ethics between friends refers to the "pacify the world" component. For Confucius, as for Trinh, the most worthwhile activity one could engage in was to improve one's own character because doing so would automatically improve one's family, community, nation, and the world.

A Lack of Confucianism Attributable to Autocracy

The Vietnamese people's shameful ignorance of authentic Confucianism, Trinh argued, was attributable to centuries of despotic rulers and corrupt mandarins who deliberately misinterpreted Confucianism to justify their despotism.[35] Trinh provided a lengthy critique of Vietnam's monarchical tradition and put forth three main criticisms.

First, Vietnamese kings promoted a corrupted version of Confucianism. They tricked their subjects into thinking that it was Confucian to obey the ruler submissively and blindly. To restrict and control the people, the kings "selected from among the sayings of Confucius and Mencius ... passages that would carry ambiguous meanings that they could take advantage of in making laws." The kings "called themselves 'Son of Heaven,' but at the same time regarded themselves as human beings" and in an intimate relationship with the people "as sovereign, father, husband." Thus, "when the ignorant people in the villages hear that the king is related to them, they respect him without realizing that if he is infuriated he might have their three families/generations murdered. Father, teacher, and husband, in contrast, do benefit us and would not do such evil things."[36] Absolute monarchy in East Asia and Vietnam was maintained by teaching that "from the moment one comes into the world, one must perform one's duty as a subject toward the king." Unfortunately, many were unaware that "the relationship between the king and his subjects should be a mutual one." The kings thought only of how to suppress the people's intellect in order to keep the throne exclusively for their descendants, and they did not know that "if the people were ignorant, the country remained weak." Expressing a Social Darwinistic assumption that it is natural for the strong to conquer the weak, Trinh reasoned that, because "the people were so ignorant and weak that they could not rise in rebellion, it is understandable that foreigners would encroach upon their countries."[37] Autocrats also used corrupt interpretations of Confucianism to violate people's rights. The court made laws against "having talents but not allowing the king to use them."[38] Political speech was prohibited because kings feared people would stage a revolution if they were well versed in politics. Swords were confiscated, melted, and recast into monuments to prevent the people from using them to rise up against the king. Fearing that scholars would challenge them, kings had them buried alive.[39] Trinh lamented that "the people's life and death are decided unilaterally by the king, and we have no rights to defend ourselves. We should ask ourselves why this is so!"[40] In promoting a corrupt version of Confucianism, the autocrats prevented the people from learning the actual teachings of Vietnam's ancient ancestors: Confucius and Mencius. In China and Vietnam, during the previous two thousand years of dynasties, "there has been a decline in the practice of Confucianism," each ruler being less Confucian than the ruler before him.

> When one looks into the history of monarchy in East Asia, one finds that ... since the Qin dynasty [221–206 BC], though the East Asian countries would consider they were practicing Confucianism, in actuality there was nothing Confucian in the policy practiced. Only one or two things remained in the family traditions, and, apart from that, the absolute monarchs relied on Confucianism only to exert pressure upon their peoples.[41]

Even scholars "have allowed the morality that had been left by our ancient ancestors to drain away down-stream."[42]

Second, habituation to autocracy prevented the Vietnamese from having a sense of nationalism or patriotism. "The people understand if someone tells them, 'You must be loyal to this person, or respect that person,' but if anyone mentions the name of Vietnam and tells them, 'That is your motherland, you must love it,' they do not understand because they cannot touch it with their hands or see it with their eyes."[43]

The Vietnamese will gossip if a family has children who are addicted to gambling, "but if one talks about the 'loss of national independence,' not a single soul cares." Trinh declared, the "poison of autocracy has fatally injured the patriotism of our people."[44]

Trinh's third criticism of the monarchical tradition was that Vietnamese kings were to blame for the Vietnamese people's ignorance of world trends. Trinh remarked that Vietnam, China, Korea, and Japan belonged to the same culture. All had monarchies, all venerated Confucius, and all faced European encroachment. However, he wondered, how was it that only Japan "was able to abandon the Old Learning and adopt the New Learning, and within a mere forty years it was able to join the ranks of the world powers?" The answer was that, unlike Vietnam, Japan did not "close their eyes to condemn the new civilization (the European one) as barbaric" but rather learned from the West during the Meiji period. "The world trends are unrelenting. Those who go with them are sailing with the wind, and those who go against them are pushed away and trampled on like grass."[45] Unlike Japanese rulers, Vietnamese rulers, such as King Tự Đức who reigned from 1848 to 1883 refused to learn from the West.[46]

In short, autocrats cherry-picked parts of Confucianism to justify their despotic rule, preventing the people from learning Confucianism's genuine teachings. As a result, the Vietnamese had a poor conception of the proper ethics between ruler and subject, of rights, of patriotism, and of the outside, modernizing world. It was no surprise, then, that Vietnam fell to French rule. In order to regain strength for self-determination and a more respectable status in the world, Vietnam had to restore its proper Confucian moral foundation. But how was this to be done?

Western Ethics

Trinh turns to Europe for solutions. It would be instructive, he said, to "compare our ethics to European ethics." He observed that in contrast to Asians who had five ethical spheres, Europeans had three: familial (proper behavior toward one's family members), national (proper attitude or love toward the idea of one's nation, i.e., patriotism), and social (proper behavior toward all human beings, first to those of one's nation and, eventually, to everyone outside one's nation).[47] Trinh viewed these ethics as stages of development, beginning with the familial and advancing toward the goal of cosmopolitan social ethics. Yet, in Vietnam, the ethics of the Five Relationships had "disintegrated so badly only because the autocratic monarchs have practiced incorrectly the teachings of Confucius and Mencius."[48] Since the Vietnamese performed poorly in their five ethical spheres, they should simply switch to Europe's tripartite model: family, nation, and social. Doing so would not be difficult because three of the five Asian ethics already took place within the family.

Regarding familial ethics, Trinh explained that Europe and Vietnam had historically started with similar family ethics, with the exception that in Europe, "according to the law, at age twenty-one, when boys and girls become adults, they can leave their parents and live on their own, assuming duties and responsibilities according to national ethics, and the burden for the family thus becomes lighter." Thus, Trinh saw Europe as having advanced beyond familial ethics. Europe's "social movements" and "numerous thinkers" had "begun contemplating means to break the stuffy family bondage so that everyone in the same country would be equal, i.e., both the rich and the poor are to be educated and to live in the same way, putting an end to the enormous gap that exists between them today."[49] In contrast, as Europe began moving beyond familial ethics to think about the nation, Vietnam still struggled to advance even in family ethics. Vietnamese children in both wealthy and poor families had "to breathe the authoritative atmosphere in their family." When these children grew up and entered society, how could they "possibly escape that submissive and servile mentality?"[50] Simultaneously, Trinh lamented, children did not fulfill their duties of filial piety. Furthermore, he argued against a hierarchical relationship between husband and wife if both did not respectively exercise proper conduct, arguing instead that it should be the case that "where the wife is wiser than her husband, she will be in charge of that family."[51]

Regarding national ethics (by which Trinh means patriotic feelings toward the idea of one's country), Europeans had developed patriotic consciousness whereas the Vietnamese had not. In Europe, "national ethics have been developing since the sixteenth century, when monarchism was still in vogue. Europe's monarchs at the time were like ours, that is, recklessly autocratic." European kings suppressed their people "by colluding with the church, saying that the king was God, acting on behalf of God . . . that the king was not the same human race as the people, and therefore the people must respect him."[52] Yet "numerous philosophers clarified the distinction between the nature of a monarch and a nation." As a result, people in Europe came "to understand the importance of a nation and to place less emphasis on the family."[53] In contrast, Vietnamese "national ethics from the ancient times to the present day have been confined, parochially, to the two words 'king' and 'subjects.' There has been nothing about 'people' and 'country,' because the people have not been allowed to discuss national affairs." Contemporary Vietnamese "do not realize what popular rights [dân quyền] are, what love for their country is, and what their duties are."[54]

Lastly, with regard to the social (global) sphere, Trinh argued that in Europe, the age of nationalism began to give way to social ethics after the international wars, particularly World War I, when the "great politicians, great philosophers, and great educators all came to realize that the age of nationalism has passed and cannot be maintained, giving way to the age of social ethics."[55] Trinh viewed Europeans as more developed in their social ethics—if not yet toward all human beings, then at least in the way they treated their fellow nationals—because "they compete only within the law. They help one another with respect to public justice and maintain a sense of respect for each other's interest." In contrast, "it is a shame that our people, though having to work throughout their lives, cannot look after their basic personal needs and prepare for their old age, let alone think of society or humanity. How could we not respect the Europeans if they are so superior to us?"[56] Contemporary Vietnamese "are much more ignorant about social ethics than about national ethics." Instead, the ancestors of the Vietnamese "understood that we have to help one another. For this reason, there are sayings, such as 'It is impossible to break chopsticks when they are in a bunch.' . . . Our people lost their sense of solidarity and public interest because, in the past three or four hundred years, the students in our country craved power and official position."[57] In short, Trinh believed that Europe was further along in the evolutionary stages of ethical development and closer to the goal of cosmopolitan social ethics than the Vietnamese.

Trinh's infatuation with Europe was clear. But rather than call for an abandonment of Vietnamese culture and wholesale adoption of European attitudes, he assured the Vietnamese that adopting European ethics would in no way contradict or impinge on Confucian morality but rather would preserve and revive it. After all, while morality stays the same, ethics can and should change to preserve morality. He considered it a shame that "so-called Confucian scholars" in Vietnam had refused to learn from Western ethics.

They "do not know anything about Confucianism. Yet every time they open their mouths, they use Confucianism to attack modern civilization—a civilization that they do not comprehend even a tiny bit." With the exception of a few youths, there "is no one who cares to compare the Western learning with our 'Old Learning' and to single out what is good and what is bad so that our people may judge and select the path for their future."[58] The proper task for the Vietnamese, then, was to learn from the West in order to develop and strengthen their ethics in these three spheres and thereby restore (or bring in) proper Confucian morality.

Liberalism and Democracy as a Means to Confucianism

Trinh essentialized Western civilization, viewing it as fairly monolithic and unified by the predominant ideology of liberalism, a word he translated to Vietnamese as *tư tưởng tự do*—"ideology of freedom" or "the thought of freedom." For Trinh, liberalism was the mental attitude that naturally buttresses democracy, which he understood as a form of government and political institutions that institutionalized and maintained the spirit of liberalism. Trinh did not decouple liberalism and democracy. For him, together, they constituted a sort of "Western ethics package." Let us start with how he understood liberalism and how he thought it would improve national and social ethics.

Liberalism

In the West, liberalism is a widely contested concept. Yet, in general, its core seems to be a concern for safeguarding individual liberty (even though exemplary liberals have been deeply critical of received individualism). Trinh misinterpreted or had a naive interpretation of liberalism because he ignored individual rights. Trinh's liberalism was centered on "popular rights" (*dân quyền*), a term that he invoked often and in opposition to the autocratic rule to which Vietnam had been historically subject. Popular rights included the right of freedom of expression, particularly the freedom to publicly criticize anything without being punished. Trinh was convinced that Europeans valued popular rights because while he was in France he saw numerous public statues of philosophers who had argued in favor of popular rights and against tyranny. Writing to the emperor of Vietnam, Trinh said of Paris that along its long boulevards and in the large public squares, you must have seen the bronze statues commemorating the philosophers and the heroes who risked their lives in defense of freedom. You must have seen the pillar that reaches up into the clouds; atop it stands a Goddess who holds in her hand the flame of Liberty radiating in four directions. That is the Goddess of Liberty, who illuminates the whole world and has no mercy for any tyrant monarch on earth.[59]

Liberalism was a product of European history, he believed, particularly of rebellions against tyrannical monarchies led by philosophers who argued for popular rights. By following this European tradition of respecting popular rights, the Vietnamese could have a better sense of "the people" and the fact that their country belonged to them. Naturally, this would improve their patriotism, or national ethics.

Trinh drew attention to the public far more than to the individual. Terms such as "public rights," "public interests," and "public expression" appear often in his writings, in contrast to terms like "individual rights," "individual interests," and "individual expression." Trinh's liberalism was a mix of what we might think of as classical liberal concern for rights without the emphasis on individualism, and classical republican concern for civic duties. Yet, while downplaying individual rights, he did not totally dismiss them: "In France, if a person of power or the government uses authority to repress an individual or an association, people make an appeal, resist, or stage a demonstration until a fair solution is reached. Why are people in France able to do so? It is because they have associations and a public awareness that promote their common interest."[60]

Even here, the collective was held up as being more important than the individual. Even the defense of individual rights, he argued, required collective action and "associations," which are permissible and promoted in a liberal society. By collectively defending individual rights and promoting the common good, the Vietnamese, Trinh believed, would improve their social ethics.

It should come as no surprise that Trinh downplayed individualism. While theorists today may view sovereignty of the autonomous rights-bearing individual as a core tenet of liberalism, for Trinh such an idea would have seemed outlandish and out of character for Europeans and their "superior" morals and ethics. David Marr shows that the term for "individual" (*cá nhân*) did not enter the Vietnamese vocabulary until the first decades of the twentieth century. Initially, "Individuals were often compared with cells in the body, each one having a legitimate role in sustaining and enhancing the vitality of the organism, but meaningless and incapable of surviving on their own." The introduction of the term *individualism* brought awareness of the danger of "individuals acting in a selfish, short-sighted manner, which could jeopardize the larger order of things. Such persons were said to be witting or unwitting perpetrators of 'individualism' (*cá nhân chủ nghĩa*)."[61] Trinh may have been unable to conceive of an ideology that would uphold the individual as sovereign, and he would have viewed individualism as a defect rather than as constitutive of the logic, of liberalism. Trinh described aspects of Western ideas that he did not favor as mere deviations that could be remedied by "true" principles of Western ideas. "In European society there are drawbacks, such as excessive freedom between men and women, high rates of divorce, enormous gaps between the rich and poor, and people who are unemployed or overworked," and "fanatical nationalism" has made wars "incessant." However, "the Europeans have remedies to deal with them." That is to say, "there are philosophers and educators who devote themselves to remedying the evil effects, so that their morality and ethics will be uplifted day by day. In contrast, in our country only the good is shown and the bad is hidden, and thus the situation increasingly grows worse."[62] Liberalism is ultimately better even if it includes individualism because it respects open discussion of the "good and bad," which can then remedy the bad of liberalism and restore communal values. In a society where critique is permitted, "there are those in the upper and middle classes who have social concerns, and great politicians, philosophers, writers, and educators make appeals, write books and plays, publish newspapers, and deliver speeches to denounce social evils."[63] Only this kind of society, not a society that hides "the bad," such as Vietnam, could foster proper morality. In borrowing from the West, the Vietnamese ought to be "purposeful and selective, only adopting that which is worthy of adoption."[64]

Trinh seemed to think that respect for popular rights in Europe had the effect of fostering admirable behaviors with respect to the common good. The morality and ethics of Europeans "are high because they have been influenced by liberal ideas ever since the Greco-Roman age." The European "public sentiment is very enthusiastic, and their character is highly dignified."[65] They "help one another with respect to public justice and maintain a sense of respect for each other's interest."[66] Trinh thought that these behaviors were a direct result of liberalism in which the people were valued and exercised their rights. If the Vietnamese were to also respect popular rights, they, too, could improve in familial, national, and social ethics.

Trinh made several moves to implement liberalism in Vietnam. Recognizing the importance of free-market competition, he advocated the creation of "commercial societies" and stressed the importance of competition within constraints of the law, as well as creating his own company, as mentioned. Recognizing the importance of discussion and deliberation as part of a proper liberal democratic society, he advocated for the creation of a Public Speech Society and a New Learning Society. Moreover, he even wanted the Vietnamese to adopt European fashion, and so he advocated Short-Hair and Short-Clothes Societies, as we saw in Chapter 2. As early as 1906, Vinh Sinh writes, "Phan Chu Trinh began to promote short haircuts; for a man to have his hair cut short became a powerful symbolic act that represented courage, modernization, and eventually even rebellion."[67]

Democracy

When it was no longer possible for European kings to mislead their people with the deception that they had a divine right to rule, "popular rights became stronger in Europe and the monarch's power was diminished."[68] Thus, Trinh argued, all nations in Europe except those "whose people are still ignorant" now practiced democracy. To Europeans, "there is no need to explain 'why it is called democracy'; but in our country, this is not so." Not only did the Vietnamese "dare not think about the question of 'whether or not we should have a king,' but they act as if a person raising this question would be struck by a thunderbolt, buried under rocks." When the Vietnamese could understand democracy, they would "realize that those who have been called kings and officials since the olden days are, after all, just their representatives acting on their behalf, and if they cannot do a good job, there is nothing wrong with chasing them away."[69]

Trinh advocated democracy as a form of government necessary to institutionalize liberalism and, to do so, provided his fellow Vietnamese with a brief on the history of democracy in the "West," covering ancient Greece, Roman law, and the British system. He went on to describe the political structure of France, explaining that the lower house, the National Assembly, was the most important and had legislative power, that the senate was elected by an electoral college, and that the president was elected by the two houses.

He mentioned that the president took an oath in front of the two houses in which he promised not to betray the people and not to be partisan, and that if he was, he would be subject to impeachment. Trinh explained France's system of checks and balances, and said that there were two political parties in the National Assembly. And "if the leftwing party holds the majority of the seats, the rightwing party will be the watchdog and be ready to level criticism; therefore, it is difficult to do anything outrageous." Moreover, government officers "possess only administrative power," while "judicial power is entrusted to judges who have the required training and qualifications," and these powers "are separate, not controlled by a single person."[70]

Whereas a monarchy is a "government by men," a democracy is "government by laws," and the laws are created by representatives of the people.

> [The] rights and duties of everyone in the country are well described by the laws—like a road on which lines have been drawn clearly, so that you can walk freely, there is nothing to stop you, and you may go on as far as you like, as long as you do not violate the rights of others. This is because before the laws, everyone is equal, regardless of whether they are officials or common people.

In short, he said,

> we see that democracy is far better than monarchy. To govern a country solely on the basis of the personal opinions of one individual or of an imperial court is to treat the people of that country as if they were a herd of goats—their prosperity and joy, or their poverty and misery, are entirely in the hands of the herder. In contrast, in a democracy the people create their own constitution and select officials, who will act according to the will of the people to look after their nation's business.[71]

Adopting the rule of law and a constitution would improve social ethics by improving a sense of "public justice."

The Way to National Dignity (Confucianism)

If implemented in Vietnam, Trinh believed, liberalism and democracy would allow Confucianism to find its fullest expression because true morality—the unchanging qualities of a good human being—did not shape the ethical spheres in the Confucian formula (self, family, nation, world) in a strictly forward causal chain. In other words, while morality shaped the ethical spheres, the ethical spheres could also cultivate morality. The individual related to the family, nation, and world at any moment, and was in turn affected by them just as they could affect them. Thus, a change in ethics would produce a change in morality. By adopting liberalism and democracy, social and national ethics would improve, thus improving Confucian—or true—morality. An improvement in social ethics (proper behavior toward those inside and outside the nation) while national ethics (patriotic feelings toward one's country) were still weak would also improve national ethics because half of social ethics is about improving relations with fellow nationals, which would improve patriotism. Therefore, if the Vietnamese learned to love and respect their fellow Vietnamese (half of social ethics), they would simultaneously improve their patriotism (national ethics) and family ethics. Trinh hoped that eventually, once they were equal in power with other nations, the Vietnamese could move beyond nationalism and practice social ethics that would be inclusive of all individuals, inside and outside the nation, emulating Europeans who "not only worry about those in their own country, but also about all others in the world as well."[72]

According to Trinh, democracy was guaranteed to exercise the people's moral self-cultivation, in contrast to the gamble one could take with monarchs who might or might not promote self-cultivation. "Self-cultivation is such a crucial aspect, one which Confucius insisted the people and the monarch must practice." If a country "were fortunate enough to have a wise and heroic king ... that country would enjoy prosperity and peace as long as that king was on the throne." However, if the king were a despot, the country would collapse.[73] Monarchy was a form of government that "may be liberal or harsh, depending entirely on the joyful or sorrowful, loving or unloving, mood of the king, and it is a form of government in which the laws exist for nothing."[74] Evidently, Trinh did not detest monarchy in principle, but only in cases of bad monarchs. Unfortunately, Trinh thought, Confucius was silent as to what the people should do if the monarch was uncultivated, corrupt, and oppressive. Thus, Trinh viewed democracy as picking up where Confucianism had left off. Democracy could aid one's moral self-cultivation. This was apparent when he attempted to reconcile what may initially appear to have been conflicting claims about equality made by Confucius and Mencius. Trinh wrote that Confucius was "very fair [bình đẳng], teaching that the monarch and the people are both equally important [quân dân tịnh trọng]." In contrast, Mencius famously wrote that "the people are the most important element; the spirits of the land and grain are the next; the ruler is insignificant." Trinh argued that Mencius made this prodemocratic claim only in response to the rampant authoritarianism of rulers during Mencius's time. "Because the kings of the vassal states had become so autocratic, [Mencius] advocated democracy." Therefore, for both Mencius and Trinh, it was out of situational necessity and in the context of autocracy that they offered democracy as a solution. For them, democracy was not inherently desirable or good, but rather an appropriate response that would counter autocracy and alleviate the spiritual malaise of a people who had lived under an autocracy. Trinh wrote, "It is regrettable that [Confucius] did not say what the people should do if the monarch does not love the people." Mencius also "does not mention what the people should do if they question the monarch."[75] It is in this uncomfortable silence from Confucius and Mencius, in which they have no advice to give, that Trinh picks up where they left off, reasoning that democracy is the way to bring back (or to bring in) long lost (or never understood) Confucian values.

Given that ethics (which include forms of governance) can change, "at present, in order to meet the trends of the time, we should replace autocratic monarchism with democracy."[76] Trinh's "engaged comparative political theorizing" is most apparent here:

> Montesquieu said, 'The people who live under an autocratic monarch have no ideas about morality and see their social status as their chief source of pride. It is only under democracy that there is genuine morality.' For this reason, in order to have a genuine democracy in our country, we should take this opportunity to break the tyrannical chain and bring in liberal ideas [tư tưởng tự do] from Europe as a medicine for our people.[77]

Addressing potential concerns that adopting European values would displace traditional Confucian values, Trinh argued that European democracy would enhance, not contradict, the teachings of Confucius. "If your Majesty opened the Five Classics and the Four Books, could you find an indication that autocracy should be promoted? If your position is above everyone, you should place your heart below everyone—that is the essence of Confucianism." For Trinh, democracy was "a wonderfully efficacious remedy against the autocratic disease" of Vietnam. "To bring in European civilization is to bring back the teachings of Confucius and Mencius... The introduction of European civilization would not cause any harm, but it will help to enhance the teachings of Confucius and Mencius."[78] Therefore, learning about democracy was actually a way of resurrecting the long forgotten (or perhaps never understood) ideals of Confucius and Mencius. For Trinh, liberalism and democracy were the means to the goal of Confucianism and thus national dignity.

To liberalize and democratize, Trinh believed that Vietnam needed inspiring philosophers of its own. European thinkers such as Voltaire, Rousseau, and Montesquieu, he wrote, had "contributed to unshackling their compatriots from autocratic rule" and only "Confucius, Mencius, Mozi, Laozi, or Zhuangzi... in ancient China might be compared" to those European men. However, from the Qin dynasty [221–206 BC] on, "there has been no person of such caliber" in Vietnam. Phan Chu Trinh asked his compatriots: "In our country at present, is there a person who may be called moral philosopher? Even since the time of the Lê dynasty, is there anyone who may be called a moral philosopher like those I mentioned?"[79]

Conclusion: How to Learn from Others

In sum, Trinh argued that (1) liberalism and democracy were part of a package of properly Western ethics, (2) liberalism and democracy were compatible with Confucianism, and (3) the Vietnamese should adopt liberal democracy to fulfill Confucian ideals. Trinh's conclusion was based on his limited understanding and idealization of liberalism that downplayed individualism. However, his (mis)reading and romanticization of the West was a creative and productive one from which we can gain valuable lessons.

Trinh offered a method of learning from foreign "others." This method is different from the one that, according to Leigh Jenco, was used by Chinese reformers grappling with how to learn from the West in the latter half of the nineteenth century. Soon after Protestant missionaries introduced Western knowledge into China, Chinese reformers argued that all Western knowledge, particularly of scientific and technological methods but also of "parliamentary political systems," actually had Chinese origins.[80] The "China-origins" thesis may sound outlandish, and much of it did turn out to be false. However, Jenco argues that the thesis was more than just rhetoric or cultural chauvinism. It performed the political work of authorizing the use of Western knowledge in a way that made the use of Western methods an innovation of, rather than a departure from, traditional Chinese learning. By characterizing Western knowledge as actually having Chinese origins, the Chinese Yangwu reformers were able to be truly disciplined by Western knowledge rather than merely incorporate it as a variant of what they were already doing. Jenco took from this the lesson that political theorists in the West ought to do something like a China-origins thesis if we are to see foreign, particularly marginalized non-Western, thinkers and knowledge as "think partners who help us to develop a practice we see ourselves as sharing with them," that is, to be truly disciplined by them, rather than viewing them simply as "targets of representative inclusion." The ironic outcome, Jenco says, is that by "integrating Western science into an existing frame of discourse, these reformers end up displacing the repositories of (largely Confucian) past thought that once lent definition to *ru* [scholarly] learning, and contribute instead to the evolving criteria of a very different kind of knowledge."[81]

Instructive comparisons may be made with Phan Chu Trinh's "Western learning." Unlike the Chinese reformers, Trinh never claimed that Western liberal democracy actually had "Vietnamese origins." He was explicit that those ideas came from the West and he adopted them in a way that still disciplined his learning. Trinh's glowing admiration for the West is in contrast to Chinese reformers such as Feng Guifen who viewed the West as "barbarian."[82] To be sure, Vietnamese rulers, such as the emperor Tự Đức, also saw Europeans as barbaric, which Trinh criticized. However, whereas a "China-origins" claim may have been appropriate in China whose "Qing empire matched the British one in its 'universalistic pretensions,'"[83] Trinh never made any kind of "Vietnam-origins" claim, which may have had to do with Vietnam's relative lack of pride and power as compared to China and Vietnamese awareness of their peripheral status. Trinh and many other Vietnamese intellectuals at the time lamented Vietnam's shameful lack of great thinkers as compared to China and Europe. They were well aware of Vietnam's long history of borrowing from Chinese culture and of the difficulty of locating anything "originally" Vietnamese.

The approach Jenco advocates "may not involve manufacturing 'Western' origins for that disciplinary continuity," but "it would require us to act as if such knowledge is part of our own heritage."[84] However, we may also act like Trinh who had few qualms about viewing foreign ideas as foreign, and therefore we do not need to act as if such knowledge is part of our own heritage in order for us to learn from it. If we are not so prideful, we may just as easily act as if such knowledge comes from the outside and still be disciplined by it.

Moreover, it may be useful to idealize and romanticize foreign knowledge, explaining its perceived drawbacks as defects rather than as an inherent part of the logic of foreign knowledge. This does not require "orientalist fetishization" but simply a disposition that assumes the Other might be doing some things better than we are. By doing this, we may be able to import the creative distortion to our own context in order to revive our own faltering tradition. This kind of cultural appropriation need not harm anyone, even when done by the more powerful who perceive their own traditional ideas to be inadequate.

Just as Trinh explores how liberalism and democracy might improve his cherished Confucian tradition and therefore bring national dignity to Vietnam, we (citizens in Western liberal democracies) might consider conducting more scholarship of the "Confucian democracy" kind mentioned at the beginning of this chapter, in which Confucianism is examined for ideas that might improve our cherished liberal and democratic traditions. For example, Brooke Ackerly does this when she suggests that we in the West might find useful the Confucian expectation that all people are capable *ren,* a virtue perhaps best translated as "care." If we design our institutions to help develop this virtue, perhaps a healthier kind of democracy—and even liberalism—can flourish. This does not require attempts to make Confucianism (or any other "foreign" idea) compatible with liberalism (or any other of "our" ideas). It would just require that we assume that foreign ideas can be valuable to us and that they may educate, inform, and perhaps even fix what needs fixing in our own traditions.

Trinh died from natural causes a few months after his final two speeches. His funeral in 1926 saw an unprecedented surge of people—reportedly 100,000—into the streets of Saigon.[85] It was, for the Vietnamese, the closest they ever had to a truly national funeral. He never saw his project of reviving Confucianism through liberalism and democracy realized, a project that by the 1930s, was displaced by Marxism–Leninism. Nevertheless, he had introduced a powerful new political vocabulary—democracy, liberalism, constitution, separation of powers—to the mental universe of the Vietnamese. Bui Ngoc Son has argued that "the Democratic Republic of Vietnam in 1945 and the subsequent enactment of the first written constitution in 1946 are the denouement" of movements led by Trinh.[86] Today, it remains an open question as to whether the countless street signs that adorn his name evoke his memory or his exhortation to liberalize and democratize Vietnam.

Phan Chu Trinh's relationship with Phan Bội Châu was, in Trinh's words, at first "one of friendship. At the end, it was one of enmity."[87] But this is evidently not how Châu saw it. In March of 1927, on the first anniversary of Trinh's death, Châu reflected on their relationship:

> Alas! Would he be willing to forgive me? When I sent him off from Hong Kong, on his return to Vietnam from Japan, he held my hand and told me his last feelings. "From the nineteenth century onward, the countries in the world have competed against one another more fiercely than ever. The fate of a country must be left in the hands of a large number of people. I have not seen any country survive in which the people's rights were lost. How can you uphold monarchism at this moment?" When he said that, I did not have a reply for him. Today more than twenty years have passed, and the more I think about what he said, the more I feel he is right. I know that what I considered or what I examined is nothing as compared to his thought! If he were still alive, we would ask him to lead us. Nowadays, those who worship him, those who love him—aren't they only watching his statue, or picking up sentences from his writings, and imagining that they are patriotic? We must know that [Trinh's] name will last forever because he had real principles and real spirit.[88]

We have seen how Trinh harnessed the national shame of lacking a Confucian moral foundation for productive ends, hoping to goad the Vietnamese into fulfilling their duty to become dignified and morally upright people. A generation later, a young man named Nguyễn An Ninh, nearly thirty years Phan Chu Trinh's junior, would also shame his own compatriots for Vietnam's lack of great thinkers. However, Ninh would propose channeling shame into something more radical than reviving Confucian morality through Western ideas. Whereas Trinh saw Confucian morality as key to national dignity, Ninh viewed Vietnamese reliance on Confucianism as a source of shame.

PART II
WHAT SHALL WE DO WITH TRADITION?

4
Nguyễn An Ninh's Tagorean Call

Today, Bến Thành Market is a large, lively, bustling area in the center of Hồ Chí Minh City (formerly Saigon). An important symbol of the city and a center of economic activity since the seventeenth century, the building was built in 1859 by French colonial powers and nowadays receives thousands of visitors each day. Exit through the doors on the west side of Bến Thành and you will arrive at the T-shaped intersection of Phan Chu Trinh Street and Nguyễn An Ninh Street, astir with motorbikes and street vendors, lined with shops selling jewelry, organized tours, and clothes.

There is some irony here. In the 1920s, the two men whose names now christen these streets shamed their own country for lacking "great" national figures. A century later, the Vietnamese consider them to be the "great" Vietnamese figures of the kind that these two men were exhorting their compatriots to become. And yet, they had very different visions of what it would mean to construct national dignity. For Trinh, Vietnam was mired in shame because its Confucian tradition was sick, and the solution was to revive it with the medicine of European ideas of democracy and liberalism. However, for Ninh, the true source of national shame was their reliance on foreign ideas in the first place and their inability to construct their own intellectual tradition.

Trinh and Ninh spent a significant amount of time in France. When Ninh traveled to France to study law, he met with Trinh, Hồ Chi Minh, and two other Vietnamese colleagues (Phan Văn Trường and Nguyễn Thế Truyền) at the apartment located at 6 Villa des Gobelins in Paris where they debated Western ideas that they had been soaking in and considered how the Vietnamese might use these ideas to assert their national dignity. Collectively, these men were nicknamed "the Five Dragons" (*les cinq dragons*).

Shortly after his initial return to Vietnam, on an October day in Saigon in 1923, twenty-three-year-old Ninh stood before a large crowd of fellow young Vietnamese and gave a fiery speech, delivered in French. He shamed his own country for its poor intellectual output compared to other nations: "At present, as India and Japan provide thinkers and artists whose talent or

The Architects of Dignity. Kevin D. Pham, Oxford University Press. © Oxford University Press 2024.
DOI: 10.1093/9780197770306.003.0005

genius radiates alongside the talents and geniuses of Europe, Annam is still only a child who does not even have the idea or the strength to strive towards a better destiny, towards true deliverance."[1] Nguyễn An Ninh wanted his countrymen to feel ashamed about Vietnam's past and present intellectual weakness, but his speech was supposed to motivate them to become "great men" rather than drive them to despair. Their task, he exhorted, was to muster a creative spirit to "guide the footsteps of the people and enlighten their path. We need artists, poets, painters, musicians, scientists to enrich our intellectual heritage."[2] In short, the Vietnamese needed to assert their self-respect. He explained the reason why he was speaking to them:

> to show today's youth how, above all things, it can only count on itself to rise to the level in which man, conscious of his own strength, begins to be conscious of his dignity. It is to show that the youth's hitherto disheartening struggle to obtain knowledge, to preserve his own pride and dignity, only continues to be met with unexpected and varied discouragement imposed by stronger forces. In the necessary process that the youth must endure to arrive at consciousness of itself, it will find that when it wants to assert itself, it will be met with talents proclaimed with trumpets, false gods raised amidst fictitious glory.[3]

In other words, Ninh said, it was up to the youth to work for their own sense of self-respect and self-worth. This should be their primary task, he argued, necessary to counter the shameful tendency of Vietnamese people to blindly follow others: the "populace, trusting appearances, turned away from noble and laboriously acquired talents." Rather than apply their own intellect rigorously to transform themselves, they had been lazily deferring to Confucian elites and following those who proclaimed wisdom but themselves only parroted Confucius without even understanding him. In Vietnam "more than anywhere else," Ninh argued, "proud and noble students have to climb a long ordeal. And what explains this? What is the cause of all this? It is ignorance. It is the thick and heavy ignorance of the masses." The task for the youth was to think, listen, and learn for themselves, not copy those who appeared to be intelligent.

This speech became one of the most influential in Vietnam at the time, and Ninh would soon become one of the most influential Vietnamese anticolonial intellectuals of French colonial Vietnam, embodying the attitudes and aspirations of an entire generation of Vietnamese youth coming of age during the height of French rule.[4] As the Vietnamese revolutionary-turned-scholar Trần Văn Giàu (1911–2010) put it, Nguyễn An Ninh "was revered by the people, our students, a lively, popular, heroic man, eloquent as he spoke at rallies and gatherings, sharp in the newspaper column, not afraid of the West... a man of the masses, a man of the people.... In the eyes and hearts of the people of Saigon... Nguyễn An Ninh is a revolutionary, deserving of recognition, honor by stone steles, bronze statues."[5]

In the generation before Ninh, Phan Bội Châu and Phan Chu Trinh were among the first Vietnamese to become acquainted with Western ideas from Chinese translations of Japanese translations. Neither knew how to read French well, and both would remain firmly Confucian in their moral and worldview. In contrast, Nguyễn An Ninh (1900–1945), three decades younger than Châu and Trinh, was fluent in French and read French texts in their original. Educated in the best French schools, Ninh and the intellectuals of his generation were more savvy about Western ideas and distanced themselves from traditional Confucianism. Yet, this loss of a sense of rootedness led them to a spiritual malaise that he and Phạm Quỳnh would seek to rectify.[6]

Whereas Trinh shamed the Vietnamese by describing their low morals and ethics in comparison to Europeans and exhorted them to return to a more authentic Confucian morality, Ninh used shame to motivate his compatriots to abandon the Confucian tradition and to construct a brand-new national identity, which he thought would be much more dignifying for the Vietnamese than relying on a tradition based on a foreign thinker. Phan Chu Trinh, in turning to Confucius to construct an authentic Vietnamese identity, resembled the humanists of the European Renaissance who set out to study Roman antiquity. But once the humanists believed they properly understood the past, "their impulse to copy it led them into pedantic academicism; and that in turn provoked a revolt against the past by writers like Bacon and Hobbes, who asserted that modern men ought to stand on their own feet and think for themselves."[7] Like Francis Bacon and Thomas Hobbes, Ninh asserted that modern Vietnamese ought to stand on their own feet and think for themselves.

Ninh was more explicit than Trinh in using shame. Shame can be debilitating, leading one to despair and self-abandonment. People who feel too much shame about their own country may want to flee to other countries rather than stay to improve their own country. Some analysts have argued that *pride*, not shame, is necessary to be productive. The American philosopher, Richard Rorty, argued that "national pride is to countries what self-respect is to individuals: a necessary precondition for improvement." In contrast, national shame, Rorty stated, could "make energetic and effective debate about national policy unlikely."[8]

Yet, as we have discussed, political theorists have overlooked the fact that the kind of national shame matters. If national shame refers to the shame a nation feels because of its reprehensible actions toward outside (weaker) groups—which is what most scholars mean by national shame—then national shame can be seen as an emotion that threatens to unravel the national identity. For Rorty, the new cultural left in the United States has been unfortunately mired in this kind of shame. They find pride in American citizenship to be an "endorsement of atrocities: the importation of African slaves, the slaughter of Native Americans, the rape of ancient forests, and the Vietnam War."[9] Scholars have long discussed how Germany might deal with its shameful actions toward Jews.[10] And in Israel, the "New Historians" have challenged traditional versions of Israeli history to bring attention to the harm Israel has inflicted on the Palestinians.[11] Others have written about the national shame of detaining refugees or incarcerating aboriginals.[12]

To be sure, it is equally intuitive that national shame can be based on something that has been done to the nation rather than by it. Koreans, and particularly Korean "comfort women" during the Asia–Pacific War (1937–1945),[13] the inhabitants of occupied Palestine,[14] and many others have experienced a sense of dishonor or humiliation stemming from being occupied by another power and subsequent atrocities. This kind of shame has been overlooked in political science in general.[15] Nguyễn An Ninh and the other Vietnamese thinkers examined in this book offer an account of national shame different from these, one arising not from bad acts toward others or from being humiliated by others, but from a sense of their own national inadequacy.

For Ninh, Vietnamese moral, cultural, and intellectual inadequacy was not an inherent condition, nor was the Vietnam nation condemned to be forever inferior. The problem was not metaphysical or biological, but deeply related to the historical processes that constituted Vietnam's situation: lingering Chinese cultural dependency and material hardship under French colonialism.[16] Fortunately, he thought, there was a way out and one leading to national dignity.

Nguyễn An Ninh's emancipatory account of national shame follows a logic. (1) A person may feel shame because they acknowledge that their national ancestors failed to create a robust cultural stock for their nation. (2) This shortcoming in cultural stock created a bad situation (e.g., it weakened the country, making it vulnerable to foreign conquest). (3) Given that the person had a sense of national identity (as evidenced by their use of "we" to refer to themselves and fellow nationals), they had a national responsibility to redeem national shame by engaging in creative self-remaking and constructing a new "culture" for the purpose of nation-building, so that their national identity could become worthy of pride.

It is well known that pride connects individuals to the achievements of others, some of whom might be dead. Consider statements of national pride such as "*we* made the desert bloom" or "*we* won the war" declared by people who were born long after their co-nationals made the desert bloom or won the war.[17] Pride can sustain the national identity over time. Similarly, shame can connect the individual to the shortcomings of others, some of whom might be dead. The difference is that while pride can help sustain the national identity over time, national shame can help motivate the *creation* of national identity from scratch.

In this chapter, we take three lessons from Ninh: (1) national identity can be based on national shame, not just pride; (2) national shame can refer to feelings of inadequacy as compared to other nations, and not just to the shame from harming outsiders; and (3) national responsibility can refer to the duty to assert the nation's dignity, and not solely for redressing harms done to others. In Ninh's case, national responsibility means the duty to creatively remake the self for the sake of nation-building and national self-determination.

A Brief Biography: Nguyễn An Ninh

Born in 1900 in Saigon, Nguyễn An Ninh was raised in a family engaged in anticolonial activity. His father translated Chinese historical novels and helped to manage a Vietnamese language newspaper that spread anticolonial ideas, and his uncle and aunt were active in anticolonial politics. His father had Ninh educated entirely in French language schools. After graduating from the lycée Chasseloup-Laubat in Saigon, Ninh worked for a newspaper and then went to Hanoi on a scholarship where he enrolled in the School of Medicine, after which he switched to the School of Law.

In 1920, Ninh asked to go to France. His father gave his permission, selling some land to fund his trip and, according to legend, asked Ninh to never forget his duty to his country. In France, Ninh attended the lycée of Bordeaux for a *baccalauréat* (because the Indochinese *baccalauréat* that Ninh had been awarded was not valid in France), after which he went to Paris where he enrolled in the Sorbonne to study law. In Paris, he joined Phan Chu Trinh, Hồ Chí Minh, and other Vietnamese expatriates who belonged to the *Groupe des Patriotes Annamites*. On his bookshelf could be found works by Nietzsche, Rousseau, Plato, Kant, and Tolstoy, as well as a photograph of Rabindranath Tagore.[18] After receiving his law degree, Ninh traveled to Belgium, Austria, Germany, and Italy and returned to Vietnam in 1922 to marry the daughter of a wealthy landowner. He soon went back to France to obtain a doctorate, but he lacked the necessary funds. Ninh therefore worked in France for newspapers as a proofreader and editor, and eventually, without enough money and upon his wife's request, returned to Vietnam in 1923.

Upon his return, he gave his now famous speech "Aspirations of Annamite Youth" in Saigon and created his newspaper, *La Cloche Fêlée*. He remarried in 1924 and returned to France in 1925 where he translated Rousseau's *Social Contract* into Vietnamese. In the company of Phan Chu Trinh, Ninh left France and returned to Vietnam in June 1925.

That year, Phan Bội Châu was on trial. Ninh said of Châu: "The only crime he can be accused of is to have loved his country too well." In March 1926, Ninh was himself arrested by colonial authorities for his anticolonial activity, imprisoned, and released in December of that year on the condition he give up politics. At the beginning of 1928, Ninh went to his village Mỹ Hòa in Saigon and became interested in religion, particularly the Cao Đài sect, a religion that professedly incorporates elements of Buddhism, Confucianism, Daoism, and Christianity. Ninh didn't join the Cao Đài, but he shaved his head, became vegetarian, and spoke constantly of Gandhi and Tagore.

Meanwhile, Ninh's followers formed a mutual aid organization called the Nguyễn An Ninh Secret Society, which became known to the French police in March 1928. It's unclear how involved Ninh himself was with the organization, but he was arrested again that year, served three years in prison, and was released in 1931. He would be arrested again in 1936, 1937, and for the last time in 1939, after which he was detained in Côn Đảo Prison (where Trinh was imprisoned a few decades earlier) until his death in 1943.[19]

Radicalism

By the time Nguyễn An Ninh was born in 1900, France had been extending its control over Vietnam for four decades. Many educated elites were now beginning to doubt the adequacy of Confucianism *as it had been practiced* as a social philosophy for Vietnam. The prevailing explanation for Vietnam's fall to France, as mentioned, was Social Darwinism. Its emphasis on struggle and competition negated the ideals of equilibrium and harmony long held by Confucian elites, but thinkers like Phan Chu Trinh, as we have seen, reframed Social Darwinism to argue that the Vietnamese had to struggle to achieve Confucian ideals to make their country stronger.

For Nguyễn An Ninh and other youth of his era, it indeed seemed that the fate of the country depended on what culture, ideas, and values it would adopt as its own. They would not have been fully convinced by the claim that "the West won the world not by the superiority of its ideas or values . . . but rather by its superiority in applying organized violence."[20] Many Vietnamese assumed that Western material superiority must have had something to do with their supposedly superior culture, ideas, and values. For many, the only way Asians could equal the West was to master Western ideas. They debated the merits of an eclectic range of political philosophies in order to find the ones most suitable for their goal of self-determination. Like Phan Bội Châu and Phan Chu Trinh, Ninh's generation was entranced by Giuseppe Mazzini's argument that education and activism must advance simultaneously,[21] by Montesquieu's notion of democracy as loving laws and one's country,[22] and by Abraham Lincoln's example of developing inner virtue.[23] In their stay in Japan, Vietnamese students studied Japanese, Chinese, and Western ideas. Equating independence with survival, patriotic literati, Hue Tam Ho Tai wrote, "believed that they were engaged in a desperate race against annihilation as a people and a culture."[24] This is why, as we have noted, schools such as the Tonkin Free School promoted debates about what and how to learn from the West, and what should be done to strengthen the Vietnamese people spiritually, intellectually, and culturally. The assumption was that doing so would bring greater material and political power. Part and parcel of this new educational movement was the imperative to construct a sense of national identity, which was then only incipient.

The question of how to construct a national identity where there was none was deeply related to the question of where the Vietnamese should get their moral guidance. By the 1920s, Social Darwinism's influence was diminishing and was being supplanted by the rising influence of "radicalism," a term Hue Tam Ho Tai used to describe a kind of iconoclasm and the marriage of the personal and political in response to colonialism.[25]

A primary reason for this growing "radicalism" was that young, educated Vietnamese were growing more alienated from the French and Vietnamese accommodationist elites. Natives held advisory roles but couldn't vote on budgets or quotes to pay for the corvee labor. Colonial authorities refused the native elite any real decision-making power. This young generation was increasingly politicized and nationalist. They were skeptical and resistant to French and Vietnamese authority, as well as to the authority of their fathers. They were attracted to anarchistic ideas. Those who traveled to China and Japan were more likely to encounter collectivist styles of anarchism, and those who went to France were more influenced by individualist strains of anarchism owing much to Friedrich Nietzsche. The most influential figure of this period was Nguyễn An Ninh. His writings in his newspaper *La Cloche Fêlée* urged young Vietnamese to engage in a mental struggle against themselves, their family, their environment, and the colonial system.

Unlike Social Darwinism, radicalism was influenced by anarchism and was preoccupied "not with survival and competition but with freedom and the relationship between the individual and society."[26] At this time, many young Vietnamese saw a "symmetry between the national struggle for independence from colonial rule and their own efforts to emancipate themselves from the oppressiveness of native social institutions and the deadweight of tradition."[27] In order to dignify their nation, young Vietnamese believed they first had to dignify their individual selves by breaking free from stifling tradition and family. Conservative Vietnamese elites would, of course, criticize them for this attitude, and so would French authorities. One day, the governor of Cochinchina, Maurice Cognacq, asked Nguyễn An Ninh to come to his office and gave him a warning, one that Ninh would try to defy: "There must not be intellectuals in this country. The country is too simple. If you want intellectuals, go to Moscow. Be assured that the seeds you are trying to sow will never bear fruit."[28]

After his time in France from 1920 to 1923 and upon receiving a law degree from the Sorbonne, Ninh returned to Vietnam and created, edited, and wrote for *La Cloche Fêlée*, which made its debut on December 10, 1923.[29] This newspaper is where we find most of Ninh's writings and speeches. It is full of exhortations to compatriots to fulfill their national duties, one of which was the "duty to translate this journal to our brothers who are interested in it and who do not read French. It is your duty to spread the ideas expressed in this journal around you. It is your duty to make the people aware of all the injustices, of all the dishonesties of which our race is a victim."[30]

For Vietnamese youth, Ninh was the archetypal patriot intellectual. However, his patriotism stemmed not from national pride, but from a passionate sense of responsibility rooted in national shame. The few historians who have written about Ninh have not framed him as being primarily motivated by national shame, so this chapter offers a new interpretation of Nguyễn An Ninh.[31]

Before we discuss how Ninh harnessed national shame, we should be clear that he was a firm anticolonialist, rejecting colonialism on the basis of equality and self-determination. His critiques of colonialism are found in the writings he addressed to French citizens in the metropole, informing them about their government's unjust actions in Indochina. He expressed his anticolonial commitments in three ways.

First, Ninh thought colonialism as a civilizing mission was unjust because no people is inherently inferior. Even if the colonizing nation hypothetically really was superior, he still would not have supported colonialism because he deplored mimicry and imitation and he believed that only internal, personal struggle gave meaning to anything. Yet Ninh thought that the French were not actually superior. France, he wrote, "which has granted freedom and rights of the citizenship" to Frenchmen who, "till yesterday, were still slaves, imposes slavery on a free people who already possessed a civilization at a time that the French were living in caves."[32] The Vietnamese people, once superior, were now subjugated by a colonial force and ideology that falsely proclaimed European superiority: "The European prestige is based neither on the moral nor the intellectual superiority of the Europeans over the Asians. It is based on the color of skin alone."[33] Moreover, this "European prestige" held that "a European, as idiotic as he can be, could be a boss over a Vietnamese, and the inverse is inadmissible." He continued: "It is the European prestige that kills justice in the courtrooms; that prevents the judges from giving the same sentence to a Frenchman and a Vietnamese indicted with the same offense."

Second, Ninh believed that the French civilizing mission was a sham from the beginning, providing mere justification for exploitation—"it was not to carry out a sentimental deed that France came to Indochina"—and that those Vietnamese who "have talked about France's humanitarian ideas, in order to humor the colonialists, are as naive as those Europeans who believe in the civilizing mission of Europe."[34] Referring to a recently published work titled

"The French Miracle in Asia," he asked: "What is this miracle? It is a miracle indeed to be able in a short time to bring a people with a low intellectual level down to deeper ignorance, and to bring a people with democratic ideas into complete servitude."[35] That Ninh believed the Vietnamese had "democratic ideas" prior to French colonialism is an interesting contrast to Phan Chu Trinh who believed the Vietnamese were ignorant of democracy and needed to democratize.

Those who officially represent France in Indochina, Ninh wrote, "can only speak of the construction of costly railroads, ruinous underwater cables, . . . in short, of the excessive exploitation of Indochina in both senses of the word." Ninh was also aware of the harm French colonialism was inflicting on the French themselves, quoting Rabindranath Tagore: "Those who take pleasure in dominating foreign races abdicate little by little their own liberty and their own humanity in favor of the mechanisms that are necessary to keep other peoples in servitude."

Lastly, Ninh was aware of and expressed outrage at a wide range of human rights abuses by the French. Such violations justified violent rebellion as a last resort: "there are cases when violence must be accepted for it represents the only recourse."[36] Death was preferable to slavery, he said. However, before combatting "violence with violence as in a bulls' fight, the Vietnamese youth of today, fully conscious of its responsibilities towards its own society, tries first to reconcile French interest with Vietnamese wishes. It tells the mother country—which is too far away from Indochina—the truth about what happens in this colony." Thus, he addressed the French people in the metropole, appealing to their purported sense of right by citing France's Declaration of the Rights of Man and of the Citizen of 1789, and explaining how these rights were denied in Indochina.[37] The French regime, he noted, violated several rights, including the right of Vietnamese to travel freely in their own country and the right to freedom of thought by censoring Vietnamese newspapers. For several consecutive issues of *La Cloche Fêlée*, each issue displayed on one of its pages in large text two or three articles of the Declaration of the Rights of Man of 1789, until all seventeen articles were presented. In one place, he wrote that he had heard that some Vietnamese had been afraid to subscribe to *La Cloche Fêlée* given its anti-French tone. This was "too bad," he said, but he understood that they did not yet have the power to revolt against despotism. He exhorted them to at least defend the rights they had obtained and to try to rebel against tyranny and despotism: "Any concession you make today is binding on your heirs. Live in servitude and serfdom if you like, but you have no right to mortgage the liberty of your children."[38] Despite Ninh's criticisms of France, implicit in his appeals to the French metropole was his admiration for France's noble ideals of rights. Ninh detested one kind of France (a colonial France) and admired another France (a republican, rights-loving France). However, when speaking not to the French but to his fellow Vietnamese, his exhortations were replete with expressions of national shame.

National Shame from a Sense of Intellectual Inadequacy

In 1923, Ninh diagnosed the central problem for Vietnamese youth as a crisis of moral knowledge stemming from the lack of an intellectual culture. Vietnamese youth were putting most of their energy into politics, he worried, "as if it was from there, and from there only, that the long-awaited great promise could come, as if the vital problem of our race were a political problem and not a social one." To be sure, Ninh was deeply immersed in politics but believed that the youth should have a clearer sense of who they were and what they wanted before engaging in it. As we will see later, Phạm Quỳnh would see much irony in this position as he believed Ninh had failed to do exactly this. Ninh believed it was his duty as an intellectual privileged to live in France to tell the youth that their deeper problem was a lack of self-knowledge that should be rectified before engaging in political struggle: "When ignorance has come to this point, the silence that encloses the lips of enlightened minds may be qualified as a crime." Vietnamese youth "is caught as if in whirling waters, not knowing toward which direction to swim. Faced with a moral choice, it does not know on which morality to base its actions and its judgments."[39] He did not believe that turning to Chinese ideas or Western ideas for prepackaged moral guidance would work.

With regard to Chinese ideas, Ninh simply believed that the Vietnamese were unable to properly understand Chinese culture because of their poor understanding of Confucius and their limited knowledge of philosophy in general. He asked the Vietnamese to consider

> the decline of Chinese culture in our country, *as if* there had been a period of flowering of Chinese culture in our country. But in reality, I wonder if Chinese culture could have acclimated to Annam. The word culture carries within itself an idea of expanse, the idea of a summit where one could reach

to enjoy broad horizons. There are many names of those whose works contribute to the intellectual education of the Chinese. And yet it seems to me when I hear them talk that our current men of letters who write in Chinese know no other name than that of Confucius.

"Culture," he argued, necessarily carried with itself an idea of expanse, but existing Vietnamese intellectuals were narrowminded, with only a shallow familiarity with Confucius and without knowledge of other philosophers. In this speech, Ninh assured the audience that he greatly admired Confucius because Confucius's ideas, "properly understood, of course, elevate man to a broad and generous conception of life. The backbone of Confucian doctrine is in the individual himself, in the improvement of himself."[40] However, "over time Confucianism in China had been transformed into an export item [to Vietnam]," a doctrine not properly understood.

It is revealing, Ninh thought, that the Vietnamese elite upheld Confucius as the apex of virtue when Confucius himself "came to bow down to Lao Tzu whom [Confucius] called his master and whose superiority he consequently recognized, despite the difference between the two doctrines." If Confucius himself "recognized the superiority of another over him," isn't this "the obvious sign of the weakness of our race, the mark of the helplessness of the finest minds back home?" The Vietnamese were praising someone who himself believed was inferior to Lao Tzu. "Indeed, how many [of us] can read Lao Tzu?"

Ninh introduced the audience to Zhuangzi, "the famous disciple of Lao Tzu" who challenged Confucius's "narrow morality" and "hindering ideas." Zhuangzi is famously known for his anarchism and perhaps more so for his skepticism—the idea that no one can know the truth.[41] Confucius tells us to follow "the way," but Zhuangzi retorts that "the way" depends on perspective and differs from person to person. Ninh's exhortation to the Vietnamese to be skeptical of received traditions and instead to become unique individuals is consistent with Zhuangzi's skepticism, which expresses a kind of emancipatory individualism. For Ninh, the personal quest for emancipation of the individual would naturally lead to emancipation of the nation from colonial rule. Yet, Vietnamese conservatives prevented this freedom: "Haven't the so-called elite fashioned by Chinese books been forced to cling to Confucian ideas like shipwrecked people to a raft?"[42]

As for French or European ideas and values, the Vietnamese should not simply adopt them without struggling on their own to make such ideas meaningful to themselves: "The future that we desire will not come to us in a dream. It is not enough to mark in gold letters on the front of public buildings: liberty, equality, fraternity, in order for liberty, equality, and fraternity to reign among us.... You claim from others things that they cannot give you ... things that you must acquire by yourselves."[43]

If Chinese or European moralities were not solutions, then it would be natural to turn to Vietnam's indigenous culture for moral guidance. For Ninh, culture was the primary source of moral knowledge for all nations. For any nation, its culture was its "soul," guiding not only its citizens' moral behavior but also allowing nations to survive in the face of foreign attacks. According to Ninh: "Any people dominated by a foreign culture cannot know true independence if they do not possess an independent culture.... Take, for example, the Chinese culture that we are still influenced by. Vanquished constantly by brutal force, conquered by barbarian neighbors, China owes its existence to its culture."[44]

Correspondingly, a nation with a weak culture had a weak "soul" and was vulnerable to foreign domination. Regrettably, Ninh thought that this description fit Vietnam. "It is not difficult to demonstrate the need for a culture for our race,"[45] he argued, because Vietnam did not possess a robust intellectual culture:

If we pile up all that we have produced in our country in terms of purely literary and artistic achievements, the intellectual lot that was left to us by our ancestors would certainly be weak compared to the heritages of other peoples. . . .The literary lot that was transmitted to us is thin and, what's more, exhales a strong breath of decadence, of sickness, lassitude, the taste of an impending agony. This is not the kind of heritage that will help give us more vigor and life to our race in the fight for a place in the world.[46]

The standards that Ninh endorsed to assess the value of a nation were not necessarily "European" (e.g., rationality and autonomy), but rather reflected concern over whether a nation had a heritage of intellectual culture, specifically literary and artistic works, and whether these works had endured to guide and invigorate future generations and inspire the world at large.[47] Ninh's view of culture was not unique but rather was common in Vietnam. He wrote: "Many people owe to their culture the duration of their name, their influence in the world, and the messianic role that they play in the world."[48] Unfortunately, Vietnam lacked a pantheon of "great men," according to Ninh, and the little culture that the youth had inherited was more harmful than good. Vietnam's standing in the world was low, even compared to other nations colonized by the West: "India, despite its oppression by the English, has its philosophers, its poets, its intellectuals, its leaders who lead actions of the masses."[49] By contrast, "Annam figures like a pygmy next to a giant, because India has a most glorious past."[50] Compared to nations like India and Japan, whose thinkers "radiate alongside the talents and geniuses of Europe, Annam is but an infant." More than mere "envy," "shame" best captures Ninh's feeling about Vietnam's dishonor and humiliation.

It is interesting that Ninh cited India as an inspiration. For Gandhi, the problem for Indians was not their lack of an intellectual culture (of this they knew they had a rich heritage), but rather a contemporary moral failing in falling prey to the desire for luxury, ease, and material gain.[51] In contrast, the problem for Vietnam, in Ninh's view, was that it lacked even the requisite foundation of an intellectual culture. Whereas "self-criticism" may describe Gandhi's approach, a deeper sense of "shame" best describes Ninh's.

National Shame as Motivation

What task, then, was incumbent on the Vietnamese given their shamefully limited cultural stock? Ninh's solution was for the Vietnamese to aim for a kind of originality generated through an energetic, personal, spiritual struggle. Their aim should be to become "great men." Quoting the Indian thinker Ananda Coomaraswamy, Ninh wrote, "the only and real importance of India for the world will be revealed in the great men India will provide to humanity."[52] Ninh wanted Vietnam to offer its own "great men"—by which he meant philosophers, artists, and poets—to the world. Unfortunately, Ninh thought, the Vietnamese might not be receptive to this idea because they were "without energy, without will, discouraged by the slightest effort," which were consequences of a lack of intellectual culture rather than natural, essential qualities. "Even if favored by heredity and by circumstance, very few of us are capable of efforts that can bring us up to the level of spirit cultivated in Europe." Yet, even so, "why shouldn't we speak of great men, since we need great men, a flowering of great men, personalities that can give status to their own people?" For Ninh, his generation's task involved creatively "finding a solid intellectual heritage that can serve as the first stone on which to build our dreams." This heritage would be solid only if it was the result of their efforts rather than the work of others: "The current generation needs new ideals, *their ideals*; a new activity, *their activity*; new passions, *their passions.*"

For ideas, Vietnam should not depend solely on China or Europe but should learn from diverse sources. "[I]n these times," he wrote, "all Asian minds must be nourished by two cultures, one occidental and one oriental." Vietnam should be like a vampire, sucking up wisdom and knowledge wherever wisdom and knowledge could be found in order to reinvigorate the nation: "What we need is curiosity under all its forms, a curiosity that is the last hope and last sign of life, that is capable of every audacity in order to quench its thirst, a curiosity that burrows, seeks, searches, and dissects everything that is life in others so as to find the remedy which will give new vigor to a weakened blood."[53]

This reinvigorated "blood" would be hybrid. Importantly, although other sources should be studied for inspiration, what the Vietnamese needed was "not servile imitations that far from liberating us attach us to what we imitate. We need personal creations that come from our own blood or works that come from an actual change within ourselves."[54] One precondition to attaining a genuine "change within themselves" was the necessity of breaking away from convention, tradition, and even their families: "It is against your milieu that you must struggle, against your family that paralyzes your efforts, against the vulgar society that weighs on you, against the narrow prejudices and hindrances that lurk around your actions, against ideals that lack vigor and nobility, that are humiliatingly base and reduce, day by day, the status of our race." Here, we see Ninh's conception of dignity as something that is collective (racial), related to status, and requires the Vietnamese people's duty to uplift their status. The greatest idealists, he wrote, "have always hitherto advised those who wanted to be their disciples to flee 'their father's house.' We, too, must flee the 'house of our father.' We must escape our family, escape our society, distance ourselves from our country. We must have a life of struggle that awakens the little vigor we have; we must have a society that reveals our true worth."

Ninh's exhortations to his fellow Vietnamese to struggle against the authority of the family and to awaken their vigor reflect his attraction to what Hue Tam Ho Tai described as "anarchism heavily tinged with Nietzschean individualism."[55] At a time when even the most progressive-minded Vietnamese felt that at least some traditional family values ought to be respected, Ninh's calls to struggle against the family, to reject the values of their fathers, were radically iconoclastic and revolutionary.[56] Only by breaking free from old and stale cultural constraints could the new generation rectify the failure of their ancestors and become great thinkers themselves: "And more than India, we need men who know the soul of our race, its needs, and what is best suited to it. We need men who guide the steps of the people and illuminate their path. We need artists, poets, painters, musicians, and intellectuals to enrich our intellectual heritage."[57]

Ninh insisted on following the example of India. His favorite figure, the man he thought Vietnamese men should strive to emulate the most, was Rabindranath Tagore, whom he quoted approvingly: "My mind refused to be seduced by the banal intoxication of political movements of the time, empty, they seemed to me, of all force proceeding from real national conscience, totally ignorant of the country." The Vietnamese should look to Tagore who, "besides his glory as a poet, ... devoted himself to national education, creating for his students literary masterpieces in the Bengali language, the translations of which are scattered across Europe." Echoing Mahatma Gandhi who considered Tagore to be someone "who by his poetic genius and singular purity of life has raised India in the estimation of the world,"[58] Ninh urged his fellow Vietnamese to raise Vietnam's status and dignity in the world, just as Tagore did for India. One way they could do so was to implement a holistic education, similar to that of India's. In India, he wrote: "the first seven years are entirely devoted to Sanskrit, religion and physical culture; the next twelve years in Western literature, science, laboratory work. ... The most striking feature of this system is the return to the impersonal and philosophical concepts of culture which have always characterized the East, and the combination of ancient wisdom and practical knowledge of the modern age."[59]

If Vietnam were to have its own enlightened education that combined ancient wisdom and practical modern knowledge, which it should, it needed to develop Romanized Vietnamese, *quốc ngữ*. Ninh admitted that his call to develop *quốc ngữ* might seem odd, considering that he himself wrote mostly in French. "When I speak of intellectual culture for our race, you may be wondering why I am not making use of our language. Of course, I don't pretend to rank among the best writers in *quốc ngữ* today." He "blushed" because of his greater comfort writing and speaking in French rather than Vietnamese. However, he spoke to them in French "to spread all my ideas, to put them within the reach of a larger audience, in order to deny the stupid suspicions that roam around my life." In other words, his use of French was to assure colonial authorities that he was not hiding insurrectionary plots. Castigating himself for speaking and writing mostly in French, he argued that the Vietnamese should be wary of using French too much because it might be "a constraint on the Annamese youth." It would be shameful for "future intellectuals whose thought will guide the Annamese race" to "go through a European culture for a deep understanding of their own Far Eastern culture." Knowing that French authorities were also reading his journal, Ninh addressed "compatriots" but subtly cajoled the French for financial support to develop *quốc ngữ*:

> [I]t is through *quốc ngữ* that we can hope to help the greatest number of our compatriots to understand France and to make this country a second France, the "France of Asia." But there are many obstacles in the way of the Westernized Annamite who wants to write in newspapers in their mother tongue. For us, the biggest obstacle is in our scarce resources—or more correctly (we must admit it without false shame) in the lack of financial support. We have only our intelligence, our will, and our love to put at the service of our country. What we lack we provide to the extent that our young energy, ready to do anything to fulfill its dreams.[60]

Ninh's exhortations to develop *quốc ngữ* through newspapers (despite the lack of resources), to break from tradition, to learn from diverse sources, and to become "great men" can be read as the "national responsibility" he prescribed for Vietnamese youth. According to the philosopher Bernard Williams, any notion of responsibility requires that a link be made between someone who causes a bad state of affairs (whether they intend to or not) and the later self who knows the meaning and consequences of the act.[61] Yet, how can someone who merely identifies imaginatively with the members of their nation be responsible for what those members do, or, in Ninh's case, did not do? The answer lies in the use of "we" statements. An individual's ability to say "we have been conquered"—and mean it—is, in the words of the political theorist Farid Abdel-Nour, "evidence of their success (by whatever mechanisms) in extending their sense of communal belonging to persons they have neither met nor are likely to meet or hear about."[62] Ninh makes a link between Vietnam's ancestors (whose act of omission—not creating great intellectual works—caused a bad state of affairs) and the present generation of Vietnamese who know the meaning and consequences of the act of omission. Thus, for Ninh, the "task that is incumbent on the present generation is heavy."[63] This generation had a "mission. And who better than us to take on this mission?" His generation was a "sacrificed generation" that should "think of our task and not our happiness, that we should contribute all our efforts to a better future." Only by fulfilling these responsibilities could the Vietnamese eventually conceive their national identity in terms of pride: "Today's youth must avoid above all talk of the fatherland and of patriotism. They must concentrate all their strength on seeking themselves. The day they find themselves, the words fatherland and patriotism will have become greater words, more elevated, more noble."

These words, he said, were probably surprising to the Vietnamese, ringing a "strangely new note to your ears, an accent hitherto unknown," because they had been habituated to obeying authority and tradition. Yet, they could be worthy of dignity if they would break from authority and tradition to fulfill their responsibility to creatively remake themselves, and thus their society. He reminded the Vietnamese that "society is a group of human beings," and it was up to each person to fulfill their duty of asserting Vietnam's dignity:

> The sum of the values of individuals makes the value of the group. Society is always in our image and in our resemblance; if we are ugly, it will not be pretty. The social environment is only worth what the individuals within it are worth. You want your place in the sun, your part in the well-being of humanity. You want to live, and you know that to live is to act. You want the society of which you are a part to be as active as any other society, and to have the well-being that they enjoy. More than that, you want freedom. Above all, you want justice. But you must be prepared to create it. And you know a job will never get done if no one starts it. Well, compatriots, you have embarked on a path that does not allow you to easily turn back. Think of working for society, of preparing a future less burdensome than the present, of a social environment where generations will follow you, and your grandchildren will be happier than you. Of course, it's never too late when it comes to doing the right thing. A family has already been established. Children are there to feed, raise, and educate. The future is your responsibility.

The Vietnamese wanted freedom, he noted, but before calling for freedom, the youth must pause to ask themselves what freedom really meant to them: "we dare to speak of political autonomy, of freedom. We make the hollowest speeches, the craziest demands which further waste the strength of the race. What freedom are you asking for? What will we do with it? Does the child who isn't even yet sure of his steps need the whole earth to learn to walk?"

Ninh himself did not offer a clear explanation for what freedom really was. It was something to be struggled for, something that required self-striving, but he never spelled it out. Much like the *dao* of the Taoists such as Lao Tzu and Zhuangzi whom he admired, freedom was ineffable but required skill and was recognizable. One cannot ever say what it was, but one can talk about it and know it when one sees it. Presumably, freedom involved at least the end of colonialism, but, for Ninh, one had to struggle to end colonialism through the hard work of fulfilling one's national responsibility.

For Ninh, as well as for other thinkers featured in this study, there is an essential continuum between individual freedom and collective freedom. Ninh approvingly quoted Charles Maurras on the importance of collective striving and institutionalizing progress, not just making it a matter of personal development. "Their personal progress will not be enough to determine a progress of manners. . . . Only the institution, enduring indefinitely, makes the best of us last. Through it, man is dragged on; his good act continues, consolidates itself into habits which are constantly renewed in new beings who open their eyes to life."

One might criticize Ninh's "national responsibility" for placing undue emphasis on individual answerability while overlooking the realities of France's capitalist expansion and imperialism.[64] However, Ninh called for Vietnamese answerability while also being fundamentally anticolonial and well aware of the historical realities of French imperialism and the brutality of French colonial power. Far from being the act of an apologist for French colonialism or a victim of false consciousness, his call for national responsibility was part of his anticolonialism. Ninh, Trần Văn Giàu argued, was "a man of deep character who hated colonialism. The more Ninh directly understood the French people and the political and ideological views of the French democratic and revolutionary philosophers, the more he hated imperialism."[65]

For Ninh, the Vietnamese had to develop their own national language, but this did not mean that also learning the French language alienated them from their Vietnamese roots. "We are not among those who, in order to learn to speak French poorly, give up their mother tongue." The knowledge that France had given them, "far from distancing us, from detaching us from our race, makes us come back to it."[66] Colonialism had not taught the Vietnamese to hate themselves or to be ashamed of themselves. On the contrary, it taught the Vietnamese "to love the people from whom we came" and "to work fruitfully for the race from which we come." By asserting that colonialism did not cause the Vietnamese to feel ashamed of themselves, Ninh reclaimed shame for the Vietnamese. Their use of shame would be on their own terms, independent from what colonizers did or said.

Conclusion

The early 1920s was a period flowering with liberal and anarchistic ideas, philosophical experimentation, and new political vocabularies. By the 1930s, this "radicalism" would be replaced by another radical tradition: Marxism–Leninism. Ninh studied Marxism, and his journal even translated *The Communist Manifesto* into Vietnamese, but, according to Hue Tam Ho Tai, there was no sign that he ever became a Communist.[67] Yet, this new ideology would appeal to many who, like him, became convinced that the French would never commit to serious reform. In late November 1925, Ninh called for violent revolution:

> [L]iberty is to be taken; it is not to be granted. To wrest it away from an organized power, we need to oppose to that power an organized force.... When we ask for reforms, we acknowledge the authority of the established regime. But if they are refused to us, let us know how to organize ourselves. Let us not put any faith in the policy of association that is much talked about these days. To associate, at least there must be two sides and only equals. Let us say to the government to wait until we have the same liberty and the same rights as those with which it wants us to associate.[68]

The following year was a tumultuous one in Vietnam. On April 24, 1926, Nguyễn An Ninh was sentenced to eighteen months of imprisonment for his critiques of French injustices in *La Cloche Fêlée*. When this sentence was announced, Ngô Văn wrote, "students of Saigon, from the primary school at Phú Lâm in Chợ Lớn and from everywhere in the province to Bến Tre, Mỹ Tho, Vĩnh Long, Cần Thơ deserted their classes en masse. More than a thousand among them were expelled."[69] The French closed down Ninh's newspaper, angering his followers. Recall that it was also in that year that Phan Chu Trinh's funeral brought out thousands into Saigon. And shortly after

Trinh's death, workers went on strike across the country. Vietnamese accommodationist elites refused to join the movements that year.

One such "accommodationist elite" was Phạm Quỳnh, Ninh's contemporary and another intellectual giant of that period. Quỳnh attacked Ninh personally. Whereas Ninh believed that the Vietnamese shamefully clung to "Confucian ideas like shipwrecked people to a raft"[70] and should struggle to create new ideas and philosophies for themselves, Quỳnh believed that neglecting Confucian tradition was tantamount to taking their anchor away during a storm. Once lost and adrift, the Vietnamese would be far from having any sense of self-worth and self-respect. For Quỳnh, it was tradition that provided the strongest source of national dignity. It is to him that we now turn.

5
Phạm Quỳnh's Cultural Resistance

On a spring evening in 2018, I happened upon a bookstore in downtown Hanoi. I was not looking for anything in particular, but a thick orange book sitting on a shelf near the entrance caught my eye. I was stunned when I saw the name of the author: Phạm Quỳnh. It was a Vietnamese edited volume of his essays from his journal *Nam Phong*.[1]

I had known from my reading of Vietnamese history that *Nam Phong* was a journal set up in Vietnam by the French government as its official mouthpiece for colonial propaganda from the late 1910s to the 1930s. Its lead editor, Phạm Quỳnh (1892–1945), was an infamous pro-French collaborator, described by some nationalists and historians as "obsequious," "servile," and a "French lackey."[2] For his treason, Quỳnh was among the first to be executed by Việt Minh revolutionaries when they took power in 1945.

The volume I held in my hands was recently published: 2018. Was the Communist Party of Vietnam now allowing colonial propaganda and the writings of traitors to the revolution to be published? This did not match with what my Vietnamese family members, some of whom fought on the side of the anti-Communists, told me: the Communist Party in Vietnam today prohibits the writings of those who do not toe the Party line.

Phạm Quỳnh was certainly reviled by the revolutionaries, and it is easy to see why. I recalled Hue Tam Ho Tai's description of Quỳnh's obsession with stability at any cost and of his uncritical support of French violence in the name of restoring order. She attributed these words to Quỳnh: "Since violence is not within our power, we trust that the government will know how to use it for the common good. We believe that the violence of France is always impartial and vigilant: it will strike hard and strike in the right place."[3]

How could the ideas of a defender of colonial violence be published and sold in a bookstore in Hanoi, the historical base of northern Vietnamese Communist revolutionaries, considering that hostility to Phạm Quỳnh and his ideas, writes Tai, "was the driving force behind northern progressivism"?[4]

When *Nam Phong* closed down in 1934, a journal called *Mores,* the chief vehicle of progressive thought in North Vietnam, "announced the news as if it were a joyous event."[5] David Marr, the historian who provided the most influential English-language interpretation of Quỳnh in his 1981 book *Vietnamese Tradition on Trial*, refers to Quỳnh as one of the "colonial regime's most faithful servants"[6] and suggested that Quỳnh's collaboration with the French was a kind of "prostitution" that mirrored Quỳnh's defense of the prostituted heroine in the famous Vietnamese poem "Tale of Kiều."[7] In the poem, a woman ends up selling herself to get her father and brother out of debt and to prevent them from going to jail. Young Vietnamese men and women, Marr writes, saw Quỳnh's defense of Kiều as part of a "poisonously deceptive" strategy aimed at keeping the Vietnamese population weak and submissive, as if they had no choice but to "sell themselves" by collaborating with the French for the greater good of modernizing Vietnam.[8]

While many have branded Quỳnh as a traitor, others in Vietnam have simply decided to ignore him; anthologies of literature in Hanoi following the August Revolution of 1945 fail to even mention him, which is notable given the fact that *Nam Phong* was the most important and widely read intellectual and literary journal from its inception in 1917 to 1934.[9]

I opened the orange book to read the inside flap of the cover: "Phạm Quỳnh is a pioneer. He has made important contributions through using the national language script and promoting the construction of a national education system.... He also actively translated and spread the essence of Eastern and Western ideas with the aim of enlightening the Vietnamese people and fostering the nation's traditions and national soul."[10] I flipped to the editor's introduction: "The essays demonstrate an amazing writing and thinking ability, a serious spirit, hard work, and a trusting heart.... It has been 100 years since the inception of *Nam Phong*... but this scholar's contributions to the development of modern Vietnamese culture are still a milestone of special significance today."[11]

It started to make sense. Although Marr casts Phạm Quỳnh in a negative light, Marr did give faint praise to Quỳnh's nationalism and his desire to promote Vietnamese literature. "The best that can be said," Marr writes, "is that *Nam Phong* transliterated a significant number of *nom* [Chinese script] poems which, while not usually of folk origin or particularly threatening to the status quo, were deeply appreciated by readers of diverse political persuasions."[12] Although Marr suggested that young people saw Phạm Quỳnh's defense of the prostitute in the *Tale of Kiều* as a strategy to keep the Vietnamese submissive, some Vietnamese nationalists like Mạc Phi (1928–1996) argued that such a conclusion would be absurd because Quỳnh resisted colonial discourse by proudly asserting the value of Vietnamese culture and language at a time when French colonialism was trying to erase them. Mạc Phi argued that it

> is necessary to clearly see the malicious plot of the French colonialists to make young Vietnamese people, students, and intellectuals forget their mother tongue, worship the French language, worship French culture, and despise Vietnamese cultural heritage. At that time, all high schools used French in all lectures, and Vietnamese was only used in the subject "Vietnamese" (Annamite) for about two hours a week! . . . *Nam Phong* contributed to awakening a sense of respect for the Vietnamese language and Vietnamese cultural heritage in society.[13]

Along these lines, Hue Tam Ho Tai argued that "Phạm Quỳnh was not concerned with political representation, which was unavailable to natives of the protectorates, but with finding solutions to the acute cultural malaise from which, everyone now realized, the nation suffered."[14]

Another thing that makes praise of Quỳnh in the introduction of that orange book less surprising is the fact that there is an emerging generation of scholars who have shown that Phạm Quỳnh's role in colonial Vietnam was more ambiguous than earlier generations of historians have portrayed. For example, Sarah Womack argues that Quỳnh used the power of the colonial state for his own agenda and, in doing so, complicated assumptions of value regarding his interactions with the colonial state.[15] Gerard Sasges has even portrayed Phạm Quỳnh as somewhat of a resistor. Contrary to Hue Tam Ho Tai's claim that Quỳnh was unconcerned with political representation, Sasges shows how, in an anticolonial move, Quỳnh represented Vietnamese natives at Indochina's Grand conseil des intérêts économiques et financiers [Grand Council of Economic and Financial Interests] in 1931 and succeeded in stopping the colonial regime's attempt to renew their monopoly on the production of rice alcohol. "The [principle of] indigenous representation," Phạm Quỳnh argued, "is hostile to all monopolies."[16] Yen Vu, has shown how Phạm Quỳnh's "speaking French and borrowing of colonial discourse—this mimicry—unravels the rhetoric upon which the French colonial empire gathered its strength."[17]

The orange book that I held was a proud Vietnamese assertion of Vietnamese culture and identity. And the fact that it was in a bookstore in 2018, with a stylish cover design, was evidence that Phạm Quỳnh's writings were playing a significant role in postcolonial, postwar Vietnam. Nowhere in the introduction of the volume was it mentioned that Phạm Quỳnh was a collaborator or traitor. Rather, he was portrayed as an architect of national dignity.

This chapter is an effort to explain why, despite being a pro-French collaborator with the colonial regime, Phạm Quỳnh's writings are praised, or at least permitted, by the heirs of Vietnamese revolutionaries. It is a familiar case of the victors of war recasting history in ways useful to postwar projects, emphasizing some things and choosing to remain quiet on others. But, more interestingly, it is a case of how material from which victors conduct selective remembering can complicate the traditional binary of collaborator versus resister, which is so often used to make sense of colonized subjects.

Phạm Quỳnh, frequently portrayed as a collaborator, is best understood as an architect of Vietnamese national dignity. Although he collaborated with the French, he used his privileges as editor of a French-sanctioned journal to assert a Vietnamese culture against Western cultural hegemony. In effect, he subversively resisted Western cultural imperialism at a time when colonizers were teaching the Vietnamese that their culture was inferior. As for Quỳnh, he shamed his compatriots not for lacking an indigenous intellectual tradition, but for failing to assert it against Western culture while also harmonizing with it. This chapter shows how, for Quỳnh, there were two major obstacles to national dignity. The first was internal to the Vietnamese people themselves. Vietnamese youth, he thought, were experiencing a debilitating "moral malaise" caused by a sudden influx of Western ideas and the subsequent retreat of Vietnamese ideas. The solution, he recommended, was to shame the Vietnamese for failing to appreciate the greatness of their own cultural productions. By asserting the value of Vietnamese culture, namely, Confucian morality and the Vietnamese vernacular language, both Vietnamese and Western culture could be harmonized rather than allowing Western to dominate Vietnamese culture. He was like Phan Chu Trinh in this respect, but different because of his more forceful critiques of Western liberalism, democracy, and science.

The second obstacle to national dignity concerns the relationship between the Vietnamese and the French. Quỳnh acknowledged that colonial violence created a degrading, unequal relationship between the French and the Vietnamese. But the solution was not revolutionary violence. Rather, it was to appeal to France's own professed principles of liberty, equality, and brotherhood, and to exhort the French to shift from what he called a "policy of force" to a "policy of consideration" (*politique d'egards*). Furthermore, Quỳnh exhorted the Vietnamese to do their part in creating a reciprocal relationship between them and the French by harmonizing Eastern and Western values.

Quỳnh had his blind spots and, from our perspective, he seems naïve about France's intentions. Yet, he seems less so considering the promises that Albert Sarraut, the governor-general, made at the time.

Some Colonial Reforms

Recall that a revolt broke out in 1908 against corvée demands and taxes, leading to the shutdown of the Tonkin Free School. French officials, aware and nervous of the growing restlessness and indignation of the Vietnamese under colonial rule, debated in Paris from 1908 to 1911 as to how French policy in Indochina might be reformed. They came to agree with Phan Chu Trinh that "French policy will fail unless it is a pro-indigenous one,"[18] and they concluded that the only way for French republicans to be true to their values and to quell a revolution was to offer legal guarantees of the Vietnamese people's rights.[19] Thus, they decided to send Albert Sarraut to Indochina to be the French governor-general from 1912 to 1914 and from 1917 to 1919. Sarraut, seeing reform as necessary to prevent upheaval and to preserve the empire, argued for a more enlightened, liberal, humanist colonialism. Later reflecting on his years as governor-general, he wrote that France

> has long repudiated the brutal conception of the old colonial pact based "on the eternal inequality of the races and on the right of the strongest to control others solely for the interests of the conqueror." The only right she wants to recognize is the right of the strong to protect the weaker. The France which colonizes does not work only for itself; its advantage merges with the advantage of the world; its labor must benefit the colonies, whose economic growth and human development it ensures. Thus, the French colonial operation, designed for the good of both parties, will no longer be the spoliation of one race by another, but rather an association, according to a happy formula which has become the motto of our colonial policy.[20]

Consider Sarraut's remarks above in light of arguments for why colonialism is morally wrong. Two common ones are the nationalist argument (that self-determination ought to be respected) and the territorial rights argument (that territorial rights ought to be respected). However, the political theorist Lea Ypi has argued, convincingly, I think, that these two arguments are ultimately untenable and that the wrong of colonialism is ultimately colonialism's instantiation of an unequal and nonreciprocal political relation.[21] Indeed, colonial domination and exploitation entails an unequal and nonreciprocal relationship. A major source of Vietnamese indignation during French colonialism was precisely the absence of equal and reciprocal politics (understood as discussion with others over what is best for the common good) between the French and the Vietnamese. In that sense, colonialism was fundamentally an antipolitical relationship. The French, with their monopoly on power, simply refused to allow the Vietnamese to engage in equal, reciprocal discussions with them over what was best for the French and Vietnamese in Vietnam.

Yet, with Sarraut coming to power as governor general, many Vietnamese, including future Communist revolutionaries, were optimistic and hopeful. He seemed to be promising that the French would make the (non)political relationship between the French and the Vietnamese more equal and reciprocal. Sarraut's promise was to "increase native representation in the existing local assemblies, create native representation in assemblies where it does not yet exist, and enlarge the native electoral body that will designate its representatives in such a way that the native representatives are increasingly the direct emanation of the population and no longer the administration's delegates."[22] Unsurprisingly, French settler politicians resisted these proposals as well as giving more natives the right to vote, knowing that reform would have likely meant *legally* expelling the settlers.[23] All the same, Sarraut pronoted some judicial reforms favoring individual and indigenous rights, advocated educational reforms such as presiding over the closing of the old Confucian exam system (which, by then, was largely detested by Vietnamese), and opened new educational programs to induce native elites to cooperate with the French.[24]

Sarraut promoted freedom of expression to win over hearts and minds, but he reserved such freedoms solely for trusted members of the Vietnamese elite, which his team recruited and placed at the heads of the major government-backed newspapers in Vietnam. In 1917, Louis Marty, a Frenchman who was the director of France's operational intelligence in Indochina, recruited Phạm Quỳnh to set up the most influential intellectual journal of the period: *Nam Phong* (Southern Wind) in Hanoi.[25] The journal was to promote *quốc ngữ* writing, and Sarraut and Marty viewed the promotion of *quốc ngữ* as a possible alternative outlet for nationalistic energies that might otherwise galvanize into anticolonial sentiments. Intended to promote the official views of the French colonial government, *Nam Phong* was entrusted to Phạm Quỳnh, providing him a degree of freedom unavailable to other Vietnamese journals at the time.

A Brief Biography: Phạm Quỳnh

Phạm Quỳnh was born in Hải Dương in North Vietnam in 1892. His father was a Confucian scholar who attained a degree in the state examinations. Quỳnh's parents died when he was young, so he was raised by his paternal grandmother in Hanoi where he attended a school for interpreters. He graduated in 1908 when he was sixteen and then worked as a translator at the École française d'Extrême Orient. His talent as an interpreter and his work with the Sûreté made him seem like a good candidate for the French colonial regime's class of loyal, indigenous collaborators, under the leadership of Albert Sarraut. They turned to Confucian elite Vietnamese, like Quỳnh, who would not be content, David Marr writes, "to simply exist on colonial sinecures or sit around writing classical poetry.... What was needed, in short, was a carefully supervised yet stimulating alternative to the outlawed movement."[26] Soon after leaving the École française d'Extrême Orient, Quỳnh became the assistant editor for the *Đông Dương tạp chí* (*Indochina Review*), led by the French-selected editor Nguyễn Van Vinh. Vinh was known for his attacks on Vietnamese literati who neglected to study the French language and failed to appreciate French ideas. According to Vinh, the Vietnamese were harming themselves by learning about the West through Chinese translations of Western ideas and texts: "It is hard enough to select primary French concepts and ideals that are digestible to Annamites, but if one picks these things up via Chinese books and Chinese characters, with pieces carved off the top and the bottom and strange ingredients added here and there, then it is not just a matter of indigestion or choking, but of being poisoned."[27] The Vietnamese should no longer depend on Chinese translations (often of Japanese translations) to learn about Western ideas, Vinh argued. What they needed was a class of Vietnamese Francophone elites to replace the traditional Vietnamese literati. Phạm Quỳnh agreed. Francophone elites, Quỳnh believed, should sift through Western texts and provide interpretations of ideas they considered harmful or beneficial to the Vietnamese masses.

Soon after Quỳnh's stint at the *Indochina Review*, the French officials asked him to found a new review. He agreed. The first issue of *Nam Phong tạp chí* (*The Southern Wind journal*) was published on July 1, 1917. The journal was explicitly supposed to be an organ of propaganda for the colonial state. Yet, Phạm Quỳnh as editor was "given a degree of freedom from censorship that was remarkable for its time. In return for oftentimes fawning praise of the French administration—and all things French, for that matter—Phạm Quỳnh was given the freedom to discuss ideas and politics that was only to be exceeded when press censorship was relaxed during the Popular Front years of 1936–1938."[28] It became one of the most widely read and influential journals of its day. The scholar Vũ Ngọc Phan described how the journal was used in its heyday: "Many young intellectuals could use articles from *Nam Phong tạp chí* as a foundation, in order to address the deficiencies that persisted in their studies. There were even those who used *Nam Phong* as a textbook, essentially in order to be able to amass the ideas of East and West."[29]

Quỳnh was also politically active. In 1926, he attempted to create a political party, the Việt nam Tấn Bộ Dân Hội (Vietnamese People's Progressive League), aimed at gaining Vietnamese support for reforms and also to stem the rising tide of the radicalism led by Nguyễn An Ninh.[30] Quỳnh wanted the party to collaborate closely with the colonial regime to raise the moral, intellectual, and economic standards of the country. Although this was a reactionary aim, the party attracted many people, such as those like Phan Bội Châu who were suspected of anticolonial activism. For these reasons, Alexandre Varenne, the governor-general at the time, refused to approve it.[31] Quỳnh also became involved with the Association for the Intellectual and Moral Formation of the Annamites (Hội Khai Trí Tiến Đức), a state-sponsored organization aimed at uniting Confucian and French-trained elites. In 1932, Quỳnh was appointed the secretary of Emperor Bảo Đại's new cabinet in Huế. After the French rejected calls for reforms to grant more power to the imperial government, some members of the cabinet resigned. However, Quỳnh stayed on and would act as minister of education and minister of the interior until 1945. That year, Việt Minh revolutionaries seized power. Shortly after, they arrested Phạm Quỳnh at his home, took him to the forest, and executed him along with Ngô Đình Khôi and Ngô Đình Huân, a brother and a nephew of Ngô Đình Diệm, the future leader of anti-Communist South Vietnam. The men were buried in unmarked graves.[32]

The Problem of Moral Malaise and the Solution of Cultural Assertion

Like the thinkers discussed in the previous chapters, Phạm Quỳnh was troubled by an apparent moral disorientation among Vietnamese youth. Although he believed French colonialism caused this disorientation, he shamed the Vietnamese for not doing anything to reorient themselves. Unlike Phan Bội Châu, Quỳnh abhorred violence and favored stability and order above all else. Unlike Phan Chu Trinh, Quỳnh was far more cautious about importing ideas from the West. And unlike Ninh, Quỳnh was far more philosophically conservative.

In a 1926 article titled "Moral Malaise" published in *Nam Phong*, Phạm Quỳnh personally attacked Nguyễn An Ninh as embodying the moral malaise of his generation. Ninh's calls to his peers to abandon their tradition and family to re-create their identities anew were not only vague but also dangerous, thought Quỳnh. Quỳnh pointed to how Ninh himself had admitted to being full of self-doubt and anxiety, all the while pretending to be confident enough to lead a whole generation. It was the blind leading the blind.

> Let's take an intelligent and sufficiently cultured subject, for example our compatriot Nguyễn An Ninh with whom the whole press from North to South has been so busy in recent days. We have perhaps not noticed enough this passage from his letter to the Attorney General: "Since the age of 18, I have been tormented by a spiritual evolution working incessantly in me and which often makes me doubt myself, my ideas, my actions. I have been tempted many times by the religious life. These anxieties explain my decision to give up everything to rest." Here is a man amid spiritual crisis, who does not yet know how to resolve this crisis, who doubts his strength and the effectiveness of his actions, who in short is far from having faith in himself, and who dares to lead a whole people to the conquest of their freedoms! The Buddha, when he was still seated under the "bodhi" tree before having received "enlightenment," did not dare to "turn the wheel of dharma." Our young compatriot Ninh showed himself more in a hurry: without waiting for enlightenment, he began to "spin the wheel" and at such a speed that it

made him tumble. Mr. Ninh is certainly a worthy man; his mistake is that he did not wait until he had completed his spiritual development before taking action. But what should we think of the thousands and thousands of his admirers who saw him as a leader? They have to be in terrible disarray to place their trust in a man who has made the sincere admission that he still doubts himself, his ideas, and his actions. This is really very serious.[33]

Quỳnh's criticisms of Ninh as being "in the midst of a spiritual crisis" and as someone "who doubts his strength" and yet "dares to lead a whole people to the conquest of their freedoms" display Quỳnh's adherence to the Confucian imperative that the most worthwhile activity that anyone could be doing with their time was to improve their own moral character and sort themselves out before setting out to lead others. The youth's faith in Ninh's leadership, Quỳnh argued, reflected the fact that the young generation lacked "personal power, strength, temper of character, that vigor of spirit and that moral virility which, more than intelligence and knowledge, would make them 'men' in the full sense of the word."[34] The irony here is that Ninh lamented the same thing.

But whereas Ninh believed that the cause of this malaise was blind adherence to Confucian tradition, Quỳnh thought that much of the cause was Western cultural imperialism. Vietnamese youth, "exclusively formed in the French schools and completely detached from the old ancestral disciplines," were despondent, Quỳnh argued.[35] To be sure, young people in general, all over the world, were prone to despondency, he said. "From 18 to 20, when youthful spring love begins, they are confused and unable to look clearly at the world and distinguish reality from fantasy."[36] The young were hormonal and lacked experience, and so were naïve and didn't yet know how to manage their expectations for themselves and the world. However, this general phenomenon was made worse in Vietnam due to colonialism's impact on the national culture: "The situation in our country is that of transition," in which "old traditions are almost in ruins and new ones have yet to be established."[37] Young Vietnamese people judged others but lacked standards for doing so. They evaluated things without knowing what to use as evidence. And this was because of the imposition of new Western ideas and a concomitant lack of confidence in Vietnamese (East Asian) culture: "obliged to bow down to Western power, Eastern wisdom has at first fallen back on itself. The East wondered anxiously which way to turn. Sometimes suspicious of itself, the East was hesitant and puzzled."[38] This doubt in Vietnam's own ideals prevented youths from developing a sense of national dignity that could be achieved through exercising their Confucian morals and being cautious about certain Western values. Every step taken "in the acquisition of modern Western science marks for man a setback in the field of moral and spiritual values."[39]

Westerners, Quỳnh believed, were motivated by the "ideal of power." To "tame the forces of nature to put them at the service of man, the westerner invented science."[40] This desire to predict, control, and dominate nature "multiplies the means, creates the needs, excites the appetites, and, carrying the will of power to its highest degree, makes the Western man overflow from his natural environment and throws him to the conquest of the world."[41] Anticipating Max Horkheimer and Theodor Adorno's influential book, *Dialectic of Enlightenment,* which would be published about a decade later, Quỳnh saw the West's emphasis on reason, science, and their desire to control nature as potentially self-destructive. This desire for power was pernicious, he thought, and one could easily see it in the recent mass slaughter of the First World War in Europe. "The misdeeds of science without conscience have never appeared so clearly to Orientals as during the immense massacre of which the whole of the West has just been theater. If all Western power with its murderous science only ends in this vast collective madness, how can Orientals avoid feeling sorrow for the loss of their ancient wisdom?"[42]

Worried that Vietnamese youth, seeking to emulate the West, would fall to a similar destructive fate, Phạm Quỳnh urged them to turn instead to their "Eastern ideal" and to nurture and assert it. The Eastern ideal is an "ancient wisdom," conducive to a "happy quietude."[43] It is in perfect contrast to the Western ideal of power, he argues. Unfortunately, the Eastern ideal is in retreat: the massive introduction of ideas and conceptions of the west and the subsequent destruction of the ancient moral framework of the east resulted in a general imbalance of minds. Thanks to this worsening imbalance, our minds are stuffed with words and formulas, stuffed with foreign theories and doctrines poorly assimilated or even unassimilable, ... provoked by the most intemperate individualism or the most disheveled romanticism.[44]

Quỳnh's insistence that the Vietnamese resist harmful Western ideas bears similarity to the concept of *gharbzadegi* (westoxification) developed decades later by Iranian thinkers like Jalal Al-e Ahmad in response to Western intrusion into the economic and cultural life of the Middle East.[45] Ahmad used the term to describe a kind of "illness or intoxication; a foreignness or strangeness that takes over the cultural and political body."[46] He warned Iranians of the

West's "mechanosis," by which he meant Western power and use of machine life to extract resources from Iran and also produce harmful new desires for consumption. Phạm Quỳnh was similarly disturbed at how the Vietnamese were "rushing at an increasingly rapid rate" toward "this mechanical civilization."[47] Furthermore, Quỳnh was concerned that the Vietnamese were moving toward the most harmful Western idea of all, one that sought "only profit and happiness for each person, making each person's personality the center of the universe, what we call 'individualism.'"[48] Taken out of context, Quỳnh's assertions may sound fitting for contemporary leftists who oppose neoliberalism.

Quỳnh admitted that the "libertarian and individualistic theories that come from the West are certainly not without attractions" that are understandably "often irresistible" to the Vietnamese who had "barely escaped the rigors of a patriarchal organization over which absolutism reigns triumphant." However, Quỳnh concluded that it was "best to incorporate [such theories] cautiously." Individualism and liberal theories from the West

> can give a positive character to old traditional ideas that tend to discount individuals a bit too much by inscribing them completely within the family unit or the community and in this way often hinder the full development of the personality. But if they act alone without the solid base of good traditional training, these theories may cause dissolution and destruction. The delicate matter of the dosage must be respected, as it requires much foresight and tact and can be the work only of an elite truly conscious of its role as initiator and guide.[49]

Quỳnh's elitism shines here. Rather than reject Western ideas wholesale, the Vietnamese should incorporate them slowly and carefully but only after elites (like him) decided on the proper dosage and kinds of liberal ideas to administer to the masses. For Quỳnh, Japan was proof that elite-led filtering of Western ideas could be beneficial. Japan, he argued, attained a "synthesis of the ideals of the Occident and the Orient, and of ancient moral tradition and modern scientific culture."[50] Key to Japan's success was Japan's "farsighted elite" who "took up with ardor the task of educating the people."

Quỳnh's philosophical conservatism resembles that of Edmund Burke, the grandfather of the conservative tradition in the West. Like Burke, Quỳnh favored slow, gradual change, arguing that "[we] must ensure that in the process of constant progress, society remains stable and peaceful."[51] Like

Burke, Quỳnh envisioned society not as a contract to which individuals gave their rational consent, but as a sacred, involuntary chain of generations. He was concerned with preserving the social fabric in which individuals were connected, in which the tapestry as a whole, not the individual threads alone, was beautiful. Furthermore, Quỳnh and Burke aimed for order, stability, and harmony, and they saw radical ideas, innovation, and lack of restraint as obstacles to these goals. Quỳnh's Burkean desire for order and stability led him to rely on the French to provide it in Vietnam as the Vietnamese underwent a cultural transformation. Quỳnh's Burkean conservatism, while anti-imperialist in the realm of ideas and culture, called for participation with the powerful colonial state to ensure order.

To stem the tide of Western individualism, Quỳnh exhorted the Vietnamese to assert their traditional Confucian values, starting with the family. "The smallest, strongest, and most enduring union compatible with nature is the family.... Families in European societies have passed through a dangerous period" due to the movement of "individualism" (*chủ nghĩa cá nhân*). But "apart from them, everyone who maintains the good, old ways of thinking knows that the family is a secret harbor to save us in the storms of these times."[52] Here, Quỳnh was expressing a normative desire rather than describing reality. This is how families should be, he thought. Furthermore, he was not calling for a return to the stifling patriarchal family, but for a fusion of familial and liberal values, because while family *can* be a safe harbor, it can also be overbearing and stifling, Quỳnh admitted. Confucius's "patriarchal organization of society and state, modeled on the family monad ... has certainly aged and no longer responds to the current state of modern societies, even those which have just left the patriarchal stage as Annamese society.... This conception no longer accorded with the current evolution of societies."[53]

These outdated perspectives, Quỳnh thought, were the primary reasons why, in contemporary Vietnam, Confucius "does not seem to have interested his readers; no one has approved or contradicted him; and I doubt very much that his articles, written with great concern for style and documentation, have had as many readers as the small bit of recent news about the two tennis champions who have been promoted to the rank of national heroes."[54] Vietnamese indifference to Confucianism, Quỳnh thought, could be attributed to stereotypes of Confucianism as being shrouded in inaccessible scholarly talk. However, it would be a mistake to dismiss Confucianism entirely, he argued. Quỳnh's aim was thus to "free it from all the scholastic apparatus which surrounds it" and update it for modern times.

The way to do so, he said, was to present the core essentials of Confucianism in a clear and simple way that anyone could understand. To this end, he declared that Confucius simply aimed to "maintain social order and human peace based on the practice of humanity and justice, respect and propriety." Writing this in French, Quỳnh made an interesting decision here to include the term *justice*, which seems to reflect his desire to balance Eastern and Western moral traditions. Those familiar with the Confucian moral tradition know that "justice" is not an important or even a relevant concept in Confucianism.[55] Rather, the guiding ideal in Confucianism is "harmony." According to Quỳnh, order and peace can be summed up in the word "harmony." To achieve harmony, Quỳnh says individuals should develop their "social or sociable tendencies," what Confucius has called *ren* (sometimes translated as "care"). In doing so, one's "nature is thereby improved and, in whatever society in which he is called to live, he will be able to behave as he should, avoiding unnecessary conflicts with other men and above all seeking peace and harmony."[56] One must refrain from egoistic instincts and practice four Confucian virtues, he argued: respect, propriety, benevolence, and equity. The latter two are the "fundamental virtues of Confucian ethics." These qualities and virtues "are within the reach of all men; they require no superhuman effort, no extraordinary courage." While some people will be able to better achieve these qualities than others, all should try to practice them. Quỳnh evoked Confucius's famous Golden Rule: "To love other men as oneself and to act towards them *comme il convient*, which is to say as one would like them to act towards you, isn't this all of morality?"

To appreciate these Confucian teachings, Quỳnh argued, one should "have in mind the state in which the world and civilization would fall if the worst instincts of man were allowed free rein." Quỳnh's "state of nature" thought experiment, here, is evocative of Thomas Hobbes's. But Quỳnh's solution was not an absolute sovereign leviathan, nor was it self-interested and rational consent that gave rise to legitimate government. Rather, the solution was to assert the best of Eastern (Confucian) wisdom and to marry it with what elites like him decided were the best ideals from the West.

In an interpretive move that developed Phan Chu Trinh's project of marrying Confucianism, liberalism, and democracy, Phạm Quỳnh modernized Confucianism by turning to Mencius, Confucius's famous disciple, and comparing him with Rousseau to argue that Confucianism was not rigid but compatible with modern ideals like democracy. Mencius's ideas are,

> in the order of morality, those of the fundamental goodness of human nature, of the existence in each man of germs of goodness that education must develop, and, in the order of politics, those of the importance of the people, of the rights they have which rulers must care for, of the need to practice a policy of benevolence aimed at creating happiness for the greatest number of the masses. These are almost egalitarian and democratic ideas that permit Mencius to be regarded by modern Chinese as a kind of patron of democracy. Indeed, it can be said of Mencius that he is a Chinese Rousseau living three hundred years before the Christian era. For twenty centuries, Jean Jacques's moral and political conceptions had been so convincing and eloquent. Like the philosopher of Geneva, Mencius maintains that man is naturally good, and that society perverts him.[57]

Quỳnh recounted Mencius's debate with a man named Cao Tu on whether man was naturally good. Cao Tu argued that man was neither good nor bad, just as how it is that water naturally flows neither east nor west. However, Mencius countered by saying that humans were indeed naturally good, just as water sinks naturally. (Here, Quỳnh also invoked Mencius's famous "proof" for the natural goodness of humans: anyone who sees a drowning child will naturally feel an impulse to help the child.) However, by unnaturally striking water, one can make it splash up, which upsets the nature of water to flow down. Thus, "when man does evil, he is like water rising upward." Evil is possible, but it is against nature. Referring to Mencius's view of good tendencies as "sprouts," Quỳnh remarked that all people had "germs of virtues" which constituted "a kind of moral instinct." Good instincts prevail in most people, he thought, unless there is irretrievable decay. "It's about discovering [the good instincts] and promoting them through appropriate education. This education, everyone can undertake it himself." These passages are key to understanding why Quỳnh was so optimistic, as we will see shortly, about the French changing their policies toward the Vietnamese to supersede past colonial injustices. Following Mencius, Quỳnh thought that the French, like all people, were inherently good and that such goodness could be cultivated.

Quỳnh also evoked Mencius to make the point that the Vietnamese must undergo transformative education—to water the seeds of virtues within them—before practicing democracy. Quỳnh was not against the democracy principle but doubted that the Vietnamese were currently capable of doing it. The Vietnamese "mentality," he wrote, had been "formed by twenty centuries of Confucian education." This mentality, he said, "developed in a strict, specifically patriarchal environment." If such a mentality "remains faithful to itself," it "could not and cannot ... conceive of any form of government other than the form of government of monarchy." The recent introduction "of a vague democratic ideal imported from the West is not likely to alter this age-old mentality."[58] The Vietnamese should be wary of adopting democracy from the West too quickly, he argued, because Westerners themselves had been unable to achieve their own democratic ideals. Western democracy was made up of "a few modestly representative institutions having only the attraction of novelty," and presented "only a very questionable utility in exchange for certain unfortunate habits that their imperfect functioning inevitably implants within the new clientele," whoever that might be, Vietnamese or European.

For Quỳnh, the kind of democracy on offer from the West fell short of an ideal of politics understood as "all that relates to the government of the state, to the good management of public affairs, to the safeguarding of the higher interests of the nation." Instead, the "democracy" existing in the West, Quỳnh argued, was what we would call "populism." This kind of "democratic" politics, he wrote, came from "the demagogic societies of the West ... which consists in exciting popular passions and exploiting them, in dividing the nation into opposing cliques, in training them against each other, in making appeal to the lowest instincts of the masses to satisfy the ambitions of an unscrupulous minority."[59] In this kind of democracy, "it is the mediocre who triumph at the expense of the best, it is the most impassioned who are agitated, and it is the cleverest or the least scrupulous who profit."[60]

At the same time, Quỳnh acknowledged that the West, "in their old practice of liberty," had "antidotes powerful enough to neutralize ... the harmful effects" of this populism. In contrast, Vietnam, lacking an "old practice of liberty" was not ready for this sort of "democracy." What would happen to Vietnam, Quỳnh asked rhetorically, "if, overnight, young men just left school and decided to go into politics on the basis of foggy ideologies imported from foreign lands, and undertook to upset everything to rebuild the state and society on a new basis?" Without a proper moral foundation, the Vietnamese would end up engaging in a kind of politics that "exploits popular passions." Such politics would remain an "industry in the hands of people who live on it, who we call politicians. They maintain in society a state of continual excitement favorable to the hatching of all hatreds, all resentments, all bad feelings that sleep in the heart of the masses."

Before the Vietnamese could be capable of a better, more ideal democracy, they needed a particular kind of education:

> This education must be undertaken in a clearly moral and national sense. It must aim to train good Annamese citizens to be aware of their rights and their duties, respectful of order and the law, to know how to love their country above all and to be eager to work for its prosperity and its greatness. Based on worship of the fatherland and the race, it must, for its teachings and its principles, draw on old traditions and disciplines which over the centuries have strengthened and solidified the Annamite family and nation. It must also choose among modern ideals imported from the West and popularize those which are likely to favor the development of the individual, to give the feeling of personal dignity, passion for the public good, and the desire for more equity and social justice, in short, those likely to happily complement our own qualities or virtues.[61]

Quỳnh's ambitious program aimed to dignify the nation through harmonizing individual rights and collective duties, and the best ideas of the East and West. To achieve this program, the Vietnamese must "love their country above all," and this love could be expressed through loving the Vietnamese language and literature.

For Quỳnh, the national identity was ultimately found in the Vietnamese vernacular language and its literature. It was for this reason, he wrote, that he had "devoted all my fervor and love to my mother tongue. I swore a long time ago to sacrifice my whole life to this task: to build a literature with our language so as to give to our country an independent national literature ... and to see to it that our people would no longer have to suffer the pain of learning and imitating everything from foreigners."[62]

Drawing on Ernest Renan's writings on nationhood, Quỳnh argued that the nation was "above all a soul, a spiritual principle."[63] Vietnam had a national essence, Quỳnh argued, which was embodied in the Vietnamese language.[64] By developing and refining Vietnam's language, its "soul" could therefore be developed and refined. Thus, the promotion of *quốc ngữ* (romanized Vietnamese) was among the central points of his education program. In *Nam Phong*, he created a dictionary to propose new words in *quốc ngữ*. In the introduction to his vocabulary development project in the first issue of *Nam Phong*, he wrote: "Our national language at present is poor. We do not have enough words to express important ideas," and he went on to present new Vietnamese words based on Chinese and French: "despotism," "skepticism," "epic," and so on. He imported foreign concepts from French and Chinese, which he thought could lend more richness and nuance to the Vietnamese language. Because he believed that Confucianism was the basis for Vietnamese culture and sustained the social order, he argued that Chinese rather than *nom* (Vietnamese in Chinese script) should be the source of all *quốc ngữ* vocabulary relating to important topics such as politics, law, philosophy, and religion.[65]

Aside from constructing a national language, Phạm Quỳnh drew his readers' attention to Vietnam's most famous piece of literature, *Tale of Kiều* by Nguyễn Du, published in the early nineteenth century, to generate national pride and confidence. He exhorted the Vietnamese to study and appreciate the Vietnamese classic epic poem. "Amazingly," he remarked, "all kinds of people in our country, from men of literature and intellectuals to the ordinary worker, from the royal family to those who work the fields gathering mulberry, there is no one who does not love the *Tale of Kiều*, no one who reads *The Tale of Kiều* and is not moved."[66]

Quỳnh's claims about the widespread popularity of the poem may sound exaggerated at first, but it is less so when we consider just how popular the *Tale of Kiều* really (still) is among the Vietnamese people. "Virtually all Vietnamese know some parts of its plot or memorize some of its 3,254 verses," Truong Buu Lam wrote not too long ago. Lam remembered when "on the benches of elementary school, we were assigned long passages out of it to learn by heart. I never needed to carry the text with me; I simply needed to hang around some adults in the village. While they busied themselves with menial work, they would recite the assigned passage for me to repeat after them until such time as the passage was registered in my mind."[67]

There is thus truth to Phạm Quỳnh's claim that the *Tale of Kiều* is the quintessential Vietnamese poem loved by all Vietnamese. Furthermore, his claim that all Vietnamese loved the *Tale of Kiều* functioned to imagine and construct the nation, as Benedict Anderson would have it. The nation lived in the imagination, and for Quỳnh, the Vietnamese nation, as with others, was best imagined through literature:

> European and American countries value writers more than emperors, because the work of the spirit is more valuable and precious, and its influence

is deeper than temporary political careers. The names of King Louis XIV and Napoleon I may one day disappear, but as for the names of famous writers like Pascal, Corneille, Racine, so long as there are people who study and speak French, so long as there are people who understand deep and subtle ideas, then they will never be forgotten.[68]

The Vietnamese "only have one literary book, and that book is enough to make us famous to the world," he wrote.[69] "So long as the *Tale of Kiều* endures, our language endures. So long as our language endures, our country endures. And if our country endures, there will be nothing to worry about, nothing to be afraid of."[70] Quỳnh compared the *Tale of Kiều* to the literature of China and France, two nations with the closest relations to Vietnam, he said. Chinese literature is superficial, he argues, and, of all Chinese literature, "few can compare with the *Tale of Kiều*."[71] Even though the *Tale of Kiều* was originally a Chinese novel, the Vietnamese author "transcended the traditional Chinese style." As for French literature, the *Tale of Kiều* can be compared with Racine's and Bossuet's masterpieces.

Recall from Chapter 4 how Thomas Babington Macaulay engaged in "canon formation" when he denigrated Indian literature, while upholding English literature as *the* normative embodiment of beauty and truth. In contrast, Quỳnh upheld Vietnamese literature as *a* (not *the*) normative embodiment of truth and beauty and did not denigrate anyone else's literature in the process.

For Quỳnh, the poem's protagonist, Kiều, was a role model of self-sacrifice for the sake of social harmony and filial piety. She was "forced to choose between love and filial piety, and she deliberately chose the more difficult path. She sold herself to save her father, and from then on she endured misery after misery. But like a lotus in the mud, she retained during that abjection the pure scent of her original nobility."[72]

Kiều was a role model, Quỳnh thought, because she asserted her desires, which happened to accord with social expectations of filial piety, even though it came at a great cost for her as she sold herself into prostitution. As mentioned earlier, nationalists criticized Quỳnh for using the *Tale of Kiều* to justify his collaboration with the colonial regime. He probably would have said they were not wrong. He believed that self-sacrifice was necessary for the greater good, and, in his view, collaboration with France was a necessary sacrifice because it allowed him to use their printing press and resources to develop a more robust national culture, providing a foundation for future, long-term self-determination.

To call Phạm Quỳnh a "collaborator," retaining the word's connotations from the Second World War, risks overlooking how Quỳnh asserted national dignity by rallying his compatriots around their national culture. The assertion of indigenous culture is a common theme in the writings of anticolonial thinkers. Decades later, Amilcar Cabral, the anticolonial revolutionary from Guinea Bissau, argued that when native elites asserted their indigenous culture, they restored a sense of dignity to the entire nation. Resistance against colonialism was possible, Cabral thought, "only because, while keeping their culture and identity, the masses keep intact the sense of their individual or collective dignity, despite the horrors, humiliations, and brutalities to which they are often subjected." The assertion of indigenous culture by indigenous elites did not "and could not bring about restoration of a sense of dignity to that class alone,"[73] but rather would restore a sense of dignity to *everyone* in the nation. For Cabral, it would be admittedly difficult for native elites to assert the indigenous culture because they were usually alienated from their own culture due to their proximity to the culture of the colonizer. Such proximity usually led to confusion and identity crises among elites, Cabral thought, so their goal should be to confidently rebel, commit "class suicide," and join the masses. As for Quỳnh, he was an elite, but he was not alienated from his own culture despite his proximity to the colonizer. He asserted indigenous culture, thereby restoring a sense of cultural pride to everyone in the nation, but he did not commit class suicide to join the masses.

Far surer of Vietnam's cultural greatness than Phan Chu Trinh and Nguyễn An Ninh, Phạm Quỳnh shamed the Vietnamese for not asserting their already existing dignity as evidenced in its literary tradition. They must take pride in themselves to begin a cross-civilizational dialogue with France, which, he argued, had its own great literary tradition. The greatness of Vietnamese literature was proof that "in the world, there is a certain conception of literature and art that happens to be shared among two peoples of the Far West and the Far East." Between "the French spirit and the Annamite spirit there are certain natural affinities that are interesting and should be cultivated with a view to rapprochement so desired on both sides and which must be realized by the elites of the two peoples through the intimate communication of art and poetry."[74] This rapprochement was especially necessary, according to Quỳnh, considering the asymmetrical colonial relationship between the two that has characterized the last few decades. And such rapprochement, he said, was possible.

The Problem of Domination and the Solution of Harmony

The following words seem odd coming from a supposed pro-colonial collaborator:

> When a people settles with another people as ruler and master, it is at bottom a policy of force that they apply. Having conquered the country by force, it is maintained only by force. The iron hand may be more or less a velvet glove. It remains ultimately an iron fist. This assertion may seem brutal. Unfortunately, it reflects the harsh and exact truth.[75]

Yet, Quỳnh continued,

> against this truth, something in us protests. Men belonging to two different races can encounter each other in violent shocks. There may have been at the beginning the victors and the vanquished, some bruised by their defeat, the others proud of their victory. But a half-century of common life, equally profitable for both—as is the case between the French and the Annamese—has also been able to gradually erase the memory of this bad dream.... Time is a big factor; it reconciles, it soothes. It creates between men only interests, duties, and common burdens that bring ties closer every day, which can become indissoluble. Time blunts roughness; it rounds the angles; it transforms rough stones into polished pebbles which polish more by rubbing each day. It must do its work in the relations between French and Annamese; it has done so to a certain extent. And these relationships, it must be acknowledged, have multiplied to become much more cordial and more confident than in the past. But there is still much to be done, and we must help time to complete its beneficent work.[76]

This passage is controversial. Not all of Quỳnh's contemporaries would have considered a half-century of colonial rule to be "equally profitable" for both the French and the Vietnamese. And Quỳnh may seem naïve in his hope that the passage of time can help transform the unequal, nonreciprocal political relationship of colonialism into something more equal.

Yet, Quỳnh is advancing a theory regarding how the wrong of colonialism *might* be superseded.[77] To aid the passage of time in superseding colonial injustice, Quỳnh flatters, wheedles, and guilts the French into fulfilling their own idealized, universalist pretensions. The French man, he argues, is not as imperialistic as the English, not as chauvinistic as the Italians, not as militaristic as the Germans, and not as exploitative as the Americans. Rather, the French represent "the best that western civilization has produced."[78] They are a country "of harmony and balance, serene beauty and ineffable gentleness, a country of reason and wisdom, a country of humanity and justice."[79] With that said, Quỳnh explained that the French conquered the Vietnamese

> not to satisfy imaginary needs for expansion, but only for the sake of glory, for he loves glory, and that is his only weakness. What will he do with these conquered people? Will he be content to dominate and exploit them as a vulgar colonizer does? No, because that is not its strength.... it would be infinitely better for him to follow his natural inclination and let this broad humanism within him, eager to spread for the greater good of all humanity, act freely.[80]

Like how a parent might scold their child for misbehaving and say that he is capable of being so much better than he is acting, Quỳnh scolds the French for failing to live up to their potential as moral human beings. An obstacle to mutual respect between the French and the Vietnamese, he argues, is a false sense of prestige that some French have from "the humiliation of others." It is "thus something unhealthy, I will even say inhuman, that poisons and spoils everything."[81] In contrast, real prestige, if the French want it,

> emanates from personality itself, from all its qualities and moral value; it cannot be the effect of some sort of racial pride which makes it so that when one belongs to a so-called superior race, one believes one has the right to manifest it in every respect towards men of another so-called inferior race.[82]

Note, here, that Quỳnh is very much echoing Governor-general Albert Sarraut's own progressive beliefs, as we have discussed earlier. Sarraut argued that, under his watch, "the French colonial operation, designed for the good of both parties, will no longer be the spoliation of one race by another, but rather an association."[83] Many Vietnamese, including those who would become future Communist revolutionaries, were optimistic about Sarraut's promises until such promises fell through.

For Phạm Quỳnh, mutual respect between France and Vietnam was necessary if the two peoples were to fulfill what Quỳnh saw as a cosmic duty: harmonization of the "Eastern ideal" and the "Western ideal." He identified "the famous problem of the East and the West" as being "the opposition of two principles, both of which were equally necessary and which must meet and merge into a vast unity." Quỳnh evoked the ancient Chinese dualistic concept of yin and yang to represent the ideal relation between East and West.

> If I reasoned like a Chinese philosopher, I would say that the east is the principle yin [in Annamite *âm*] and the west the principle yang [*dương*]. One represents perennialism and stability, the other strength and activity. So far, they have not met each other, having developed each in their own pole. However, their meeting may one day produce a more beautiful form of civilization for humanity. Harmonious, more humane, and more perfect.[84]

Quỳnh was using an old trope to mend colonial relations in Vietnam. The notion that the East and West expressed opposite and complementary ideals has a long history and can be traced back to Herodotus, namely, his account of the conflict between the Hellenes and Persians, which he viewed as a conflict between the heroic, liberty-loving, and dynamic West and the despotic, stagnant, and passive East.[85] For some, like Samuel Huntington, this contrast has taken the form of an eternal East–West conflict. For others, this duality carries the Romantic message of the "marriage of East and West" and the "pursuit of the ultimate unity of the human spirit which has had the misfortune to become bifurcated in the modern age, the West's 'rationalistic and ethical, positivistic and practical' mind needing to be supplemented by 'the Eastern mind [which] is more inclined to inward life and intuitive thinking.'"[86] It is in this latter camp that we can place Phạm Quỳnh. Quỳnh is like his contemporary Sarvepalli Radhakrishnan (1888–1975), an Indian comparative philosopher and "bridge-builder" between India and the West. Whereas Radhakrishnan used Hinduism to bridge Eastern and Western thought, Quỳnh used Confucianism.

Some Western thinkers, Quỳnh argued, were already doing their part to harmonize East and West by denouncing the dangers and shortcomings of Western "mechanical civilization" and showing that "a purely quantitative conception of life and progress" promoted in the West had been "insufficient."[87] These Westerners had "turned to the East, whose old philosophies they scrutinized to seek lessons of wisdom." If such a trend continued, Quỳnh thought, it would bring the West "back to a more just appreciation of the spiritual elements of civilization and give it all its human value, which resides in a harmonious synthesis of matter and spirit." Quỳnh lamented the West's "political, economic, social, and international crises" as coming "precisely from the excesses of this quantitative or mechanical civilization." However, he also praised the West's "creative dynamism," which could and should temper the Eastern ideal should it ever become too "static." Needed was a "spiritual alliance" that would "unite together European science and Asian wisdom." Just as Western dynamism could use Eastern stabilizing wisdom, he argued, Eastern stability could use some Western dynamism. He shamed the Vietnamese for having become too "static":

> Eastern wisdom, which has allowed vast human multitudes through the centuries to maintain their cohesion and unity, has been confined to the ivory tower of its old immutable principles, far from the reality of things. It no longer evolves. It has become fossilized in a way and become a principle of stagnation which condemns the societies it governs to no longer renew themselves and to live in perpetual mediocrity. The stability it gives them often resembles sleep or death. Thus, neither pure dynamics nor absolute statics are conducive to the blossoming of a truly human and complete civilization. It is from the harmonious union of European science and Asian wisdom that a new culture will be born which will be the true universal culture. This union is far from being realized, and for the moment the East–West question is essentially the struggle between these two principles, following the violent introduction of Western science into societies governed by old Asian wisdom.[88]

For Quỳnh, the "ideal would be the achievement of harmony of the West and the East, European science and Asian wisdom." He emphasizes the need to harmonize East and West to mutually enhance both. This is distinctly Confucian. As Chenyang Li described it, the Confucian notion of harmony is "a dynamic, developmental, generative process, which seeks to balance and reconcile differences and conflicts through creativity and mutual transformation."[89]

Phạm Quỳnh's pronouncements that essentialize the East and West may seem problematic today, particularly to those who, following Edward Said's critiques of "orientalism," are aware of how Western essentializing of East and West has been deployed for Western imperialist projects. However, Quỳnh's essentializing is different. He oscillates between criticizing and romanticizing aspects of "the West." And when he romanticizes the West, this "reverse orientalism" was not for imperial ends, but for Vietnamese self-assertion and reconciliation and reciprocity between France and Vietnam.

The back cover of the thick orange book of Phạm Quỳnh's writings that I found in Hanoi explains to the reader that you are

> holding in your hands just a small part of the tens of thousands of pages written throughout the life of [Phạm Quỳnh].... His calmness and carefulness permeate the pages with his clear thinking and writing style, but they still sparkle with subtle, witty, and surprisingly accurate remarks.... Even though [these writings] have been buried for a long time under the ups and downs of history, they will surely be recognized as a special milestone in the development of national culture.

Reprinted for new generations, Quỳnh's essays in *Nam Phong* have become a source of Vietnamese national dignity today. The book that I held in my hands was a continuation of what had developed throughout the 1930s as Vietnamese thinkers worked on the genre of self-strengthening literature that Phan Bội Châu, Phan Chu Trinh, Nguyễn An Ninh, and Phạm Quỳnh had begun. Quỳnh had constructed the vocabulary and intellectual groundwork that anticolonial activists would later work from. The *Self-Reliant Literary Group* [*Tự lực văn đoàn*] in the 1930s, the historian Martina Nguyễn writes, "developed an ardent belief that only Vietnamese could change their conditions and liberate themselves."[90] Although the group presented themselves as foes of Phạm Quỳnh's exhortations to revive Confucianism, arguing that such traditional ideas were no longer appropriate for the times,[91] they would use the *quốc ngữ* language that Quỳnh had developed and promoted through *Nam Phong*. As John Phan writes, *quốc ngữ* was a "vehicle for exactly the kind of anticolonial activity feared by Sarraut and Marty over the later 1920s and 1930s" and "a tool for self-strengthening."[92] In promoting a language and culture that the Vietnamese could be proud of, Quỳnh succeeded. But in promoting harmony between the French and the Vietnamese, he failed. His collaboration with the French would make him one of the first to be executed by the Việt Minh once they seized power in 1945. And the man who was central in founding the Việt Minh, Hồ Chí Minh, would have a very different view from Phạm Quỳnh about how to construct national dignity. Both looked upon Confucianism favorably, but for different reasons. Whereas Quỳnh saw Confucianism as embodying the Eastern ideal of wisdom, which should be harmonized with the Western ideal of power, Hồ Chí Minh regarded Confucian discourses of virtue-cultivation as useful for revolutionaries who wished to resist Western power. And whereas Quỳnh had faith that colonial relations could become more reciprocal over time if the Vietnamese and French harmonized Eastern and Western ideals, Hồ Chí Minh had no such faith. For Hồ, colonial relations could only end through organized resistance to expel the French from Vietnam, and the harm of dehumanization that colonialism had caused could only be rectified through implementing a new vision for Vietnamese society.

PART III
REVOLUTION AND ITS DISCONTENTS

6
Hồ Chí Minh's Rehumanizing Blueprint

It is remarkable that the first four pieces of text in the official fifteen volumes of writings attributed to Hồ Chí Minh from 1912 to his death in 1969 are Hồ's letters to Phan Chu Trinh. The young Hồ is in England and asks his mentor if they can meet in France. In another letter, Hồ writes poetry to Trinh. And, in his letter from August 1914, Hồ remarks to Trinh that, upon the beginning of what we call First World War, "fate will have many surprises for us, and it is impossible to predict who will win.... The situation in Asia will change and there will be many changes."[1]

Neither Hồ nor Trinh knew then how much they would eventually diverge, ideologically, in the following years. The mentor and the mentee would come to identify very different sources of national shame and would thus offer very different proposals for how to construct dignity for Vietnam. Both would become national heroes, but only one would have his name in the official political ideology—"Hồ Chí Minh Thought" (*Tư Tưởng Hồ Chí Minh*)—of the Socialist Republic of Vietnam that emerged in the aftermath of the bloodshed of the First (1946–1954) and Second (1955–1975) Indochina Wars.

Recall from Chapter 3 that Phan Chu Trinh saw the primary source of Vietnam's national shame as coming from within Vietnam: its own tradition of monarchic rule. Although he criticized the French colonial regime, Trinh reserved most of his anger for Vietnamese autocratic monarchs and the corrupt mandarins who supported them. They distorted Confucianism, he argued, to justify their authoritarianism and keep the people ignorant of genuine Confucian morality and ethics. This produced weakness in the Vietnamese and thus vulnerability to foreign conquest. For Trinh, Europeans had superior ethics and morals. Unlike the Vietnamese, Europeans "help one another with respect to public justice and maintain a sense of respect for each other's interest."[2] Europeans were more "Confucian" than the Vietnamese, and this was because Europeans had a tradition of promoting "liberalism" (by which he meant popular and individual rights) and "democracy" (by which he meant "government by laws") in response to their own past autocratic monarchs. If the Vietnamese wanted to strengthen themselves to construct national dignity, they had to adopt liberalism and democracy from Europe as "medicine." Doing so, Trinh argued, would improve the ethics and morality of the Vietnamese, thereby allowing for Confucianism's fullest expression in Vietnam: "To bring in European civilization is to bring back the teachings of Confucius and Mencius.... The introduction of European civilization would not cause any harm, but it will help to enhance the teachings of Confucius and Mencius."[3]

In contrast, this chapter shows how Hồ Chí Minh saw the main source of national shame as coming not from within Vietnam but from Europe: capitalism. Whereas Trinh understood "liberalism" to be a noble tradition of advocating popular and individual rights, Hồ regarded "liberalism" as a bourgeois ideology whose emphasis on individual rights enabled, while masking, capitalist exploitation. Influenced by Lenin's writings, Hồ explained that the logical outcome of capitalism was colonialism in which colonialists exploited the Vietnamese to produce valuable raw materials for industrial production in the French metropole, where the bourgeoisie there also exploited their own local workers. Thus, whereas Trinh thought Europeans were ethical among each other, Hồ thought Europeans were oppressing their own people.

Perhaps what sets Hồ apart from Trinh the most, however, is that Hồ was especially disturbed by what he saw as the capacity—and need—for colonialism and capitalism to racially dehumanize its victims in the interest of generating profit. This was apparently not as much of a concern for Phan Chu Trinh who praised Europeans for their superior morality and ethics and criticized French colonialists not for dehumanizing the Vietnamese but for giving too much freedom to Vietnamese mandarins. Furthermore, recall the scene that introduced this book. After Trinh suggested that the Vietnamese should ask calmly for their rights, Hồ responded: "Why don't our twenty million compatriots do anything to force the [colonial] government to treat us as human beings? We are humans and we must live as humans. Anyone who does not want to treat us as his fellow man is our enemy."

This chapter gives special attention to this feature of Hồ Chí Minh's political thought: his indignation over dehumanization. I interpret him as a theorist of humanization, namely, as a critic of dehumanization and an architect of rehumanization. In the first section, I will show how, as a critic of dehumanization, he explained the racial dehumanization faced by the Vietnamese as a logical consequence of capitalism and colonial relations. Hồ was also sensitive to how the condition of colonial subjugation caused the Vietnamese to, in turn, dehumanize all French people as well as the Vietnamese themselves through drug abuse and political inertia.

In the second section, I demonstrate how, as an architect of rehumanization, Hồ had a vision for how the Vietnamese could restore their dignity. I reconstruct this vision and show how its core assumption is a Confucian one: that the exercise of moral virtue will create a causal chain of dignifying social and political improvements. In this way, Hồ marks a departure and thus an innovation within Marxist traditions of thought that downplay morality. For Hồ, party leaders must cultivate revolutionary moral virtue; this would make them trustworthy in the eyes of "the people" whom they were to serve; once party leaders became trustworthy, they could effectively guide "the people" in becoming virtuous themselves; once the people were virtuous, they could use democracy as an instrument toward the goals of independence and Communist revolution. I call this "blueprint" for rehumanizing the Vietnamese "paternalistic democracy," which I do not mean as a pejorative. It is paternalistic because party leaders were to act as wise parents, and it is democratic because of Hồ's reference to the people's well-being and development as the aim of revolution.

Lastly, in the third section, I discuss how Hồ's theory of dehumanization and rehumanization contributes a few insights for political theorists. First, in contrast to mainstream discussions of revolution, Hồ foregrounded racist dehumanization as a motivation for revolution. Second, whereas Hồ would agree with left-wing critiques of liberals who equated humanity with protection of the law, Hồ would disagree with such critiques' conclusion that one's humanity could not be conferred or taken away. For Hồ, one could indeed confer or take away *one's own humanity*—one's dignity—through one's own actions. And third, whereas many discussions of rehumanization focus on intergroup recognition and forgiveness, Hồ's method of rehumanization focused on a national political project.

Before we begin, a few caveats and a brief biography are in order. Hồ remains a controversial figure to this day. In the eyes of some observers, he was an agent of dehumanization, not humanization. Consider Vietnamese American protests in Southern California in 1999 when outrage arose over a Vietnamese man's decision to display a portrait of Hồ Chí Minh in the video store he owned. Protestors held signs displaying Hồ Chí Minh's face next to Hitler's. To understand this Vietnamese anti-Communist sentiment, Tuan Hoang argues, we must consider the complex tradition of Vietnamese anti-Communism and also the experiences of those who suffered at the hands of communists. In Vietnam under the new regime, especially during the first few years after the war, many who were associated with the South Vietnam regime faced political persecution and incarceration and reported widespread torture. The memoirs of ex-prisoners "describe both systemic dehumanization and cruelty committed by individuals" acting in the name of Hồ Chí Minh's revolution. They used such words as "nightmare" [*ác mộng*], "darkness" [*đen tối*], and "hell" [*địa ngục*] and referred to camp wardens, officers, and guards variously as "animals" [*thú vật*], "devils" [*quỷ*], and "red devils" [*quỷ đỏ*].[4] And for some, Hồ was far from democratic. Consider anti-Communist politicians of the Republic of Vietnam (South Vietnam) in the 1950s who saw Hồ's ideology as autocratic and who debated among themselves over their own competing visions of democracy.[5] Yet, "humanization" and "democracy" have always been contested concepts, ideals that different ideologies interpret in different ways. Therefore, Hồ also has his supporters. Various caricatures of Hồ abound: power-hungry zealot, selfless patriot, Machiavellian apparatchik, nationalist saint, and so on.[6]

For these reasons, Hồ Chí Minh is the thorniest of all the figures we examine in this study. A cult of personality still remains around him, and the stakes of controlling his public image are very high, even to this day.[7] One way to sidestep these political minefields is for me to focus on interpreting writings attributed to him. My aim in this chapter is therefore not to assess how "humanizing" or "democratic" Hồ Chí Minh (or the Democratic Republic of Vietnam) really was, by either his own standards or by any other. Hồ never set out to create a systematic theory of dehumanization or rehumanization, and it is also not always clear how to distinguish between what may be merely "rhetoric" and what may be a theory. Yet, theory is still "happening" in his writings, a diagnosis of the cause of indignity (racist dehumanization of the Vietnamese), and a prescription of how to construct dignity (a Communist revolution that rehumanizes them).

A Brief Biography: Hồ Chí Minh

Hồ Chí Minh was born as Nguyễn Sinh Cung and would go by many names throughout his life. There is dispute about the year he was born, but his official birth year according to the Vietnamese government is 1890. Hồ's father, Nguyễn Sinh Sắc, was a mandarin and a Confucian scholar, and he was closely acquainted with Phan Bội Châu. Remarkably, Hồ Chí Minh went to sea as a mess boy on a French ship in 1911 and would not return until 1941. After traveling for a few years, including perhaps to the United States (though there is no certain evidence of this), to various ports in Africa, and to London where he worked as a snow sweeper, pastry chef, and boiler operator, Hồ arrived in war-torn France in 1917 and began working as a photo retoucher in a shop managed by Phan Chu Trinh.

In June of 1919, Hồ delivered the *Revendications du Peuple Annamite* to the delegates of the Paris Peace Conference. Following this confrontation, French authorities hired a Vietnamese informer and police agents to stake out Hồ's residence and to follow him around Paris for the rest of 1919 and on and off until 1923. Around 1920, he joined the faction in the French Socialist Party that decided to join the Third International. Thus, Hồ became a founding member of the French Communist Party.

From France, Hồ went to Moscow in 1923, a trip organized by the Intercolonial Union, and attended the first congress of the Peasant International (Krestintern) that October, joining their presidium. Then, in 1924, he went to Canton (Guangzhou) where he helped create what would become the Vietnamese Revolutionary Youth League (*Thanh Niên*), an organization of expat Vietnamese and one of Vietnam's first Communist-oriented groups. In 1927, when Chiang Kai-shek's anti-Communist coup reached Canton, Hồ left China and went back to Moscow, after which he traveled to Paris, Brussels, Berlin, and then to Siam by 1928 where he tried to mobilize ethnic Vietnamese in Siam to support the revolution. Then, in mid-1929, he went to Hong Kong where, in February 1930, he presided over the founding of the Vietnamese Communist Party. There, the British police detained him for nearly two years and then expelled him. Hồ hid somewhere in China for some time and went back to Moscow in mid-1934 where he studied at the Communist University of the Toilers of the East. He also studied at the Institute for National and Colonial Problems. Then, in 1938, he returned to southern China.

Finally, from southern China, he returned to Vietnam in May 1941 where he met with Communists and convinced them to join non-Communist parties to concentrate on national liberation before the Communist revolution. The new group became known as the Việt Minh. In 1945, Hồ also convinced the United States (Office of Strategic Services [OSS]) to give his group arms to drive out the Japanese military that had been occupying Vietnam since 1940. In August 1945, the Việt Minh entered Hanoi, and on September 2, 1945, Hồ stood before thousands of people at Ba Đình Square and declared

136   THE ARCHITECTS OF DIGNITY

the independence of the Democratic Republic of Vietnam (DRV) from colonial rule.

Hồ began his speech by quoting, in Vietnamese, the 1776 Declaration of Independence of the United States, as well as the 1791 Declaration of the French Revolution on the Rights of Man and the Citizen. "Yet," he continued, "for more than eighty years, the French colonialists have abused the flag of freedom, equality, and fraternity to rob our country and oppress our people."[8] Hồ went on to list a long train of abuses by the French colonial government and ended his speech with the decision "to mobilize all [Vietnamese] physical and mental strength, to sacrifice their lives and property in order to safeguard their independence and liberty." The next day, Hồ called for elections. Months later, on January 6, 1946, the Vietnamese in North Vietnam would vote for the first time in a general election for members of the National Assembly of the DRV.

Despite Hồ's declaration of independence, Charles de Gaulle, the new leader of a liberated France, ordered his men to reestablish colonial rule in Vietnam. However, the Chinese, whom the Allies had agreed to allow into North Vietnam to disarm Japanese occupiers, insisted that the French negotiate with the Việt Minh. French leaders accepted and, in 1946, Hồ went to Paris to engage in negotiations with the French. The negotiations failed, and in December of that year, Hồ urged the Vietnamese people to affirm their decision to commit to violent anticolonial struggle, thus inaugurating the First Indochina War.

Although Hồ's actual control over the party would wane as other figures such as Trường Chinh and Lê Duẩn took greater control, Hồ would become a symbol of the Vietnamese Communist Party and the Vietnamese Communist Revolution. Hồ died in September 1969. Against his wishes to be cremated, the party preserved his body and placed it in a tomb on Ba Đình Square, where he had declared the independence of the DRV more than two decades earlier.[9]

Part One: A Critic of Dehumanization

Bernard Fall, the influential journalist who reported on the wars in Indochina, wrote that Hồ's writings "clearly reflect the personal humiliations he must have suffered at the hands of the colonial masters—not because they hated him as a person, but simply because, as a 'colored' colonial, he did not count as a human being. This intense personalization of the whole anticolonial struggle shines clearly throughout Hồ's writings."[10] Indeed, many of Hồ's writings in the years before the First Indochina War are replete with observations of colonialism's capacity to dehumanize the colonized. Often in the form of lengthy, detailed lists, Hồ gives plenty of examples of arbitrary violence and cruelty that Vietnamese natives experienced daily at the hands of the French colonizers. This is especially common in his articles of the early 1920s in *Le Paria*, a French-language journal he helped found as a voice for colonized peoples in the French empire, and in his book, *Le procès de la colonization française* (French Colonialism on Trial), written in French and published in 1925. In an essay published in *Le Paria* on August 1, 1922, Hồ explains that "Colonial sadism is a widespread and unimaginably cruel phenomenon,"[11] a point that was to be expressed through many examples in his writings on colonial cruelty. He showed how the colonizers had dehumanized the Vietnamese in ways they would never do to their own people. For Hồ, colonial dehumanization of the Vietnamese did not merely mean that the Vietnamese were treated as animals in the way humans might treat livestock or cattle. Humans were not typically sadistic to their livestock because they viewed animals as resources and simply did not think about their well-being. In contrast, the "dehumanization" of natives, Hồ thought, entailed treating natives not only as resources but also with racist sadism and cruelty.

For example, Hồ quoted from a travel diary of a French colonial soldier who was on a boat with other Frenchmen. Vietnamese vendors in smaller boats approached them to sell fruit and shellfish and, instead of giving them money, the soldiers threw cigarette butts into their baskets and, as a "joke," threw a bucket of boiling water on the vendors.

> Then, there were screams and oars were swung wildly which caused the boats to collide. Right below me, an Annamese man was doused with boiling water. Burned from head to toe, he wanted to jump in the water, but his brother grabbed him.... Another bucket of boiling water was poured and it was the rescuer's turn to be boiled alive. I saw him struggling in the boat, his skin peeled off, revealing red flesh as he screamed like an animal. But the scene made us laugh. We thought it was funny. We had a colonial soul![12]

The French soldier notes that "in those scenes, I can only remember one thing: we are more cruel and barbaric than pirates." Hồ described an instance when French soldiers came upon three Vietnamese and asked for money, alcohol, and opium. When the Vietnamese could not make themselves understood, the Frenchmen raped, killed, and dismembered them.

> On the flat land that used to be salt fields were three dead bodies: a naked baby, a young girl with her stomach cut open, her left arm stiffly, involuntarily, raised to the sky, her hand clenched. And his body. The old man was hideously burned, and his shape could no longer be recognized, disfigured by the burning with his fat which had run, melted, and congealed with the skin of his swollen belly, grilled like the skin of a roasted pig.[13]

Sarcastically referring to cruel colonizers as "representatives of civilization," Hồ described how a Vietnamese named Tai, whose duty it was to open and close a bridge for trains, "ran out to welcome the representative of civilization who immediately shouted at him, 'You animals, why don't you open it?' Not knowing French, Tai could only answer by pointing at the red signal." This gesture angered the Frenchman who then "jumped at Tai and pushed him into a pile of embers nearby." Tai "was horribly burned, taken to the hospital, and after six days of extreme pain he died. The French official was not charged. . . . While the life of an Annamese person is considered like the body of a dog, not worth a cent, Inspector General Reinhardt received 120,000 francs in compensation for a scratch on his arm. Equality! Beloved equality!"[14] Hồ described how a Frenchman "furiously jumped out and beat an Annamese man just because he dared to be curious and had the audacity to look at this European's house for a few seconds. He beat him and finally killed him with a gunshot to the head. A railway official used a rattan whip to beat a Tonkin Chief."[15] Another Frenchman "punched and broke the skull of his driver." Another Frenchman, "a contractor, let his dog bite an Annamese man, then tied this person's hands and kicked him to death." Another Frenchman "heard a noise on the street. As soon as he opened his door, an Annamese woman ran in, followed by a man chasing her. [The Frenchman] thought it was a native chasing a girl then grabbed his shotgun and shot and killed the man. It turned out to be a European. When asked, [the Frenchman] replied: 'I thought it was a native.'" For Hồ, the "notebook" of "a series of murders where the perpetrators were our 'civilizers' and went unpunished" keeps "getting longer and longer every day. It's so painful."[16]

The above accounts are Hồ's attempts to show how arbitrary violence was inextricably linked to dehumanization of the Vietnamese. Some theorists have even argued that arbitrary violence was a key feature that made colonialism distinctively wrong.[17] In this context, arbitrariness does not mean "randomness" or "unpredictable" but something more sinister. Such violence is not merely about inflicting physical pain, but an expression of the superior status of the colonizer, the subhuman status of the colonized, a violence based on the personal whims and feelings of the colonizer. As in the case above of the Frenchman who beat Tai to death and was not charged, colonizers could inflict violence that, in the words of Frank Lovett, was "not externally constrained by effective rules, procedures, or goals that are common knowledge of all persons or groups concerned."[18] Such violence is arbitrary because, as Philip Pettit put it, the agent of such violence "was in a position to choose it or not choose it, at their pleasure."[19]

To drive home his point that colonialism dehumanizes the colonized, Hồ referred to how the Vietnamese were treated as, and sometimes worse than, nonhuman animals. In a 1941 letter to the Vietnamese people, Hồ lamented that the Vietnamese suffered under a double yoke from simultaneous French and Japanese occupation. The Vietnamese served "as buffaloes and horses for Westerners, and then became slaves for the Japanese."[20] And yet, some animals get better treatment than colonized peoples:

> we have racked our yellow-skin brains, but cannot figure out why the French people established a strange organization called the Society for the Protection of Animals. The reason why we cannot understand this is because we see that today there are still so many suffering people who are asking for people to take care of them a little but still can't get it.[21]

It remains a mystery, therefore, how Europeans could treat the colonized and "so many unfortunate human beings" worse than animals.

Ho's criticisms of racist dehumanization were not limited to the Vietnamese experience but they also extended to colonized peoples around the world.[22] He described French settlers in Tunisia who killed three natives just for grazing their sheep in their olive grove.[23] He quoted a colonial major in Morocco who told his men: "We must destroy these savages. Moroccan soil is rich in minerals and agricultural products. We, the French, civilized people, come here with two purposes: to civilize them and enrich ourselves."[24] Hồ documented colonial oppression in Martinique, French Polynesian islands, British control in China, India, and Sudan, the Belgian Congo, German extermination of the Herero and Nama peoples, Algeria, India, Native Americans in reservations in the United States, and more.[25] In

Dahomey, Hồ explained, French colonizers did everything they could to reduce the natives "to the level of animals and humiliate them."[26]

Ho's criticism of dehumanization was specifically a criticism of *racist* dehumanization. Aware that notions of racial superiority and inferiority facilitated capitalist exploitation in the colonies, he wrote: "In the colonies, anyone with white skin is considered noble and as belonging to the superior race. To maintain his status, the bottom-ranked Westerner has at least one person, a servant, who is used as a maid to do all work."[27] Here, Hồ was aware of how the category of race could be used to prevent class solidarity, as lower class Europeans were given non-European servants as an incentive to feel solidarity with those of their own race rather than with racialized others with whom they might have more in common economically. Elsewhere, Hồ approvingly quoted at length an unnamed traveler who theorized how colonial structures incentivized French colonizers to racially dehumanize the Vietnamese:

> When they arrive here, all French people have the idea that the Annamese are inferior and must be slaves for them. They consider the Annamese people as animals that must be controlled with whips. All of them became habituated to seeing themselves as belonging to a new aristocratic class with special privileges. Soldiers or colonists all believed that between them and the natives there was no other relation than that between master and servant. It seems that for them the servant is representative of the entire yellow race. You should listen to a Frenchman in Indochina talk about yellow people to see the stupidity of his arrogance.[28]

Perhaps the most famous instance of Hồ's reflections on how capitalism relied on racist dehumanization was his 1924 text titled "Lynching: a Little Known Aspect of American Civilization," which explained the lynching of Black Americans to fellow Vietnamese.[29] Despite being emancipated from slavery sixty-five years ago, Black Americans, Hồ said,

> still have to endure many terrible mental and physical sufferings, the most cruel and disgusting of which is lynching. . . . Imagine a hysterical crowd. Fists clenched, bloodshot eyes, mouths foaming. Booing, cursing. The crowd is captivated by the hysterical excitement of committing crimes without fear. They are armed with sticks, torches, pistols, ropes, knives, scissors . . . anything that can be used to kill or injure. Imagine that in the

middle of the crowd there is a pile of black meat being pushed, beaten, trampled, slashed ... over and over again until it is bloody and motionless. The torn body, the black man, is the victim. In a wave of hatred and bestiality... they tie him to a tree, douse him with kerosene.... Before lighting the fire, they break his teeth one by one then gouge out his eyes.... The black man can no longer cry out. His tongue is swollen from a red-hot iron bar pressed into it.... One cut of the knife and an ear falls off.... Someone shouts, 'Light the fire!'.... When everyone is tired of watching, they take the body down. The rope is cut into pieces and each is sold for 3 or 5 dollars. The women compete to buy them as souvenirs.... Meanwhile, on the ground covered in grease and smoke is a black skull, crushed, burned, shapeless ... seeming to want to ask the setting sun: "Is this civilization?"

It is important to note that, for Hồ, *all* such acts of lynching and racist dehumanization were the consequences of capitalist exploitation and competition:

These crimes are always caused by economic jealousy, or by seeing local black people doing better than white people, or by seeing black workers refusing to be exploited to the bone. In all those cases, the main perpetrators were never bothered, simply because they were always encouraged and spurred on by politicians, financiers, authorities, and especially the reactionary press that provokes, instigates and then covers up.[30]

In these texts, Hồ offered an analysis of what theorists would today call "racial capitalism," a term that describes not a kind of capitalism but how capitalism itself depends on racial dehumanization.

So far, we have discussed how racist dehumanization was a significant concern for the younger Hồ and that he saw it as being caused by exploitative, colonial relations. The corollary is that Hồ believed that the absence of dehumanization between two races was possible only outside of the colonial context. He received a glimpse of this when he first arrived in Marseille, France, in 1911 and was reportedly surprised to be addressed as "*monsieur*" for the first time by a Frenchman when he stopped at a café for a cup of coffee. Writing to a friend about this surprising experience of being treated as an equal by a Frenchman, Hồ remarked that "[t]he French in France are better and more polite than those in Indochina."[31] We might surmise that the experience showed him that it was possible for the French to treat the Vietnamese with equal human dignity but that it was the colonial relationship that was the obstacle. Elsewhere, Hô wrote:

> The French in France are all good. But the French colonialists are very cruel and inhumane. It is the same everywhere. At home I have seen such things happening in Phan Rang. The French burst out laughing while our compatriots drowned for their sake. To the colonialists, the life of an Asian or an African is not worth a penny.[32]

At times, Hô seemed to be more indignant about dehumanization than about colonialism itself, at least earlier in his political career. Recall the list of demands that Hô famously signed and delivered to delegates of the 1919 Paris Peace Conference following the First World War. In the list were eight demands for modest liberal rights: (1) amnesty for political prisoners; (2) equality under the law; (3) freedom of speech; (4) freedom of association; (5) freedom of travel; (6) freedom of education; (7) rule of law; and (8) representation. Contrary to popular misconception, the petition did *not* ask for Vietnamese independence from French colonial rule. If Hô sincerely agreed with these demands, this suggests that he was primarily indignant about Vietnamese dehumanization and the denial of rights that French colonizers were able to enjoy in Vietnam. It also suggests that he perhaps thought it was possible for colonizers to treat the Vietnamese with humanity while maintaining sovereignty over them. Yet, it is also possible that he delivered the list, already believing that it would be impossible to respect the liberal rights of the colonized while maintaining colonial domination.

So far, we have seen that a significant source of indignation for Hô was how capitalism (and by extension, colonialism) dehumanized its victims in order to exploit them. Yet, he was also indignant at how capitalism and colonialism, in turn, caused the Vietnamese to be agents of dehumanization as well. Colonialism not only caused colonizers to dehumanize natives, but it also produced the natural response in which the Vietnamese dehumanized all French people, many of whom were not colonizers. Just as "the French workers viewed the natives as low, insignificant, and incapable of understanding and of action," the natives saw "the French, no matter what kind of people they are, as cruel exploiters. Imperialism and capitalism do not miss the opportunity to take advantage of that mutual suspicion and artificial racial hierarchy to... divide those who should be united."[33] For Hô, mutual dehumanization was in capitalism's interest.

Furthermore, Hồ made the point that colonial monopoly over drugs and alcohol caused the Vietnamese to indirectly contribute to their own dehumanization. By consuming substances that impaired their ability to resist, that stupefied them, and made them socially and politically inert, the Vietnamese effectively facilitated the colonial project of dehumanizing and exploiting the Vietnamese. In his speech to the French Socialist Party in Tours in 1920, Hồ spoke of how the Vietnamese were poisoned: "I would like to emphasize the word 'poisoning' with opium and alcohol.... In Indochina, the colonialists try every way to poison us with opium and make us stupid with alcohol."[34] This was part of France's "Stupefying Policy" which was intended to transform the Vietnamese people who "are very studious" into ignorant, inert people through poverty, as poor people must "fight hunger before they can think about education."[35] Those living in poverty, abusing drugs, and lacking education might not necessarily be dehumanized, but for Hồ, the conscious colonial policy of keeping the Vietnamese drunk and uneducated was designed to maintain the Vietnamese as dehumanized subjects to be exploited. In a chapter titled "The Poisoning of the Natives" in his book, *French Colonialism on Trial*, Hồ lamented that there were 1,500 alcohol and opium houses for a thousand villages, while there were only ten schools for the same localities.[36] By falling prey to alcohol and opium, the natives contributed to their dehumanization.

Hồ's frustration with the Vietnamese poisoning themselves went hand in hand with his frustration over their seeming inability to organize themselves for anticolonial resistance. This political inertia was preventing the rehumanizing effects of political action. While in Guangzhou in 1925, around the time Hồ lamented drug abuse in *French Colonialism on Trial,* Hồ received a letter from a young Vietnamese man who argued that revolution had failed in Vietnam because of French brutality and that the Vietnamese should learn from Gandhi's boycott movement in India. Hồ responded:

What do you expect? Do you expect them to give us the liberty to do anything, to use all means to drive them out? Do you expect them to take no action to prevent us from attacking their own interests? Instead of blaming others, I think it is more reasonable to blame ourselves. We must ask ourselves, 'For what reasons have the French been able to oppress us? Why are our people so stupid? Why hasn't our revolution succeeded? What must we do now?' You compare us with success stories in Egypt and India, but they are like autos with wheels and a chauffeur, while we are just a chassis.

India and Egypt have political parties with members, study groups, peasant associations, and so forth. And they all know how to love their country. So Gandhi can create a boycott. Can we do the same? Where are our parties? We still have no party, no propaganda, no organization, and you want us to boycott the French?[37]

Hồ exhorted the young man, and by extension all Vietnamese, to feel ashamed for lacking what they needed—parties, propaganda, and organization—and to use such shame as motivation to rehumanize themselves. Stupidity and lack of organization are not the same as being dehumanized, but if these unfortunate qualities prevented the Vietnamese from resisting active attempts on the part of colonizers to dehumanize them, then stupidity and lack of organization effectively contributed to their own dehumanization. It was futile, Hồ eventually thought, to ask the French to humanize the Vietnamese, so the Vietnamese had to rehumanize themselves. Over decades, Hồ would develop his blueprint for how they could.

Part Two: An Architect of Rehumanization

From the early 1920s to his death in 1969, even though he never set out to construct a systematic political theory, Hồ developed a rather coherent vision for how the Vietnamese could rehumanize themselves after suffering the dehumanization of colonialism and capitalism. Just as he saw colonialism and capitalism as sources of national shame, he regarded their opposites—national independence and Communism—as wellsprings of national dignity and the promise of rehumanization. Central to his vision of how to achieve independence and Communism was an assumption that appeared thoroughly "Confucian," namely, that persistent moral self-cultivation would automatically cause social and political improvement in concentric circles outward. To be sure, there are strong Leninist and Maoist aspects in Hồ's vision, and he did not spend much time talking about Confucius, but distinctly Confucian was Hồ's constant emphasis on the need for cadres to engage in cultivating their personal moral virtue, and his assumption that doing so would create a causal chain of moral improvement outward.[38] These emphases and assumptions echo Confucius's assertions in *The Great Learning* that "the ruler will first take pains about his own virtue. Possessing virtue will give him the people." Recall our discussion of how this Confucian assumption is also key to Phan Chu Trinh's thought: "cultivate the self, regulate one's family, govern one's country, and pacify the world."

Whereas Phan Chu Trinh viewed Confucian morality as the goal that the instrument of "democracy" was meant to serve, Hồ Chí Minh viewed Confucian self-rectification and the willingness to subject themselves to the party as instrumental throughout the entire revolutionary process. It was a means to achieve democracy, which, in turn, was a means to achieve national independence and, later, Communism. And whereas for Trinh "democracy" was a liberal "government of laws," Hồ's "democracy" was an illiberal form of government in which a revolutionary party ruled in the name of the people and served their interests.

I call Hồ's vision for rehumanization "paternalistic democracy." It was paternalistic because Hồ believed the chain of causation must begin with members of the vanguard Vietnamese Communist Party who were to act as the people's "parents" because the people were akin to undeveloped children in need of moral and political guidance. And it was democratic because of Hồ's constant reference to "the people" and their well-being as the principal object of concern, the point of all political, social, and economic endeavors. To be good "parents," cadres must first rehumanize themselves by cultivating their own revolutionary virtue. Only then could they effectively guide the masses to improve the latter's virtue and instrumentalize democratic processes toward anticolonial resistance and the postcolonial socialist project.

We shall discuss this process of "rehumanization" by focusing first on Hồ's exhortations to party members, namely, how he thought they should conceptualize the ideal relationship between them and "the people," and what their responsibilities were to effectively serve the party in its claim to serve the people.

Party members, Hồ argued, must conceive of themselves as "servants" of the "people" who were, in turn, the party's "masters." In a speech to intellectuals at Thanh Hóa Province in February 1947, Hồ asked, "What is the Government of the Democratic Republic [of Vietnam]?" and he answered: "From the nation's President to the village official, it is the public servant of the people. The people are the masters, so the government must be its servants."[39] Similarly, in a speech to the National Assembly in March 1955, he declared: "Our regime is a democracy, that is, the people are the masters, and the government is the people's loyal servant. The government has only one purpose: to serve the fatherland and the people with all their heart and strength."[40] The Vietnamese term I have translated as "master" is *chủ*, which appears in the term *dân chủ* (democracy). *Dân chủ* can be translated literally as "the people are the masters," but *chủ* can also mean "principal," so that democracy means "the people are the principal." Hồ's use of the term *dân chủ* was closer in meaning to the latter than the former. The people were not "masters" who gave commands and orders. Rather, they were simply the first order of importance and had agents or representatives acting on their behalf. Thus, the *dân* (people) were akin to precious, beloved children whose well-being was the *raison d'être* of the party; they were immature and undeveloped and must be educated by their more knowledgeable—though less important—elders.

While there are many debates in political theory about when state paternalism is justified in liberal democracies, Hồ's paternalistic democracy had more in common with the experiences of developing nations around the world whose government leaders saw themselves as a moral and intellectual vanguard who must educate the uneducated masses.[41] "Our country was invaded so therefore our people are backward and impoverished,"[42] he wrote. Vietnam was an "ignorant and impoverished country" that "must be turned into one with a high culture."[43] The point of revolution, he argued, was to transform an undeveloped people into a developed people. Revolution, as he succinctly defined it, was "destroying what is bad and building what is good."[44] To help carry out this revolution, the party must "train new people and new cadres for the resistance war and nation construction. We must thoroughly eliminate all colonial relics and the servile influence of imperialist culture. At the same time, we must develop good traditions of national culture and absorb new progressive world culture, to build a Vietnamese culture that is national, scientific, and popular."[45]

During this process of destroying slavish habits and constructing progressive culture, the party must constantly think about the preciousness of the people and the potential power they held. "There is nothing more precious in the sky than the people," Hồ declared to a university classroom in 1956. "There is nothing stronger in the world than the united force of the people. In society, there is nothing more beautiful and glorious than serving the interests of the people.... The socialist and people's democratic state only cares about benefiting the people, first and foremost the working people, helping them to make progress, materially and spiritually, making sure that in society there are no people exploiting other people."[46] Here, Hồ presented "the people" in three ways: first as "precious," then as a potential source of power to be used in a resistance war against counterrevolutionaries and to build socialism, and lastly as the object of development. Because of colonial subjugation, the people lacked and therefore required "progress, materially and spiritually" and must learn to not exploit each other, and it was the state that must teach them how to achieve these aims.

By positioning the party as the people's wise servants and "the people" as precious children, Hồ could agree with two opposing positions on the classic political philosophical question of whether democracy was desirable, and thus could resolve tensions between those positions. On the one hand, advocates of democracy argued that throughout history, a few rulers had advanced their personal interests at the expense of the many, so the solution should be to make the citizens the rulers (as well as subjects of their rule). Yet, critics of democracy argued that most people were ignorant, incompetent, and unfit to rule, so democracy could be dangerous, and there should be some form of meritocracy or aristocracy instead.

Hồ agreed with both positions. For Hồ, the French colonial government clearly advanced its own interests at the expense of the Vietnamese people, so the solution should be "democracy" in which the Vietnamese "people," not the French, ruled the Vietnamese. Rather than frame this argument as nationalist or ethnic, Hồ framed it as being about democracy. At the same time, he saw that the Vietnamese people—having been dehumanized by colonial oppression and politically immature since precolonial times—were unfit to rule and in serious need of development (educational, moral, economic, cultural, political, and social) and so must be rehumanized by a virtuous, professional revolutionary class: the Vietnamese Communist Party.

So, what were the tasks for the party? How could they effectively lead the people? For Hồ, the answers can be summed up in his exhortation for them to cultivate their *đạo đức cách mạng* ("revolutionary morality").[47] To become a true revolutionary, Hồ said, one must focus on "the four words of Industry [*Cần*], thrift [*kiệm*], integrity [*liêm*], and righteousness [*chính*]."[48] Elsewhere, Hồ focused on and explicated five revolutionary virtues: "humaneness [*nhân*], righteousness [*nghĩa*], knowledge [*trí*], courage [*dũng*], and integrity [*liêm*]," saying that, together, they made up "revolutionary morality. That morality was not conservative morality. It was a new morality, a great morality, not for personal fame, but for the common good of the Party, nation, and humanity."[49] The scholar Bui Ngoc Son argued that these "five components of revolutionary virtue were fundamentally derived from the familiar cardinal moral values of classical Confucianism."[50]

Hồ maintained that these virtues would endow a person with "humaneness," which consisted of "loving deeply and wholeheartedly assisting one's comrades and compatriots." Yet, the sentence that followed was: "That is why the cadre who displays this virtue wages a resolute struggle against all those who would harm the party and the people." While one might interpret waging "resolute struggle" against enemies as going against "humaneness," one might also interpret such a struggle as a self-composed, righteous struggle. Confucius did not advocate loving one's enemies, nor did he think one should repay hatred from one's enemies with virtue. Rather, he thought that one should "repay hatred with rightness, and repay virtue with virtue."[51] Ho also said that the revolutionary "will not hesitate to be the first to endure hardship and the last to enjoy happiness. That is why he will not covet wealth and honor; nor fear hardship and suffering, nor be afraid to fight those in power."[52] "Concerning the virtue of *liêm* [integrity], Hồ cites Confucius: 'A person who has no *liêm* is less than an animal.'" What Hồ meant by *liêm* was the virtue of integrity without which one cheats and steals. And those who cheat and steal, the old metaphor goes, are behaving as less than human. For Hồ, these exhortations to cadres were meant to make the cadres loyal to the party first and foremost. But given Hồ's insistence that the party was a "servant" of "the people," Hồ saw loyalty to the party as being synonymous with loyalty to "the people." Furthermore, Hồ's moral instructions were only for cadres, not for ordinary Vietnamese. Yet, his hope was to "raise the political and moral level of our people," as a side effect of cultivating cadres' virtue.[53]

What makes Hồ's use of Confucian emphases on improving moral character particularly unique is his use of it to extend Marxism beyond the material to the moral. In other words, Hồ supplemented Marxism with its missing moral vision. Marxian conceptions of material exploitation and alienation—such as one's forced labor serving as a mere means for someone else's material colonial ends, thereby preventing one from realizing one's 'essence'—informed Hồ's understanding of dehumanization. However, by emphasizing Confucian ideas of moral and character building for revolution, Hồ helped to "correct" for the "vulgar" Marxisms of the twentieth century that denied human agency by emphasizing economic determinism. Hồ added humaneness into his engagement with Marx and Marxists like Lenin and Mao. From many Marxian perspectives, moral work-on-the-self was not a significant end or even a means. In fact, Marx made this explicit: "communists do not preach morality at all.... They do not put to people the moral demand: love one another, do not be egoists, etc."[54] Rather, the aim for many Marxists was to build a revolutionary party that could win control of the state and implement land reform and other materially redistributive policies. Any effects on ethical character formation were then believed to be *caused by* material distribution of resources, not vice versa. But Hồ did preach morality, and he did so by grafting Confucianism onto Leninism: "We should improve our character by reading the works of Confucius, and in terms of revolution, we need to read the works of Lenin."[55] Hồ's insistence on the importance of revolutionary morality is a major innovation within this Marxist tradition of thought.

To be sure, Hồ certainly did not think that moral self-cultivation was enough to rehumanize the Vietnamese. The whole point of moral self-cultivation was to generate social capacity to implement Marxian material property arrangements, such as land redistribution: "It is necessary to thoroughly reduce rents, reduce interest rates, and confiscate land that the French and Vietnamese collaborators took from us to temporarily give to poor peasants and families of soldiers, to improve the lives of peasants and raise their morale for Resistance War."[56] While material arrangements had to be changed, such change was only possible, he insisted, by first transforming one's self: "If you want to make a revolution, you must first revolutionize your character."[57]

For any party member who shirked their duty to work on their moral character, Hồ accused them of *chủ nghĩa cá nhân*, or "individualism." Well into the Second Indochina War, Hồ reminded the party that those afflicted with "individualism" were selfish and more concerned with their private interests than the party's. They "are afraid of hardships and difficulties, fall into corruption, depravation, waste, and luxury. They are greedy for fame, profit, and positions of power."[58] "Individualism" was one of the primary obstacles to revolution, Hồ thought, and the best way to combat it was through the practice of "criticism and self-criticism," a practice coined by Stalin and made famous by Mao. "Criticism and self-criticism must be honest. Having a fault and not pointing it out is no different than someone having an illness and not telling the doctor."[59] In contrast to those exhibiting "individualism," a morally upright leader cared about the party and made theory fit practice, which was crucial, Hồ thought, because if party members' thoughts and actions were not in agreement, "it would be like two crooked lines or an orchestra in which 'drums play one way and trumpets play another.' It would be impossible to lead the masses and make revolution."[60]

The day after Hồ declared the independence of the Democratic Republic of Vietnam on September 2, 1945, he gave a speech outlining the "urgent tasks of the state of the DRV." In this speech, he explained that party members and the people were politically unfit because they had been kept ignorant by the colonialists, so the party had to simply practice at self-rule so that they could guide the people: "After eighty years of oppression, exploitation, and the French colonialist policy of keeping us ignorant, you and I are not familiar with techniques of administration. But that doesn't worry us. We study while working and work while we study. Surely, we will make mistakes, but we will correct them."[61]

Similarly, in a speech on the eighth anniversary of the 1945 August Revolution, Hồ exhorted cadres to "try their best to study and correct themselves, develop their strengths, correct their shortcomings, wholeheartedly serve the people, and correctly comply with the policies of the Party and Government."[62] Specifically, party members must "strive to study Marxism-Leninism" and "strengthen ideological education in the Party."[63]

Once party members habituated themselves to using criticism and self-criticism to improve their moral character, they would by consequence become leaders whom the people would trust. And trust was crucial, Hồ thought. He remarked that in some places, the people complained about local officials more than praise them. Those local officials "are not only not loved by the people but are despised and hated by them."[64] And the reason why those officials were hated, Hồ wrote, was because they were arrogant and "do not understand the mission and policies of the Viet Minh, so when they have some power in their hands, they abuse it." Thus, he told party members, "If you want to be loved by the people, if you want to win the hearts of the people, you must do your best to do anything that is beneficial to the people, and you must do your best to avoid anything that is harmful to the people." Furthermore, he added: "towards all people in all walks of life, we must have a flexible and tactful attitude, know how to compromise, and respect people's personalities.... In short, if you want to be loved by the people, if you want to win the hearts of the people, you must first love the people, put the people's interests above all else, and have a spirit of impartiality."

To be "loved by the people," party members "must volunteer to join cooperatives and must be exemplary in production.[65] In a speech to leaders in Hà Tây Province in February 1967, Hồ said that all cadres and party leaders should "set an example" and develop "revolutionary ethics." For example, the party could protect handicraft workers' ownership of their means of production, guide and help them "improve their way of doing business," and encourage them to "organize production cooperatives on a voluntary basis." For industrial and commercial capitalists, Hồ said: "the State does not abolish their ownership of the means of production and other assets but tries to guide them in activities to benefit the country and people in accordance with the State's economic plan. At the same time, the State encourages and helps them reform according to socialism through public-private partnerships and other forms of reform."[66]

Here, we see Hồ's insistence that the party must persuade, guide, and encourage the people to align their private interests with the general will, a notion he may have gotten from reading Chinese translations of the works of Rousseau.[67] Echoing Rousseau's famous declaration that men must be "forced to be free," he told party members that they must know "how to make people enjoy their democratic rights, how to use their democratic rights to dare to speak and act."[68] To build good collectives and cooperatives, the party "must make everyone voluntarily participate, we must discuss democratically and calculate fairly and reasonably."[69]

There was yet another positive consequence of the people trusting the party, Hồ argued, which was that this trust made it possible for the people and the party to have a *reciprocal* relationship. Ideally, the "people" and the party should recognize each other's status as master and servant, and relate to each other in a reciprocal, dynamic manner, fulfilling their respective duties to contribute to the mutual enhancement of the other. While the party was supposed to serve its master by providing expert guidance, the people should do its part by helping the party do its job by offering gentle and constructive feedback, not angry and malicious criticism. Expelling the government should only be a last resort if the government continued to harm the people after efforts to help it were exhausted: "If the government harms the people, the people have the right to expel the government. But when the people use servants to work for them, they must help the Government. If the Government is wrong, it must be criticized, but not scolded."[70] To sustain this master–servant relationship, the master must be friendly in giving criticisms to his servant, motivated out of care rather than desire to scold so that the servant wanted to continue serving the master.

Another reason why it was so important for the party to gain the people's trust, Hồ argued, was that only with the people's trust could the party guide democratic processes among the people toward anticolonial resistance and the Communist revolution. For Hồ, democracy must serve as an instrument for revolution, and he was aware that there was no guarantee that democratic processes—left alone without guidance—would serve anticolonial or revolutionary ends. Thus, in a 1954 text, Hô reminded the people that democracy meant

> our state today is in the hands of the people against imperialism and feudalism. It is a people's democratic dictatorship. The people are four classes: workers, peasants, petty bourgeoisie, and the national bourgeoisie. Under the leadership of the working class and the Party, those classes unite and elect their own government. For the people, democracy is practiced. As for the imperialists, feudalists, and reactionaries, practice dictatorship against them and suppress them.[71]

Adopting Lenin's perspective, Hô viewed democracy as a "dictatorship of the proletariat" in which those who were part of the revolutionary "people" were free to deliberate to make decisions among themselves, while those who were considered counterrevolutionaries were to be repressed. As Lenin put it: "Simultaneously with an immense expansion of democracy for the people, and not democracy for the money-bags, the dictatorship of the proletariat imposes a series of restrictions on the freedom of the oppressors, the exploiters, the capitalists."[72] Hô would echo this notion in a speech to party members in 1956, where he said that the National Assembly was tasked with developing "democracy with the people and dictatorship against the enemies of the people.... Expanding democracy goes hand in hand with strengthening dictatorship to make our government increasingly truly the government of the people, serving the people and fighting against the people's enemies."[73] He would go on to frequently remind the party that they "must be truly democratic with the people, and dictatorial with the counterrevolutionaries and those who sabotage the people's interests."[74] There must be democratic freedom, but only to an extent. For example, there "must be strict adherence to the policy of respecting freedom of belief for all religions.... But religious activities must not hinder people's production, nor must they contravene the State's policies and laws."

Again echoing Rousseau who famously declared that those subject to the general will were "forced to be free," Hô described why democracy must be constrained: "Do not misunderstand democracy. If no decision has been taken yet, then feel free to discuss. But once a decision has been made, there can be no further debate. Any discussion should only be discussion of how to implement the decision quickly and effectively, not suggestion to not do it. These excessive acts of freedom must be banned."[75]

It was the party that must prevent democracy from becoming unruly and devolving into "excessive acts of freedom." Thus, while some of Hồ's assertions about democracy—namely, his calls for a democratic constitution and elections—may at first sound liberal in the sense of advocating a neutral government that prioritized individual autonomy, closer inspection shows Hồ's worry that the people, left on their own, might not become revolutionary. Therefore, the party must guide the democratic process first toward anticolonial ends, and then, once the colonizers had been expelled, toward Communist ends.

First, Hồ instrumentalized democracy for anticolonial ends. Hồ declared the independence of the DRV on September 2, 1945, but the French would not leave North Vietnam until 1954. For Hồ, democracy had to be instrumentalized to finish the task of expelling the French. A day after he declared independence, he called for democratic elections, explaining that the Vietnamese were

> first ruled by an absolute monarchy, then by an equally tyrannical colonial regime, so our country did not have a constitution. Our people do not enjoy democratic freedoms. We must have a democratic constitution. I recommend that the Government organize a general election with universal suffrage as soon as possible. All eighteen-year-old citizens have the right to run for office and vote, regardless of wealth, religion, lineage, etc.[76]

He reminded the Vietnamese that the whole point of calling for a democratic constitution and elections was to garner support and legitimacy for Vietnamese resistance against French attempts to hold onto their colony:

> Soldiers use guns and bullets to fight the enemy, but politically, the people use their votes to fight the enemy. A ballot is as powerful as a bullet. Tomorrow, our nation will show the world that we are resolutely united, resolutely fight against colonialists, resolutely fight for independence. Tomorrow, our people will freely choose and elect people worthy to represent and shoulder the responsibility of the country.[77]

Through majority rule, a "general will" would be discerned, and he had faith that the "general will" would be anticolonial. Hồ's recommendation would be followed, and on January 6, 1946, the Vietnamese in North Vietnam voted for members to the National Assembly of the DRV. A day before the election, Hồ declared: "Tomorrow is a day that will put our nation on a new path. Tomorrow is a happy day for our people because tomorrow is general election day. Tomorrow is the first day in Vietnam's history that our people will begin to enjoy their democratic rights."[78]

Once French colonizers were out of the picture in North Vietnam in 1954, Hồ could focus on ensuring that the party would guide democratic processes toward Communist revolution. In a report to the party in December 1959, Hồ again began with what might at first sound like calls for a liberal democracy:

> All citizens aged 18 and older have the right to vote, and those 21 and older have the right to run for election. Elections are conducted according to the principles of universality, equality, direct and secret voting. The people have the right to dismiss National Assembly and People's Council deputies if those delegates prove unworthy of office or the people's trust. That principle ensures the people's control over their representatives.[79]

However, Hồ emphasized that the party must foster democratic processes *while also* guiding the people ideologically: "Our election system implements democracy while also realizing national unity." The DRV state "promotes democracy to a high degree," and this was how it could "mobilize all the people's forces to carry the revolution forward. At the same time, we must concentrate to the utmost to unify and lead the people to build socialism."[80] Democracy was thus a balancing act for Ho. The people must have the ability to deliberate and decide, but they must also be guided away from the wrong decisions and toward correct (revolutionary communist) decisions.

To show that Hồ's paternalistic democracy was the right path toward Communism, he offered reports on progress made. For example, on the second anniversary of Hồ's declaration of independence, he reported on improvements in education:

> In addition to building new high schools and universities, training talented people, and developing the arts, thanks to the Government's efforts and the wisdom of officials, we destroyed the French policy of keeping the people ignorant. In two years, we taught more than four million men and women to read and write, and many villages and communes have become literate.[81]

There are also successful examples of the party properly guiding democratic processes. In an essay published in March 1967 in the *Nhân Dân* newspaper, Hồ listed numerous examples of democratic deliberation in the workplace that succeeded due to the party's guidance. For example, a cooperative of fifty households in Quảng Bình needed to build 700 shelters. It was

> a huge and difficult task to handle. Officials took the initiative to present the task clearly to all cooperative members and encouraged everyone to discuss it democratically. After consensus was reached, everyone enthusiastically competed and was ready to help each other. They worked day and night. Large families helped small families. . . . As a result, in just two days, more than 700 shelters were completed, and everything met the standards. So, thanks to democracy, difficult things become possible.[82]

The few examples above, Hồ wrote, demonstrated "that practicing democracy is the universal key that can solve all difficulties" and that "imbuing everyone with the spirit of collective mastery" generated results. Such democracy could advance the socialist project, thereby rehumanizing the Vietnamese, he thought, as long as virtuous party members led the way.

Part Three: Insights for Theorists

What might we gain from Hồ's critique of dehumanization and vision for rehumanization? First, Hồ put racist dehumanization front and center as a motivation for revolution. This differed from many works on revolution that overlooked the desire to humanize the racially dehumanized as a core aim of revolutionaries.[83] Famous theorists of revolution, such as John Locke, cite the state's failure to protect natural rights as a justification for revolution, not the state's failure to recognize its subjects as human beings with natural rights to begin with. Americans who revolted against the British complained of "taxation without representation" and revolutionaries in the French, Russian, and Chinese revolutions pointed to social, political, and economic inequalities as their justifications for revolution. But racist dehumanization was not a major factor in these movements. In many of these cases, revolutionaries spoke out against moral inequality—the violation of the idea that all humans are deserving of the same dignity and respect, but they did not emphasize, as Hồ did, moral *exclusion*—"when individuals or groups are perceived as outside the boundary in which moral values, rules, and considerations of fairness apply."[84]

We might follow Charles Mills's logic of the "racial contract" and say that American and French revolutionaries were outraged over what they saw as violation of an assumption of equality between those who ultimately saw each other as "white" and as superior to nonwhites. Thus, although Europeans experienced conflicts among each other, European expansionism and colonialism, Mills argues, led whites to "regard one another as moral equals who are superior to nonwhites and who create, accordingly, governments, legal systems, and economic structures that privilege them at the expense of people of color."[85] Mills calls this historical reality a "racial contract," as opposed to the "social contract" which is merely a thought experiment commonly assumed to apply to all human beings. In this view, the American and French revolutions were instances of white outrage over the *violation* of the "racial contract," namely, its expectation of moral equality among whites. In contrast, Hồ Chí Minh was outraged at the *existence* of the racial contract.

To be sure, Hồ Chí Minh is not the only example of a revolutionary who cited dehumanization as a reason for revolution. The Haitian revolution, for example, was clearly motivated by indignation over racist dehumanization. And Hồ would agree with Aimé Cesaire's remark that colonialism turned "the indigenous man into an instrument of production . . . colonialism = 'thingification,'"[86] and with Frantz Fanon who wrote about how French colonial dehumanization of Algerians "turns [the Algerian] into an animal. In fact, the terms the settler uses when he mentions the native are zoological terms. He speaks of the yellow man's reptilian motions, of the stink of the native quarter, of breeding swarms, of foulness, of spawn, of gesticulations."[87] The *Wretched of the Earth* can be understood as providing solutions to the problem of dehumanization.[88] A difference between Hồ and Fanon, however, was that Hồ believed that Leninist vanguardism could rehumanize the dehumanized while Fanon did not.

Second, contrary to some leftist critics of dehumanization, Hồ argued that one could indeed confer and take away one's own humanity. One leftist critique of discourses of dehumanization was that some liberals equated humanity with "protection of the law." Such liberals equated illegal oppression and violence upon human beings with the dehumanization of those human beings. While the objective of these critical assertions, Samera Esmeir argues, is "to expose the radical evil that illegal violence can institute," they are also problematic because they "establish an equation between the protection of the law and the constitution of humanity, effectively granting the former a magical power to endow the latter" while also reproducing colonial logics that argued that precolonial states, in lacking a law-based regime, left its subjects dehumanized and thus in need of modern (European) legal reform.[89] By establishing such an equation, Esmeir writes, such liberals "reproduce a particular conviction that humanity is a status to be recognized and conferred, or seized and taken away." Thus, Esmeir thinks it is wrong to think of humanity as a status that can be recognized and conferred or taken away. She wants us to challenge "the idea that humanity is a matter of endowment, declaration, or recognition." The task, she argues, is "not to recognize the other's humanity, for, like dehumanization, that task risks repeating colonial juridical logics. What is needed is the forging of concrete alliances with human beings who await not our recognition but our participation in their struggles."[90]

Hồ Chí Minh would agree with Esmeir that humanity should not ultimately be a matter of recognition. Indeed, Hồ saw that it was futile to demand that the French recognize Vietnamese humanity. Furthermore, Hồ would have welcomed foreign participation in the struggles of his followers. However, where Hồ might diverge from Esmeir was that Hồ *did* think that humanity could be conferred or taken away. Namely, he thought that the Vietnamese could confer or take away their own humanity with their own actions. If one has been dehumanized by a colonial soldier, one can rehumanize oneself by cultivating revolutionary morality and mobilizing for resistance and the socialist project, just as easily as one can contribute to one's own dehumanization through using opium, by cheating and stealing because one neglected their duty to cultivate integrity (*liêm*), or by simply doing nothing in response to colonial dehumanization. For Hồ, Vietnamese humanity could very much be conferred or taken away, not by law-based regimes, but by whether party members and the people engaged cultivating revolutionary virtue for anticolonial and Communist projects.

Third, Hồ's proposal for rehumanization focused on an internal political project, a focus that marks a departure from typical discussions of rehumanization. Discussions of rehumanization often emphasize how culprits of dehumanization (groups that have dehumanized other groups) can rehumanize their "other" by using their imagination to overcome indifference to the other's pain. If we have dehumanized others, we can use our imagination in ways that "render these people's lives, and their suffering, joys and sorrows, tangible and visible to us as the joys and sufferings of a human being."[91] As for discussions of how victims of dehumanization can rehumanize themselves, scholars have pointed to the power of forgiving their perpetrators to rehumanize oneself.[92]

Hồ's plan for how Vietnamese victims of dehumanization could rehumanize themselves is an internal practice, however, one requiring neither imagination from the colonial dehumanizer nor Vietnamese forgiveness of their dehumanizers. For Hồ, rehumanization was less a matter of imagination or forgiveness and more a commitment to ideology, expressed through daily struggles of self-rectification and political work, or what I have called "paternalistic democracy." He believed this commitment would bestow dignity upon its own members—regardless of how French colonizers and counterrevolutionaries thought and behaved toward them.

What I have called Hồ's paternalistic democracy may have theoretically rehumanized the party and the "people" that the party was meant to serve, but it may also have produced new challenges. First, Hồ did not make it clear when or if "the people" would ever "grow up" and lose their status as undeveloped "children" in need of guidance. The people were to remain under the tutelage of the party indefinitely. I have not meant "paternalism" in a pejorative way here, but such paternalism can become frustrating to those who are the object of it. Second, citizens may choose to refuse their "child-like" status and call for greater freedom of speech and freedom to criticize the government. Although Hồ had urged the party to "have a flexible and tactful attitude" toward "all people in all walks of life," to "compromise," and to "respect people's personalities," his exclusive conception of "the people" also risked dehumanizing those considered outside such membership. Throughout his life, Hồ saw that the Vietnamese "people" were at war with enemies, both external (France, Japan, and the United States) and internal (Vietnamese collaborators, landlords, capitalists, and intellectuals of the Nhân Văn Giai Phẩm movement). His paternalistic democracy was always to be used as an instrument against enemies of "the people." Yet, a problem this perspective poses is that those who hold this view of democracy may become paranoid and see enemies everywhere where there might not be any. Some, such as a man named Nguyễn Mạnh Tường, will make this criticism. To him we now turn.

7
Nguyễn Mạnh Tường's Montaignean Solace

One morning in Hanoi in 1957, Nguyễn Mạnh Tường (1909–1997) heard a knock on his door. A friend who happened to be a government agent had come to inform him that authorities in the Communist Party had decided to incarcerate him. Although he never became a party member, Tường was respected by the party because he was an impressive intellectual—the first Vietnamese to attain two doctorates from France—and he had been a proponent of the anticolonial cause for many years. However, his recent criticisms of the party had apparently crossed the line. At first, Tường considered hiding, but he quickly decided against it: "The police have put its agents, spies and informers everywhere. Besides, such an attitude seems degrading to me: I would feel as if I were renouncing my convictions and ideas. What would the communists, who used to pay homage to my dignity, think?"[1] Convinced that he would spend the rest of his life behind bars, Tường began gathering his essential belongings: "I am resigning myself to my fate and, in anticipation of a journey without return, I fill my suitcase with underwear and woolen clothes." He looked around his home and wondered what else he should bring. At last, he decided on one book that he would have with him for the rest of his days: "I also put in a copy of Montaigne's *Essais* from the Pléiade collection, together with paper, pens, ink, and pencils! I want to occupy my forced and endless spare time with some kind of intellectual work, to save myself from the insanity of imprisonment. Perhaps my jailers will have the humanity of not taking away this viaticum of which I greatly need."[2]

Tường had a large collection of literature to choose from. Why did he choose Montaigne's *Essais* as the only book to accompany him to (what he believed) could be a lifetime in prison? A clue is in the way Tường refers to the *Essais:* a viaticum—the last Eucharist for a dying man.

Three years earlier, Vietnamese Communists had finally expelled the French, and Tường was looking forward to creating a new Vietnam with his compatriots. But now he faced the prospect of a life alone. To cope, he would turn inward to himself. But he would bring along Montaigne, the revered sixteenth-century inventor of the essay, someone who in order to retain his humanity during the inhumanity of the wars of religion in his France had also turned inward to himself. Through Montaigne, Tường would nourish his own dignity, shame the Communist Party, and articulate ways toward attaining postcolonial national dignity.

Nguyễn Mạnh Tường is different from the other five thinkers we have met in the previous chapters in a few respects. Whereas the others formed their mature thought while under French colonialism, Tường developed his mature thought after Vietnamese independence. Whereas the others were responding to the denial of Vietnamese dignity by the French colonizers, Tường was reacting to the denial of Vietnamese dignity by the Vietnamese Communist Party.

In succumbing to dogmatism and fanaticism, Vietnamese Communist revolutionaries, Tường believed, were unwittingly losing the very national dignity they had been fighting for, failing to build a dignified Vietnam after achieving independence, and producing a new kind of national shame. Party leaders were becoming unthinking "robots" and were preventing the Vietnamese people they purportedly served from developing individual personalities, which Tường saw as necessary for both individual and national dignity. Far from helping the people, he believed, party leaders were degrading themselves and their country.

Paradoxically, Tường believed that the way for Vietnamese national dignity to be regained was for the Vietnamese to collectively affirm and nurture individual dignity. Barred from participating in politics with the Vietnamese, Tường sought to do his part in constructing national dignity by turning inward to reflect and write, with the hopes that his writings would be read by and thus inspire other Vietnamese to create a "new Vietnamese man" who cherished inner freedom.

This chapter shows how Nguyễn Mạnh Tường offered a distinctly Montaignean understanding of the challenges facing Vietnamese Communist revolutionaries after they achieved independence for Vietnam. We shall focus on four things he thought the Communists were promoting that were bringing new forms of national shame upon Vietnam: (1) anti-intellectualism, (2) paranoia, (3) logomachy (argument over words), and (4) conformity. He shamed the Communists for these self-imposed obstacles to their own goal of socialist revolution. Tường used Montaigne to make sense of these obstacles to national dignity and to offer ways to surmount them. To overcome the shame of anti-intellectualism, the Vietnamese needed diverse perspectives; for the shame of excessive paranoia, the Vietnamese needed democracy and law; for the shame of being caught in logomachy, the Vietnamese needed to pay attention not to words but to the people's needs; and for the shame of conformity, the Vietnamese needed freedom of thought.

Informing Tường's intellectual project was his immersion in French cultural and intellectual classics. Like some of the other thinkers in previous chapters, Tường believed that national dignity was not viable without a consolidated cultural framework. For Tường, the cultural framework that Vietnam was lacking, and that it needed, was a *humanist* one. Tường may be likened to other dissidents such as Czesław Miłosz and Václav Havel who also sought to describe and resist the mentality of dogmatic Communists. Havel also defended humanism and seemed to be describing Tường when he explained how an ordinary person might revolt against the totalitarianism of self-proclaimed Communist governments: "He discovers once more his suppressed identity and dignity. He gives his freedom a concrete significance. His revolt is an attempt to live within the truth."[3] Now that Vietnam was free from colonizers, Tường thought it was time for the Vietnamese to relax their social bonds, time to turn inward to their unique individual selves to seek happiness and self-fulfillment. They should promote a philosophy of free judgment and tolerance of different ideas. They should liberate themselves from the dogmatism that may have united them to overthrow the French but was now stifling free thought and bringing a new kind of shame on the Vietnamese. For Tường, it was Montaigne who could help with this.

A Brief Biography: Nguyễn Mạnh Tường

Nguyễn Mạnh Tường was born in 1909 in Hanoi where he learned French at a young age and attended the Lycée Albert Sarraut. In 1925, when he was sixteen, he attained his baccalaureate in Philosophy. He went to France in 1927 and, through a scholarship, studied law and literature at Montpellier University where, in 1932, he became the first Vietnamese to earn two doctorates in those fields. From 1933 to 1936 he traveled throughout Europe, to London, The Hague, Brussels, Berlin, Athens, Rome, Istanbul, Vienna, and Madrid.

Upon his return to Vietnam in 1936, he taught French literature at the Lycée du Protectorat and the Public Works College (Ecole Supérieure des

Travaux Publics). He then left teaching and became a practicing lawyer in the late 1930s and 1940s.

From 1945 to 1956, he received praise from the Communist Party for his devotion to the anticolonial and revolutionary cause, such as for when he donated to the party three buildings that were his family's heritage.[4]

In 1946, Hồ Chí Minh asked Tường to prepare a government position paper to be used at the Franco-Vietnamese Đà Lạt Conference. From then on, Tường joined the underground resistance. In 1951, a representative of the Vietnamese Communist Party asked him to join the party but he declined. Eventually, he agreed, upon the representative's urging, to join a different party: the Socialist Party of Vietnam. Still, the Vietnamese Communist Party relied on Tường to represent them at international conferences in Beijing, Vienna, and Brussels in the 1950s.

His prestige with Communist authorities rose higher when he gave a speech in Vienna in 1953, radioed to the world, urging intellectuals all over the globe to support the resistance in Vietnam.[5] For this, Communist authorities appointed him professor at the Pre-University School in Thanh Hóa and later professor at the pedagogic school in Hanoi. The party also seated him on ten executive committees.[6] However, Tường's standing with the party, and his life, took a sharp turn when the Communist Party put him through a series of trials in 1957.

In October 1956, he gave a speech at a conference in Hanoi, marking the moment that would eventually lead to his excommunication and to his rise as a leading figure in the Nhân Văn Giai Phẩm movement, which called for greater freedom of expression. In his speech, he addressed the mistakes made during the land reform campaign and called for legal and democratic reform. Following this, he was banned from practicing law and, from 1957 onward, he was isolated in Hanoi. In his words, he was "kicked out of all the places I was working. And the cruelest thing was isolation.... For decades, no one dared to come see me."

In 1989, the party, "for the first time in history," he says, "announced the birth of liberalism." He then "took advantage of the opportunity to apply for a passport to go to France." He did not think his application would be approved due to his political past, but, he writes, "to my great surprise, in just two months I had a passport and visa." In France, he was welcomed by his French-Vietnamese friends and gave interviews and talks at universities and TV stations. He died in 1997 at his home in Hanoi.

In addition to *Un Excommunié*, which describes his life in isolation in Hanoi from 1955 to 1991 and his criticisms of the party, he produced works in French that reflected on the relationship between East and West. For example, his *Sourires et larmes d'une jeunesse* (1937) features stories of young Vietnamese who, after living a while in France, either chose to stay in France or returned to Vietnam, and he describes the internal conflicts they experienced as individuals torn between two cultures.

Fallout from the Land Reform

From 1954 to 1956, the party implemented land reforms during which land was taken from landlords and redistributed to poorer peasants.[7] Yet, in this process, a number of those who were humiliated and executed were later found to be innocent and as poor as anyone else. The fallout of the controversial land reforms would become an important turning point that would give fuel to existing anti-Communist sentiment. According to Bui Tin, more than 10,000 people were killed, "most of them Party members or patriots who had supported the Revolution but were reasonably well off."[8] The party recognized these mistakes and undertook a program to "rectify errors." The party encouraged criticism from intellectuals. Nguyễn Mạnh Tường accepted an invitation to speak, which occurred on October 30, 1956, in Hanoi.[9] In his speech he criticized the party for its lack of democracy and rule of law to protect individual rights.

The party leaders claimed to have no problem with his criticism, but they did not like the fact that Tường's speech was leaked to the rest of the world and had fallen into the hands of the enemy. Vietnamese correspondents in Rangoon sent it to Saigon where it was published in full in many papers.[10] Party leaders argued that the speech was exploited by capitalists to further attack Communists and Communism. Such criticism, they insisted, was supposed to be given in private. They scolded Tường: "You are surely aware of the damage you are doing to the cause of our communist State. You will tell me that dirty laundry must be washed. Yes, it must be, but within the family! But you are putting it on display in broad daylight!"[11] But Tường argued that the leak was not his fault: "Regarding the fact that a copy of my text was taken and sent abroad during these times of the Cold War when the slightest faults and errors of communism are shamelessly exploited, I cannot be made to bear responsibility."[12]

Tường never ended up going to prison. In the end, some of the higher-ups in the party decided against incarcerating him, opting instead to permanently excommunicate him from society. But for Tường, excommunication was not that much preferable to prison:

> In my personal case, no sentence was imposed on me, neither prison nor a cell. But in the communist city there are unnamed, informal punishments that amount to a long-term death sentence. Such is the case of excommunication that political fanaticism has taken from the arsenal of medieval criminology; excommunication is the most decisive weapon of religious fanaticism. No believer is allowed to house, feed, or clothe an excommunicated who has been deprived of shelter, sustenance, clothing, and who cannot lead his life normally.[13]

Tường shamed the Communist leaders for their regressive, unmodern, antidemocratic, and religious-like fanaticism. Vietnam, he thought, had become not a democratic republic as its name purported it to be but a cult. Members were believers and nonbelievers were banished, and anyone who helped nonbelievers were also considered enemies. Tường promoted a kind of liberal ethos in response to his horror over the ethos of discipline, dedication, resoluteness, and ruthlessness that he saw animating some Communist revolutionaries.[14]

An Excommunicated

Tường described the years of his excommunication from 1955 to 1991 in Hanoi in his memoir, *Un Excommunié* (An Excommunicated), which he wrote in French. It was written "in solitude and clandestinely," but he eventually wanted to see it published for both French and Vietnamese audiences. Upon agreeing to have it published, he wrote, "I expect the worst," and if the party "inflicts on me the same treatment as on other intellectuals accused of slandering the regime, I firmly await trials whose harshness I know." If that happens, he would "begin a hunger strike until death. At 84, I have known the best and the worst of life and have no regrets about leaving this life during which I fulfilled my duty as an intellectual before the people and before history."[15] Tường's autobiography contains his frankest thoughts on the Communist Party and his political philosophy.

Even though he lived with his wife and daughter during his excommunication, he was painfully lonely. They all had difficulty finding work and were no longer granted rationing vouchers for food, so they were always hungry, trying to sell what they could to buy food.[16] His friends avoided him. Happiness was rare for him, but one day he befriended a cat on the street, and it became his pet:

> I took the animal in my hand, caressed it and felt compassion and tenderness for it. He and I are two wrecks in life, both suffering from the same hunger, victims of the same isolation, afflicted with the same fate. After going around the neighboring houses to ask if the cat belongs to them and getting negative responses, I started to thank chance, or Providence, for granting me a companion in misfortune and misery.[17]

He is evoking Montaigne's musing, "When I play with my cat, who knows if I am not a pastime to her more than she is to me?"[18] By describing his own condition as being no different from that of the cat, he acknowledges his loss of a kind of human dignity that stems from the presumed special status that humans have above animals. But because Tường and the cat share the same condition, Tường finds solace in another source of dignity, one not necessarily human but found in the idea that humans are ultimately no better than or different from animals. This is a distinctly Montaignean theme. Montaigne argues that animals possess reason, challenging the widespread belief in his day that humans are superior to animals. In doing so, Montaigne swats down human pride and arrogance, which he sees as the source of many evils. Tường does the same, and, in doing so, he finds humility to be a new source of dignity.

Just as Montaigne's hero was Socrates, Tường portrays himself as a Vietnamese Socrates who tried to encourage youth to think critically but was ultimately condemned for corrupting youth: "Since Socrates, we know that when the City wants to condemn an intellectual to drink hemlock, it accuses him of corrupting the youth! Communism has therefore revived a practice that dates back more than two millennia." A Vietnamese Socrates was needed, Tường argued, to counter the conformity and lack of critical thinking that are promoted by the authoritarian state:

> [H]istorically, the autocracy has dreamed of molding the people, especially the youth who bear the future in its image. As a result, they are

educated with every political line. The School is charged with the mission of training those who, tomorrow, will assume their responsibilities in the City. It is therefore important that the teacher trains his students to become executors of government policy. Any deviation committed in education has the same gravity as a deviation from the political line proclaimed by the leaders.[19]

But deviations were inevitable, Tường thought, if the Vietnamese were to think for themselves and develop their own personalities. Tường echoed Václav Havel who in 1978 criticized the Eastern European Communist system for becoming "so ossified politically that there is practically no way for such nonconformity to be implemented within its official structures."[20] As in the case of Socrates, the case of Tường has us ask the classic question of who has the right to educate the younger generation of the polity, which is essentially a question of who has the right to govern. Unfortunately, Tường thought, Communist leaders were like autocrats who, in dreaming of molding the people in their own image, refused to allow Vietnamese youth to develop as human beings.

Tường was not convinced that the party's only complaint against him was the leak of his speech. They were upset because their dogmatic and authoritarian tendencies prevented them from productively handling criticism, undermining even Hồ Chí Minh's exhortations to engage in self-criticism. Yet, Tường saw himself as offering a friendly insider's critique, not a critique from the outside. He emphasized that he was criticizing *Communists*, not *Communism*. He argued that he was trying to improve the party, not destroy it, starting with the criticism that they lacked intellectual seriousness: "Those who quote Marx have not read him, and if by chance they happen to take a peek at a page in Capital, they don't understand anything! The best proof of this is that the enthroned Marxists commit tremendous errors from which the people suffer, which raises doubts about their knowledge of the doctrine on which they rely!"[21] The solution to dogmatism, Tường implied, was for the Communists to actually read Marx and try to understand him. Tường was certainly elitist and more educated than most members of the party, and so one might read him here as being a snob. Yet, he insisted that his attacks on Communists were motivated out of love, not hatred. Tường envisioned mutual empowerment between Communists and intellectuals: "Communist culture forms man for the revolutionary struggle. Intellectual culture forms man for thinking and research. But the communist culture must not annihilate intellectual culture. Between these two cultures can be peaceful coexistence and, better yet, a beneficial collaboration for the respective interests of the two groups and for the entire people."[22]

Here, Tường's desire to promote "peaceful coexistence" resembled Montaigne's desire for coexistence between warring Protestants and Catholics. Like Montaigne, Tường could be understood as belonging to a long tradition of using skepticism to respond to dogmatists. Writing in the third century A.D., Sextus Empiricus (A.D. c. 160–c. 210) drew on Pyrrho's (c. 360–c. 270 B.C.) philosophy of suspending judgment, arguing that skepticism (doubt of the possibility of knowledge) was the best response to the dogmatism (the insistence on something's incontrovertible truth) of Platonism, Stoicism, Epicureanism, and Aristotelianism. Writing in the sixteenth century, Montaigne (1533–1529) drew on Sextus's skepticism, reviving it partly as a response to Catholics and Protestants killing each other over their "certainties." And writing in the twentieth century, Tường drew on Montaigne's skepticism to respond to the Vietnamese Communist Party's dogmatic devotion to Marxism–Leninism. Identifying himself as an intellectual and speaking for intellectuals, Tường wrote, "We defend ourselves with our skepticism, we attack with our irony. Our critical mind saves us from errors."[23]

Anti-intellectualism

For Tường, the first cause of Vietnam's new emerging national shame was a pervasive anti-intellectualism among leaders in the party. Tường used Montaigne's *Essais* to criticize them for this:

> I open Montaigne. It is my breviary, my viaticum. There are so many good lessons that the communists can learn, if only they were cultivated. Through the "healthy example of the Ancients" and of Montaigne, they could have learned that one should not lodge anything in one's head "by mere authority and trust," that anyone "following another follows nothing." Translated clearly, this means that one should not kneel before anybody, neither Marx nor Lenin, neither Stalin nor Mao.[24]

In this passage, Tường quotes lines from Montaigne's essay "Of the Education of Children"[25] in which Montaigne described how a tutor might properly educate his charge to become a strong thinker: "Let the tutor make his charge pass everything through a sieve and lodge nothing in his head *on mere authority and trust*: let not Aristotle's principles be principles to him any more than those of the Stoics or Epicureans. Let this variety of ideas be set before him; he will choose if he can; if not, he will remain in doubt. Only the fools are certain and assured."[26]

Tường believed the Communist Party's "certainty" and assuredness that Marx, Lenin, Stalin, and Mao held monopoly on the "truth" was foolish because it created fake personalities. Those who professed Marxism–Leninism in Vietnam, he wrote, are "lacking in personality and individuality. He is a fake and can easily be replaced by a tape recorder."[27] The "Communist mind," he argued, was narrow and happily ignorant of others it could otherwise learn from. It "carries out an operation which is completely its own: it marks out a small area of land and digs deep, without worrying at all about what the neighbors are doing!"[28] Thus, the dogmatic mind was closed off to different perspectives that otherwise would, when rubbed together, "polish" and strengthen the mind. The Vietnamese, Tường exhorted,

> must neither shut themselves up nor lock themselves in a closed world, but open themselves to the "commerce of men," "rub and polish our brains by contact with those of others," enter into this vast world, "scrutinize where we should look for to find out the good angle," and "thus, with the pieces borrowed from others," one must transform them and mix them up in order to "turn them into one's own work, namely, one's judgment." "The gain of our study is to become better and wiser." This, in brief, is what the communists should have learned in order to form themselves before governing others![29]

The quotations in this passage are lifted from the same essay by Montaigne, "Of the Education of Children," in which Montaigne argued that students should learn from diverse others through discussion, travel, and learning foreign languages.[30] Tường believed that through exposure to diversity and the truth of other ideas, one gained skepticism that any one doctrine held a monopoly on truth. By borrowing good "pieces" from diverse others and "transforming and mixing" them into one's own judgment, one would become better and wiser. For Tường, this was the true path to dignity. One who was dogmatic, on the other hand, was not worthy of respect for they had abandoned their capacity to engage the diversity of opinions in the world as well as the contradictions and complexities of their own inner self. According to Alan Levine, the inward turn that Montaigne encouraged was a kind of *proper* self-interest that benefited the world by producing tolerance and the separation of the public and private. If one is truly, properly, self-interested, one has no desire to impose oneself on others because the most pleasurable and exciting activity one can engage in is self-exploration. This properly understood self-interest is a Montaignean kind of self-exploration. It is, Levine writes, exploring and fighting "through opinions and customs that we've internalized" and taming "the anxieties, fears, and longings" that cause us to flee from our natural condition.[31] Doing so "provides one with a neverending source of wonder and delight" and allows us to achieve a tranquility that Levine calls "sophisticated simplicity[32]" For Levine, this was the most convincing justification for liberal toleration as it appealed neither to natural or divine rights, custom, and moral skepticism, nor to the claim that humans were naturally tolerant. Instead, it appealed to true self-interest. Such self-exploration was precisely what Tường did and saw as a source of dignity. Although he did it to cope with his excommunication, he also thought that party leaders should engage in it to rectify the corrosive effects of their dogmatism and to promote tolerance and separation of public and private.

Paranoia

The second source of Vietnam's new national shame, Tường thought, was the excessive paranoia displayed by the party. The party's commitment to their "Truth" led them to think that anyone who questioned the party's "Truth" was not only wrong, but hostile, even after the party allowed criticism. Paranoia set in and the party saw enemies where there were none: "The ongoing slogan reminds us that the 'enemy is everywhere and hangs up his creatures anywhere.' Maintaining general security requires vigilance in a state of alertness, the sending of professional spies to all meetings, and the mobilization of amateur or volunteer spies to wander around continuously in the streets."[33]

The paranoid party squandered manpower from using too many spies. Moreover, because all criticism was dismissed as enemy infiltration, the party prevented itself from receiving constructive criticism from the masses. During the land reform, "the worst thing was that when someone amongst the masses said that we were wrong, that we had better do something in this way or that way, we immediately shouted that this voice came from the enemy.... We still had this vague conception of friends and enemies: we saw enemies everywhere because we were too proud of ourselves and practiced self-adulation excessively."[34]

This echoes Montaigne's assertion that for humans "pride is his ruin and his corruption."[35] Because the party dismissed any critic as an enemy, the Party ended up neglecting the masses (who certainly had criticisms) for whom they were supposed to represent. The gap between theory and practice was caused by pride: "we were proud of ourselves, we believed we had a monopoly of Truth .... we did not despise the masses in theory but we did so in fact."[36] By being more self-critical in conducting their theory, Tường thought, they could be more effective in practice.

One solution to the problem of paranoia and pride, Tường thinks, is democracy. Aware that Hồ Chí Minh and the Party exalt the word "democracy," Tường notes that the Communist Party understands democracy narrowly as government *for* the people, failing to appreciate that democracy should also be government *by* the people. Tường recounts a dialogue between himself and someone from the Party who accuses him of counterrevolutionary tendencies. The accuser admits that "the communists understand democracy in the sense of action FOR the people and strive to do everything to serve the interests of the people."[37]

However, Tường responded,

> In its full meaning and effect, democracy has two functions that are inextricably linked: that of government *by* the people and that of government *for* the people. It would be shameful to play with words and pretend that government *for* the people is enough. It's a sham. If it is not the people who act and control, no one can do it for them. Under the pretext that we act *for* the people, we can commit all kinds of infamies and take measures which more or less seriously harm the interests of the people.[38]

By reminding the party representative that democracy meant governance for *and* by the people, Tường challenges the party's Confucian form of democracy and promoted a liberal form of democracy. In the Confucian tradition, the ruler was supposed to be virtuous and govern *for* the people. Nowhere in the Confucian tradition is there talk about governance *by* the people.

Governance by the people was all the more necessary, Tường argued, considering that the party was now learning about the crimes of Stalin, whom the party had revered. Because of Stalin's "pride, his self-adulation, Stalin did not allow anybody to behave democratically towards himself, and everywhere he saw enemies.... We have paid a high price, but we know now the cause of the evil which has made us suffer: We lack democracy."[39]

The party made mistakes during the land reform campaign, Tường argued, because "the rights and duties of the citizen were not clearly defined." In practice, "no one had a right to express his opinion; there were no means to present it to the authorities. He was not allowed to participate in the elaboration of the Government program." Therefore, the leaders were "permitted to commit serious mistakes, to effect a great loss of people's lives and energy, and to damage the prestige of the party and the government. Therefore, if we want now to correct our past mistakes we must establish a regime of true legality and true democracy."[40] In other words, the right to free speech must be enshrined in law. Freedom of expression was a human right, Tường argued, and could be learned from the West: "the West has offered the East a technique and conception of human rights, concerning the moderation and diversity of peoples ways of thinking and living."[41] This would provide the people a means to make their desires known to the government. However, the Communists despised law, unsurprisingly, he noted. This was somewhat understandable, he suggested, because during French colonialism and "the time of their clandestine agitation, the revolutionaries had a hard time with colonial legislation and magistrates. They therefore connected the memory of their sufferings and their sacrifices to the Judiciary and the Law, which they considered to be instruments of oppression in the hands of the capitalists." However, the revolutionaries should realize "that the instruments of oppression against the working masses can perfectly be turned into means of defense and protection of the State and Revolution..."[42] Tường claimed that the Communists hated law also because they were politicians and there was "a divergence of viewpoints between the politician and the jurist, in mental habits and intellectual practice."[43] The Communist, Tường argued, was a politician who worked in "politics," an unstable world with "fuzzy borders" between ideologies that one could cross without even noticing. In contrast, the jurist worked in the realm of "geometric rigor, rational logic, Cartesian precision, and clarity. Between legality and illegality, the dividing line is clear as between white and black."[44] These two worlds were opposed and the politician's "opportunity comes up against the judiciary and the rule of law: therefore, he decides to sweep away legislation and trample on the law."[45] Yet, this was a mistake because the absence of law led the party into its current mess. The absence of law led to innocents being punished and executed.

Clearer legal definitions, Tường thought, would also decrease the persecution of innocent people as "enemies." The Communists had a "*political* conception of the *enemy*," one that was "too shifting, too dialectical." Therefore, "we could not make any distinction between friends and enemies and we merely struck at ourselves."[46] The remedy was to "have a clear definition of the enemy and that definition must be in accordance with the penal code. And then we will be able to strike rightly at our enemies, to consolidate our revolutionary regime."[47]

While clearer definitions could guide the Vietnamese away from meting arbitrary punishment and toward democratic deliberation to discern real enemies, even definitions of "enemy" were ultimately inadequate. This is because, ultimately, the real enemy of the party is the "dogma of its infallibility."[48] Tường wrote,

> the communists should know that they have no enemies but themselves. Their enemy: it is their inordinate subjectivism which makes them believe that they are gods endowed with superhuman infallibility, installed in heaven, above the world of reality, legality, the rule of law, justice, and equity. Their folly is to believe that they are always right. Even and especially when they are wrong! This disease requires hospitalization in a psychiatric clinic!"[49]

Here, Tường was clearly drawing on Montaigne's persistent reminder that humans are fallible: "All things produced by our own reason and ability, the true as well as the false, are subject to uncertainty and debate."[50] His evocation of Montaigne here contradicts sharply with what he said earlier about the dividing line between "legality and illegality" being "clear as between white and black." This *in utramque partem* was precisely the sort of thing that Montaigne did all the time: saying that one thing was clear, and then later saying it was not clear. Tường seemed to do this on purpose, emulating Montaigne, as if to persuade his readers by his example, that it was okay to not find stability and absoluteness in anything, including in one's own arguments.

Regrettably, in Vietnam, "everyone must fill their minds" with the "fundamentalist, inviolable, immutable dogma" that "the Party is the unique holder of Truth, that it is always right against everybody else, that the duty and obligation of each 'subject' is to fight for the triumph of the Party . . . to accept all suffering, all sacrifice—even that of one's life, if necessary—in the name of the Party, for the Party!"[51]

Echoing Phan Chu Trinh's call for the popular right to publicly criticize anything without being punished, Tường lamented that party leaders "do not tolerate any discussion, any criticism of the dogmas which proclaim their permanence, their invincibility, and burn to the stake of heresy bourgeois notions of rights, justice, and innocence."[52]

Vietnamese revolutionaries such as Hồ Chí Minh were skeptical of the notion of "rights" and "justice," concepts hypocritically promoted by French colonizers. Hồ wrote with wry humor: "Justice is symbolized by a gentle woman who holds in one hand a scale and the other a sword. Because the distance from France to Indochina is so far, by the time they get there, the scales lose their balance and melt and turn into opium pipes or bottles of wine, so the poor woman only has the sword left, to kill innocent people."[53]

Tường was aware of this colonial hypocrisy but thought the Communists had allowed their suspicion of "justice" to go too far. The party leaders' belief in their infallibility opened "the door to all kinds of fantasies, insanities, freedoms, and therefore to crimes by the cadres at all levels, all the members or creatures of the Party."[54] In response to Tường's indictment of the party's dogmatism, his Communist accuser asserted: "It is clear that you have been deformed by the western culture you have received. You fall into skepticism, you doubt everything, you no longer perceive the grandeur of beings and things, you are losing yourself in the details, and no longer see the whole picture and, above all, you criticize everything."[55] To that, Tường replied: "French and western culture has made me the man that I have become. I have acquired the qualities and faults of the French spirit: the love for clarity, precision, and logic, but also a critical approach to men and problems. I don't get carried away easily and only give my approval wisely. I bow to the real, the true, the just, but I hate hypocrisy and am filled with horror by fanaticism."[56] Clearly echoing Montaigne's famous hatred for cruelty above all vices,[57] Tường was "able to see the cruelties of the communist leaders" while also being "fully aware of the crimes of the capitalist leaders."[58]

Logomachy

A third source of Vietnam's new national shame was the party's devotion to words rather than substance. The Communist Party's dogmatism was obsessed with logomachy—an argument about words. For Tường, quarrels between proponents of "capitalism" and "socialism" were really quarrels over words, preferences, and habits, not over any objective truth.

> Let us not kill ourselves over words, going to the extreme of a ridiculous logomachy. The terms capitalism and socialism have no meaning by themselves but depend on the tastes and preferences of those who use them. In the mouth of a "socialist," according to a habit which is not only inveterate but no less ridiculous and childish, one qualifies as "capitalist" all that one hates and, whoever has been given such a certification of infamy, his fate is done. When a politics of cannibals is involved, the quarrels no longer limit themselves to only matters of grammar, as Montaigne thinks, they lead to bloodshed and death![59]

By using the term *politics of cannibals* Tường was referring to the old European imperial trope that cannibals were less than human, that politics could not be conducted with them, and therefore the use of violence against them was justified. Calling someone a "capitalist" was tantamount to calling someone a "cannibal," he thought, and this could lead to bloodshed. This view is tragic since these words merely depend on the tastes of those who use them. Montaigne saw the civil wars in his native France through this lens: that most violent conflicts stem from conflicts over words and misunderstandings of them. Montaigne wrote: "Our speech has its weaknesses and its defects, like all the rest. Most of the occasions for the troubles of the world are grammatical. Our lawsuits spring only from debate over the interpretation of the laws, and most of our wars from the inability to express clearly the conventions and treaties of agreement of princes."[60]

One other frustrating aspect of this overreliance on labels such as "socialism" or "capitalism," Tường argued, was that things that ought to be universal, like "natural rights," came to be associated with "capitalism." This created the erroneous view that if "capitalism" were the enemy, then "natural rights" must be opposed as well: "Capitalism must not be given the monopoly for the application of the natural rights of man in the City."[61] Similarly, freedom of opinion was universally good, Tường thought, and he wanted to make the case that freedom of opinion could actually "strengthen ties between the Party and the people through a two-way dialogue."[62] Freedom of opinion and speech would not only

> permit the interlocutors to understand one another but also to avoid mistakes that the Party would have committed if the voice of the people had not reached it in time. Freedom of opinion, by its nature, has no democratic or socialist meaning, but any government that cares to act FOR the people

must promulgate it. If all these quarrels are about grammar, why fight over words? Is there a need for happiness to wear a socialist or capitalist label?[63]

The solution to logomachy, Tường argued, was for everyone who engaged in politics to abandon devotion to words such as "socialism" or "capitalism," and to instead focus on fulfilling the needs of the people:

> If man is the starting and end point of all education and culture, the people must be the starting and end point of all politics. Let's be realistic! Let's mock any ideology that only provides logomachy as a pretext. What are the people asking for? Not much and yet a lot. Not much because they wish for a reasonable material life: decent housing, decent food, clean clothes. In intellectual and artistic life, they only ask for the possibility to acquire instruction and culture, they want to be entertained in a healthy manner. In political life, they dream of being consulted on major issues concerning their present and future interests and of being able to sincerely express their thoughts and reflections. In social life, they demand education and the practice of morality, the purity and cleanliness of customs and mores among individuals and, even more, of those who govern. They consider that all the doctrinal quarrels and the like are purely grammatical ones, as Montaigne says. They are not concerned with whether a measure taken is capitalist or socialist. The essential thing is that it contributes to the welfare of the population: the rest is silly nonsense![64]

To make the point that political labels distract from what matters, Tường wrote about how ridiculous it was that taxi drivers in Vietnam were asked what their political ideas were before being asked about their driving skills. Another unfortunate example was that of doctors being asked what class the patient belonged to before treating the patient, allowing landowners to die because treating the landowner would cause the doctor to lose his privileges.[65]

Conformity

A fourth source of national shame and obstacle to national dignity that Tường identified was conformity. The party's devotion to Marxist–Leninist ideology demands that citizens not question the official ideology. Freedom of thought is discouraged, and freedom of expression is restricted. Since freedom of expression makes one human, "by depriving men of their use of reason and speech, the Party reduces them to the ranks of beasts, infuses in them conditioned reflexes which turn them into robots."[66] This, though, was consistent with what the party wanted: a docile and easily controlled population. Tường likened party leaders to Circé, the goddess of magic in Greek mythology who transformed those who offended her into animals: "It is not without reason that Circé transforms her prisoners into pigs whose only behavior is to jump on their trough at a given signal. All those with power dream of possessing the wand of the magician."[67] Yet, Tường recognized that while the party officially denied freedom of expression (and some would become "robotic" by sincerely believing the party's dogma), there would always be others who thought freely *in private*. Thus, public and private life in post-independence Vietnam was bifurcated. People behaved like lifeless robots in public because the party's spies were everywhere. But in private and in the company of trusted friends, people became free and alive again:

> All of Hanoi offers a spectacle of a puppet show or of mimes where people gesticulate, have fixed looks, play deaf and dumb, and act like robots driven by springs hidden inside the body. But, behind the scenes, in the rooms at the back of the shops (*arriere boutiques*), on the sidewalks, in conversations between two people, the ironical pretenses come back to life, the face regains its expressive mobility, smiles are lit up in the eyes and bloom on the lips, and, to take its revenge on prolonged silence and deliberate inertia, people thrash about like the devils, burst out laughing by mimicking the tone or mania of a leader.[68]

Tường's use of the words "*arriere boutiques*" (a room at the back of the shop) is an explicit reference to Montaigne's famous use of the term. Montaigne wrote, "We must reserve a back shop all our own, entirely free, in which to establish our real liberty and our principal retreat and solitude. Here our ordinary conversation must be between us and ourselves, and so private that no outside association or communication can find a place."[69]

The Communists effectively forced the Vietnamese into their own private *arriere boutiques*, a private space to freely be oneself. Here, Tường was describing a hidden liberalism in Vietnam, one that could not be eradicated no matter how hard party leaders tried to efface the distinction between public and private. Although Tường was aware that a fusion of public and private may have been necessary to produce the fraternal solidarity that could make anticolonial resistance succeed, he was clear in saying that post-independence, there should be respect for the separation of public and private.

Yet, the party resisted this separation. One way the party promoted conformity was through cultural production. Articles, books, plays, theaters, films, and pretty much all other cultural productions "must be in line with unconditional, absolute and tyrannical devotion to the Party. The party is not a party like any other, it is THE Party and must always be spelled with a capital P."[70] Because culture shapes one's values and habits, each person "undergoes a molding or remolding process, during which he is initiated, in defiance of all traditional human values, in the worship of a single god, in whose name permits the most monstrous ideas and most abominable actions! Man is deformed, transformed into a living robot in which all the energy of his soul and heart work for the triumph of instinct and bestiality, that is to say, that of abjection and horror."[71]

There is irony in the party's dogmatism deforming the human into a "live robot." Marxism–Leninism was initially intended to emancipate the oppressed from being tools and machines for capitalists, Tường argued, but through dogmatism and forced conformity, the party created different kinds of robots. The fanaticism of those who preached the Marxist–Leninist Gospel, wrote Tường, "turns the multitude into robots acting on outside command, upsetting minds that think!"[72] The party leader had been "baked in the communist oven." He had "alienated his individuality and even his personality, replacing it with a double of himself whose reactions are remote controlled from the outside."[73]

Vietnam was losing its dignity because through the leadership of the party, it was copying the Soviet Union and China in ideology and even in dress. Tường saw this as an erasure of Vietnam's personality:

[W]hat strikes even unsuspecting people is the total, servile submission to Soviet and Chinese big brothers! This complete abdication concerns not only the ideology, of which the Vietnamese communists advocate Soviet and Chinese orthodoxy which they defend with intransigence and harshness against the slightest expression of disrespect or discord, but it is expressed even in clothing, public or private meetings, forms of courtesy and good manners etc. . . . Việt Nam is losing its personality to become a reflection, a copy of the Soviet Union and China.[74]

Tường especially lamented conformity of clothing since he saw clothing as being expressive of individual personality:

> All the women parade in the uniform imposed by female Party cadres: white shirt and black pants. All the men disguise themselves in the outfit launched Stalin and Mao and then by Vietnamese communist leaders and cadres: jacket with an upright collar, wide pants. The women's tunic and white trousers and the men's collar and tie are condemned by communist rigor as bearing the mark of the capitalist bourgeoisie. One can cry and laugh. One laughs at seeing the whole population display the obviously simple and inexpensive uniform, which kills the individuality of the human being, their personality, the distinctive characters that allow them to be understood, sympathized with, or even communicated with.[75]

Tường had worn custom-made suits that he brought back from Peking (Beijing), Vienna, and Brussels.[76] However, unable to find work or borrow money from friends during his excommunication, he attempted to sell them for money. With no one willing to buy them, he went to a tailor's cooperative, only to have his offer declined. They said to him: "We know that your clothes are of great value. But to whom can we resell these kinds of outfits that nobody wears anymore? All we can do with them is cut them up and turn them into children's clothes. But that would be a shame! Even if we made children's clothes, which parents would buy them from us? The ordinary cadres do not have money and, even if they do, they would not give their children such clothes for fear of being criticized by their colleagues who would detect in them germs of capitalist infection!"[77]

For Tường, party leaders were faced with a choice. On the one hand, they could continue this "formalism" in which they were content with citizens behaving robotically, flattering leaders and bowing their heads to them. On the other hand, the leaders could seek to know what the people were really feeling and thinking by granting them the right to free speech. The latter was the only sane choice, he argued. Free speech "allows them to reveal what they have hitherto been hiding in their inner selves. Once diverse opinions are expressed, leaders have the opportunity to rectify their erroneous or incomplete views, to refine their decisions to make them adequate, timely and beneficial."[78]

In addition to free speech, Tường argued that the Vietnamese could reclaim their dignity through a more robust intellectual culture. Intellectual culture, he argued, "develops reason, maintains critical thinking, forms judgment, preaches realism and objectivity, advocates clarity and precision in the perception and understanding of phenomena." It promoted "logic in reasoning and greater skepticism towards the Don Quixote who ride their high horses and brag, who have no conviction, and only manifest naivety, ignorance and imbecility!" Tường got all of this, he argued, from French intellectual culture "whose benefits I recognize every day which helps me preserve, maintain, develop what is human in me, in the midst of a world undermined by conformism and servility.[79]

When Tường referred to "French culture," he was thinking of Montaigne in particular. Montaigne's idea of a private *arriere-boutique* to enable true freedom of thought was a recurring theme for Tường and crucial to resolving the challenges facing the Communists. Tường wanted the Vietnamese to preserve the authenticity of their selves. In the following passage which I quote at length, Tường provides numerous quotations from throughout Montaigne's *Essais,* referring to Montaigne as "our master" and "our author."

> And now, when faced with the communists, what attitude should one adopt to preserve the integrity and authenticity of one's own being? Let's listen to our master: "As for me, I turn my gaze inward, I fix it there and keep it busy."[80] The watchword "belong to yourself" can only be carried out at the "back-shop." "I try to make my authority over it absolute, and to withdraw this one corner from all society, conjugal, filial, and civil."[81] From this observatory where we observe ourselves, we can "be spectators of the life of other men in order to judge and regulate"[82] our own lives. . . . "In the end I recognized that the surest thing was to entrust myself and my need to myself."[83] Since we are living through difficult times, and witnessing "this notable spectacle of our public death,"[84] let us be aware that "in this confusion that we have been in for thirty years every man . . . sees himself at every moment on the verge of the total overthrow of his fortune."[85] Therefore, the only dignified attitude, even if we were compelled to take a public position, must be the one of not being "blind to either the laudable qualities in our adversaries or those that are reproachable in the men I have followed."[86] In short, let us keep our vigilance and clear perception, avoid partisanship and prejudices which affect the position we hold in a social and particularly political community. The utmost wisdom is to follow our author: "I do not know how to involve myself so deeply and so entirely. When my will gives me over to one party, it is not with so violent an obligation that

my understanding is infected by it."[87] It is to avoid infecting their understanding that a lot of intellectuals decline the offer to be admitted into the Party.[88]

Tường took from Montaigne notions of intellectual humility and honesty, as well as the idea that one should not ignore either the laudable qualities in our adversaries or the reproachable attributes of those we follow. For Tường, the kind of Vietnamese person who should be formed was one who thought for themselves. Now that the Vietnamese had achieved independence, the national fraternal solidarity that was once so necessary for resistance was no longer as necessary. To achieve national dignity, individual dignity must be respected. Of course, other party leaders would not agree, for the work of revolution was still not done. Shortly after winning the First Indochina War against the French, the Vietnamese would soon—in what became known as the Second Indochina War—be embroiled in a civil war that would involve the Americans, which would be followed by a series of conflicts known as the Third Indochina War, which had its roots in the preceding wars. For party leaders, the time to relax the bonds of fraternal solidarity still had not come. To this day, the question of when or if that time would ever come remains.

In his criticisms of the party, Tường was certainly not alone. In 1956, hundreds of other Vietnamese writers criticized Vietnamese Communist leaders for stifling freedom of thought, creativity, and speech.[89] It would not be until decades later that the liberal relaxing of social bonds that Tường advocated would be taken up. In 1986, the sixth party congress called for "new thinking" not only in economic matters, but also in foreign affairs. Vietnamese writers argued that socialist countries could grow faster if they avoided dogmatism, as the Soviet Union was attempting to do, and some argued that Marxism–Leninism should not be treated as a religion to be blindly complied with.[90]

When *Un Excommunié* was first published in France in 1992, Võ Văn Ái wrote in the introduction that "the mistakes recounted in this text in October 1956 continue to be committed in Vietnam in this month of March 1992." Regarding "corruption, waste, contempt for the public, totalitarianism, and oppression, the reader can easily compare the text of Nguyễn Mạnh Tường to the hundreds of examples reported in the official press in 1992." Tường did not "advocate the brutal overthrow of the communist regime." Rather, he was only "modestly asking that this regime be deeply reformed to have the 'genuine rule of law,' a 'truly democratic regime.'"[91] In other words, Tường was addressing what Frantz Fanon had warned about: that the postcolonial nation could become a new source of oppression. In more recent years, Tường's critiques of the party during his time have gained increasing attention and praise among newer generations of Vietnamese. A transcript of a three-hour-long interview with him was "shared" thousands of times on Facebook. As I clicked through different posts of the same interview, I saw thousands of Vietnamese lamenting his fate and praising him as a much-needed intellectual in today's Vietnam.

Conclusion

A millennium has passed since the Vietnamese won their independence from Chinese rule. Almost seven decades have passed since their independence from the French. And it has been almost five decades since Vietnamese Communists became victorious over Vietnamese anti-Communists and the United States. It might be said that, far from feeling shame, many Vietnamese in Vietnam (and surely some in the diaspora) feel proud of this Vietnamese record of defeating foreign invaders. As one taxi driver proudly put it: "Do you realize we are the only nation on earth that's defeated three out of the five permanent members of the United Nations' Security Council?"[1]

However, some Vietnamese intellectuals today are feeling shame rather than pride about the civil war in which Vietnamese slaughtered other Vietnamese with foreign ideologies and weapons. They also feel shame about how the Vietnamese victors of war have treated the Vietnamese on the losing side.[2] Like the thinkers we have examined in this book, they are using shame in new ways to motivate contemporary Vietnamese to construct new forms of national dignity. Furthermore, new generations of Vietnamese are turning to these six thinkers for ideas and guidance in making sense of Vietnam's past. What became of these thinkers? What were their fates?

Phan Bội Châu

While in Shanghai in 1925, Phan Bội Châu was arrested by French authorities and detained in Hỏa Lò Prison in Hanoi. Some accuse Hồ Chí Minh of turning in Châu to rid himself of his key competitor, to get the reward money the French put on Châu's head, or, because of the anger Châu's arrest would provoke, to stimulate anticolonial resistance in Vietnam. All such claims remain controversial.[3] By the end of that year, however, the governor-general of French Indochina, Alexander Varenne, placed Châu under house arrest in Hue. And it was there that Châu remained from 1925 until his death in

1940. During those years, he became more interested in moral philosophy and wrote more than he ever had before. Away from politics, however, he was essentially forgotten and fell into obscurity as new generations of anticolonialists took his place. In his reflections, he lamented: "My history is a history of countless failures without one single success." Yet, he hoped that his biography would be of use to future revolutionaries who "should at least study the path of an overturned chariot in order to derive instruction from failure."[4]

Phan Chu Trinh

Also in 1925, Phan Chu Trinh returned to Vietnam after fourteen years in France. He decided to stay in Saigon where he wanted to build a print shop and start a newspaper rather than travel to his native Quang Nam Province. In Saigon, he joined a campaign dedicated to releasing Phan Bội Châu from Hỏa Lò Prison.[5] Upon delivering his last two speeches in November of 1925—"Morality and Ethics in the Orient and the Occident" and "Monarchy and Democracy"—the members of the audience reportedly felt they "they acquired precious pearls." One person there reported: "It looked as if the sky that had been covered by dark clouds for many years was suddenly cleared by two rains. The sun rises on the East, shedding light at the corner of the horizon. The air is entirely different! Alas! Now reading these two speeches, whose nerves are not touched and whose are not feeling stronger than ever?"[6] At the end of December 1925, Trinh reportedly planned to visit Phan Bội Châu, who was now in Huế, but Trinh's illness with tuberculosis prevented him from going. Trinh's death in March 1926 prompted what might be called Vietnam's first national funeral. Almost a century later, in September 2022, the government of his native province held a conference to commemorate the 150th anniversary of his birth. According to an article that refers to Trinh as "representing the country's reform movement," one lesson the conference took from Trinh was that their tasks were "to arouse the energy of the people, to erase the inferiority complex of the enslaved, and to make them aware of their responsibility for the nation's destiny so that they can shoulder it together. The people's energy is only effective when they fully understand their mission through their enlightenment by a modern education."[7]

Nguyễn An Ninh

In 1926, Nguyễn An Ninh was jailed by French authorities and would be jailed several more times until he was at last sent to Côn Đảo Prison, where he died on April 14, 1943. Along with Phan Bội Châu and Phan Chu Trinh, Nguyễn An Ninh had planted the seeds for the Vietnamese revolution. But Ninh's anticonservatism set him apart from Chau and Trinh, especially in his calls upon Vietnamese youth to look beyond Vietnam's Confucian tradition for new ideas. For example, Ninh's journal, *La Cloche Fêlée*, published the first Vietnamese translation of *The Communist Manifesto* in March 1926. And according to Ngô Văn who had shared a period of imprisonment with Ninh in 1936, Ninh urged Vietnamese who had the means to "visit France or at least to become familiar with its best traditions, so as to enlarge their horizons." Ninh believed that "although France is the source of colonial oppression, there is also a spirit of liberation to be found in the land of the Enlightenment, the Revolution and the Paris Commune."[8]

In 1980, the Vietnamese state conferred upon Ninh the title of "Revolutionary Martyr." Today, major streets and schools are named after him.[9] Whether they evoke his exhortation that the "current generation needs new ideals, *their ideals*; a new activity, *their activity*; new passions, *their passions*"[10] remains an open question.

Phạm Quỳnh

As for Phạm Quỳnh, his legacy—particularly his collaboration (by conviction) with the French—remains controversial, ignored, or is now being revised. Branded a traitor and an enemy of Hồ Chí Minh's revolutionary movement, Phạm Quỳnh was executed by the Việt Minh in 1945. However, according to a story published in 2017, Hồ Chí Minh's secretary, Vũ Đình Huỳnh, reported that when Hồ Chí Minh was informed that Phạm Quỳnh had been eliminated, Hồ became silent, stretched his arms across a table, and said: "I have met and interacted with Mr. Phạm in France.... He is not a bad person!"[11] Although others have called Vũ Đình Huỳnh's account into question,[12] we might interpret such stories, as well as renewed interest in Vietnam in Quỳnh's writings, as contemporary attempts of some Vietnamese to construct new forms of national dignity by recasting former villains as heroes. Recall the introduction to the volume of Quỳnh's writings, published in 2018, that I held in a mainstream bookstore in Hanoi: Quỳnh's "contributions to the development of modern Vietnamese culture are still a milestone of special significance today."

Hồ Chí Minh

Hồ Chí Minh is, to this day, upheld by the Vietnamese Communist Party as what Jean Jacques Rousseau would have called the "legislator" for Vietnam, just as Lycurgus was the legislator for Sparta or Moses was the legislator for the Jewish people. Rousseau thought that in a good society there is no tension between private interests and the general will. But how does the general will emerge in the first place? Good institutions can shape citizens into following the general will, but the problem is that only *good* citizens can create those good institutions. "The effect would have to become the cause," Rousseau wrote.[13] "The social spirit which ought to be the work of that institution, would have to preside over the institution itself." Thus, if citizens have been oppressed and shaped by bad institutions, they cannot by themselves create good institutions.

For Rousseau, the solution to the paradox was the intervention of an extraordinary founder, what he called the "legislator" or "lawgiver," a genius individual who inspired the people with a sense of group identity so that they would be persuaded to sacrifice their selfish interests for the good of the group. The legislator has a "superior intelligence" compared to everyone else.[14] He would be "the engineer who invents the machine," Rousseau said, whereas any ruler following him was "merely the workman who constructs it and makes it run."[15] The legislator must "feel that he is, so to say, in a position to change human nature, to transform each individual (who is by himself a perfect and solitary whole) into a part of a larger whole from which this individual receives, in a sense, his life and his being; to alter a man's constitution in order to strengthen it."[16] The legislator can "persuade without convincing," by which Rousseau meant that the legislator persuades by inducing shared feelings in the citizens rather than relying alone on rational argument.[17] The legislator tells the people how to behave, what is right and wrong, and who they should strive to become. The legislator is rare, mythical, and godlike.

To this day in Vietnam, students must write "Uncle" (*Bác*) before writing "Hồ" and capitalize the first letter. His portrait is usually displayed at the front of classrooms and so, as a Vietnamese student told me, "He is always watching you, like a god." Hồ Chí Minh is upheld as a godlike figure, the "face, front and center of the communist political system and political religion in Vietnam."[18] This veneration is apparent in the gushing praise officials in the party give to Hồ. Nguyễn Phú Trọng, Vietnam's highest-ranking leader in 2021, said that Hồ Chí Minh was "a shining example for us to regularly study and follow. He is the most beautiful symbol of Vietnamese patriotism and revolutionary heroism, the radiant crystallization of morality, intelligence, courage, and conscience of the nation and the times."[19] Such expressions by party leaders are "speech acts" that serve a political function, instantiating Hồ Chí Minh as *the* source of Vietnamese peoplehood and their "general will." Furthermore, the official political ideology of the party is "Hồ Chí Minh Thought" (*Tư tưởng Hồ Chí Minh*), defined by the party as

> a comprehensive and profound system of views on basic issues of the Vietnamese revolution, the result of the creative application and development of Marxism–Leninism in specific conditions of our country, inheriting and developing the fine traditional values of the nation, and absorbing the cultural quintessence of mankind. It is an extremely great and precious spiritual asset of the Party and our people, forever illuminating the path towards our people's revolutionary success.[20]

In Vietnam, hundreds of works have been written about Hồ Chí Minh, most of them hagiographic, and, as Olga Dror puts it, they "all perpetuate the image of a staunch revolutionary leader, the father of his people, without any critical analysis of his life or work."[21]

Hồ's actual political influence in the party rose and waned as other leaders like Trường Chinh and Lê Duẩn took control. And while Hồ was persuasive to many, the authority he claimed as a founder was often assailed. Indeed, *all* foundings and founders are "underauthorized" as Angélica Bernal put it: all foundations of any political order, "including importantly their sense of authority and legitimacy, are necessarily incomplete and open to unsettlement."[22] This is no less true for Vietnam which experienced conflict and violent civil wars between (and among) Communist and anti-Communist groups ever since ideas inspired by Marx and Lenin found their way to Vietnam.[23] There are numerous other national "founder" figures from the pantheon of Vietnamese heroes and heroines—such as the Trưng sisters,

Ngô Quyền, Lê Thánh Tông, Lê Lợi, Trần Hưng Đạo, and others. However, to this day, the party upholds Hồ Chí Minh as *the* "legislator."

Nguyễn Mạnh Tường

Nguyễn Mạnh Tường is still relatively obscure compared to the others, but his significance is beginning to be recognized. In 2009, Vietnamese officials acknowledged a conference held in Hanoi to "celebrate the 100th birthday of Professor and lawyer Nguyễn Mạnh Tường," a "patriotic intellectual" who "has made many contributions to the revolutionary cause of the nation."[24] At the conference, it is reported, "many speakers proposed establishing a scholarship foundation named after him, and to collect, translate and print all of his works. Some other opinions suggested that Hanoi consider naming a street after Nguyễn Mạnh Tường to honor the great Vietnamese intellectual." Furthermore, an article published in 2021 on the website of the Hanoi National University of Education provided an overview of his life and praised Tường for donating his property to the party and for being "an intelligent, talented, and patriotic person."[25] The same article also reported that, upon Tường's death in 1997, two party leaders—Đỗ Mười (then the general secretary) and Nguyễn Đức Bình (then a Politburo member)—declared that Nguyễn Mạnh Tường "is a patriotic intellectual who has contributed a lot to the cause of national liberation, unification of the Fatherland and contributed to building Vietnamese education."

Both articles on Tường above do not mention that from 1955 to 1991, the party excommunicated Tường from society. They also do not mention his autobiography *Un Excommunie,* nor do they say anything about his criticisms of the party. As with Phạm Quỳnh, the contemporary party is selecting what to emphasize and what to downplay or ignore when it comes to figures it wants to uphold as examples of Vietnam's architects of dignity.

* * *

In the first half of the twentieth century in Vietnam, moods of shame and pride ebbed and flowed, sometimes running against, and sometimes surfing the waves of larger global trends. As David Marr put it, by the late 1920s, "both the mood of self-disparagement and the emphasis on moral rearmament were being replaced by the belief that history was moving in Vietnam's direction, and that social forces would accomplish what individual regeneration could not." Yet, this new sense of confidence and optimism was "badly shaken by the French colonial repression of 1929–32. It recovered in the Popular Front period of 1936–39. It suffered again in the Japanese–Vichy crackdowns of 1940–44. And then it burst forth as never before in the August 1945 Revolution."[26] Indeed, consider the music that accompanied this burst, particularly the songs by Lưu Hữu Phước (1921–1989). In 1944 Phước wrote "Lên đàng" (Get on the Road), a cheerful, upbeat song that evokes optimism toward a "glorious future," calling on Vietnamese youth to join the anticolonial revolution. It became the anthem of the youth and was played and sung by thousands, if not millions, in the late 1940s and early 1950s. Youth sang it in the maquis, the Vietnamese resistance against colonialism taking place in the jungle and countryside. Lưu Hữu Phước composed many other songs that the Vietnamese would sing with pride, joy, and confidence. One can still watch video footage of Vietnamese soldiers singing his "Giải phóng miền Nam" (Liberate the South) as they marched in the jungle, poised to fight soldiers from the Republic of Vietnam and their American allies.[27] Ironically, one of Lưu Hữu Phước's songs would become the national anthem for American-supported *South* Vietnam during the Second Indochina War.[28]

By 1954, Việt Minh victory at Điện Biên Phủ would even more firmly establish their sense of national pride. And such pride would be felt by other colonized peoples around the globe. Frantz Fanon, the most well-known theorist of colonialism and anticolonial struggle, said in his 1962 book *Wretched of the Earth* that the "great victory of the Vietnamese people at Điện Biên Phủ is no longer, strictly speaking, a Vietnamese victory." Fanon then posed a question: "Since July, 1954, the question which the colonized peoples have asked themselves has been, 'What must be done to bring about another Điện Biên Phủ?'" Fanon's explanation for why colonized people would sacrifice themselves to resist colonialism is a quasi-natural, Marxist one: colonial oppression would engender so much misery for colonized natives that they would naturally want to revolt. In other words, for Fanon, Điện Biên Phủ was best understood as a Vietnamese desire to finally "breathe" after suffocating under colonial exploitation and humiliation. Fanon insists that this was a simple, not a complex, matter. But this book has shown that there is more to the story.

During the Black Lives Matters movement across the United States in the summer of 2020, a quote attributed to Frantz Fanon was shared countless times on Twitter, used in online blogs, painted on murals on walls, and displayed on many signs at protests: "When we revolt it's not for a particular culture. We revolt simply because, for many reasons, we can no longer breathe."[29] The quote resonated with activists because "I can't breathe" were the last words of George Floyd and numerous other Black men killed by police in recent years.

But Fanon never said that. What he actually said is the following: "It is not because the Indo-Chinese has discovered a culture of his own that he is in revolt. It is because 'quite simply' it was, in more than one way, becoming impossible for him to breathe."[30] In a curious case of erasing the Vietnamese, contemporary American activists transformed Fanon's reference to the Vietnamese anticolonial struggle to fit their own purposes. This is not a bad thing. In any high-stakes struggle against oppression and for dignity, activists—whether Vietnamese anticolonialists in the 1920s or Black Lives Matters activists in the 2020s—creatively appropriate and (mis)interpret the ideas of authors for their own emancipatory ends.

Fanon's remark that the Indo-Chinese revolted not because they discovered a culture of their own, but because they could not breathe appears in the conclusion of his book, *Black Skin White Masks,* where he emphasizes that anticolonial resistance stems from colonial oppression *alone*: "For the Negro who works on a sugar plantation in Le Robert, there is only one solution: to fight. He will embark on this struggle . . . quite simply because he cannot conceive of life otherwise than in the form of a battle against exploitation, misery, and hunger." Fanon downplays the role of discovering or having to affirm one's own culture and past tradition for anticolonial resistance. He argues that it is not because natives find their own culture that they revolt, but that they revolt simply because they are being oppressed.

It is certainly true that Vietnamese resistance and self-assertion were motivated by a desire to escape colonial oppression, but their resistance and self-assertion were also motivated by a desire to escape their own shame, a shame of their perceived lack of an indigenous intellectual tradition or other perceived shortcomings. For Fanon, being "unable to breathe" meant suffocating under colonial repression. But for these Vietnamese thinkers in this book, as we have seen, the Vietnamese were also suffocating under their own laziness, their inability to think and act as a nation, their failure to organize, their own oppressive traditions, and so on. "Breathing" meant not only expelling French colonizers but also transforming and asserting their own selves in dignifying ways. As the political philosopher Isaiah Berlin remarked, it is not enough to appeal to common oppression to unite a group: "something more is needed—namely, a new vision of life with which the wounded society . . . can identify themselves, around which they can gather and attempt to restore their collective life."[31]

In these ways, Vietnam is not so unique. Many colonized and oppressed peoples around the globe have felt the painful and often intense emotions of shame and indignation, and their challenge has always been to channel these feelings toward productive social and political ends. This has typically meant toward projects that would generate a sense of national pride, national confidence, and national dignity. This has meant cultural assertion, violent expulsion of foreign occupation, or new ways of "worldmaking."[32] To meet these challenges, many, like these Vietnamese thinkers, have scolded, shamed, and fiercely critiqued their own people. This might appear to us in the West as self-destructive "victim blaming," but they are actually expressions of a productive, clear-eyed understanding on the part of the oppressed of what the demands of the moment are. If it was futile to blame the oppressor and there was no higher authority to appeal to, then blaming themselves was part of a rhetorical and practical strategy in their anticolonial politics and a sincere expression of their desire to self-strengthen. As Hô Chí Minh put it in a speech in 1952, "A nation that is not self-reliant but waits for other nations to help does not deserve to be independent."[33] Mahatma Gandhi said to his compatriots that "the British did not take India from us. We gave it to them." Marcus Garvey, the Black political activist who sought self-determination for the African diaspora in the early twentieth century, gave fiery speeches in which he exhorted his Black audiences to assert their sovereignty. If other nations could do it, then "Africa with 400 million Black People can do it. If you cannot do it, if you are not prepared to do it then you will die! You race of cowards, you race of imbeciles, you race of good for-nothings, if you cannot do what other men have done, what other nations have done, what other races have done, then you had better die!"

These leaders' criticisms of their own people are analogous to how parents might scold their children for not living up to their potential or asserting their dignity for their own sake. Indeed, we assert our dignity when we clean our living space, even though we might live alone and no one else will see it, or when we choose to dress well. Garvey donned a viceroy's uniform, carried a sword, and wore a plumed hat, and in doing so he transfigured an emblem of imperium into a symbol of Black power and Black dignity.[34] Although others may *recognize* our dignified appearance if they see us and treat us better for it, we can do it just for ourselves to feel more dignified. Such self-assertion is a dignity born of agency, rather than something inherent or innate.

Amilcar Cabral, the revolutionary from Guinea-Bissau who wrote in opposition to Portuguese colonialism in Africa, understood the need to assert national dignity, arguing that this could be done if native elites and native masses would unite in anticolonial struggle.[35] Similarly, Fanon observed that the persistent refusal of colonizers to recognize the dignity of colonized peoples inflicted great psychological harm on its victims, and the solution to this was self-assertion: "Since the other hesitated to recognize me, there remained only one solution: to make myself known."[36] These words could have come from any one of these Vietnamese thinkers. Malcolm X criticized fellow Black Americans for being too weak and singing songs like "We Shall Overcome" when they should instead be asserting Black national dignity:

> This is part of what's wrong with you, you do too much singing. Today, it's time to stop singing and start swinging.... We need a self-help program, a do-it-yourself philosophy, a do-it-right-now philosophy, a it's-already-too-late philosophy.... Before we can get a self-help program started, we have to have a self-help philosophy. Black nationalism is a self-help philosophy.

We see in Malcolm X, as we do in Hồ Chí Minh and other Vietnamese, the futility of demanding oppressors to respect the rights of the oppressed. For Malcolm X, key to having "a high degree of racial pride and racial dignity" was his realization that he "couldn't be anybody by begging the white man for what he had but that I had to get out here and try to do something for myself or make something out of myself."[37]

These expressions suggest that oppressed peoples have an intuitive understanding that "rights" are meaningful only to the extent that rights are backed by power, because rights are coextensive with power.[38] But although a group might succeed in generating power (the ability to act in concert) among its members, individuals in the group who are perceived to *not* be acting in concert may be punished. Vietnamese Communist revolutionaries may have generated power to expel the French in 1954, but, as we saw in Chapter 7, this would present new problems for a post-independence Vietnam when some will argue that respecting individual human rights and negative freedom should be the new paths to national dignity. Nguyễn Mạnh Tường would have agreed with Fanon who warned that, after independence, the party would help "the government to hold the people down. It becomes more and more clearly anti-democratic, an implement of coercion."[39]

As Fanon predicted, there can be new sources of national shame. Post-independence, the nation itself can be the source of oppression. Fanon warned of ongoing neocolonialism and exploitation of the indigenous, aided in part by the national bourgeoisie who "organizes centers of rest and relaxation and pleasure resorts to meet the wishes of the Western bourgeoisie. Such activity is given the name of tourism, and for the occasion will be built up as a national industry."[40] Through neocolonialism, the national bourgeoisie will "be greatly helped on its way toward decadence by the Western bourgeoisies, who come to it as tourists avid for the exotic, for big game hunting, and for casinos." Fanon also predicted that "After independence, the party sinks into an extraordinary lethargy."[41] There would be inside the new regime increasing "inequality in the acquisition of wealth and in monopolization. Some have a double source of income and demonstrate that they are specialized in opportunism. Privileges multiply and corruption triumphs, while morality declines." To some Vietnamese, Fanon turned out to be right.

While Fanon warned of these postcolonial dangers, he also provided advice to leaders of the new independent nation. Their main job, he said, should be to "reject their status as bourgeois and dedicate themselves to the peasant masses they represent." Party leaders and elites should "leave their city vocation and go to the masses to learn from the people, and they should in turn teach the masses what they have learned in Western universities." This "heroic and positive path," Fanon says, is the best way for the national elites to remain helpful to the nation as a whole.

In that apartment at 6 villa des Gobelins on that winter evening in 1919, the debate between Phan Chu Trinh and Hô Chí Minh feels familiar to many of us. In response to injustice, exploitation, domination, and racism, the young man is impatient and urges direct action while the older man is cautious and pleads for slower change. In that apartment, the seeds were sown for the First, Second, and Third Indochina Wars. It should be common intuition that if those with a power advantage fail to recognize the dignity of human beings with less power and include them in discussions over the common good, then the latter will seek to construct their dignity in other ways, violently or nonviolently, destructively or constructively. Today, various groups around the world continue to grapple with different forms of indignation and shame. While this can take productive forms, some forms of indignation can be destructive. Feelings of collective anger at losing special status, for example, and desires for a "return" to collective dignity from an imagined past can drive destructive nationalistic politics, too. Think of the case of "White working-class" Trump voters in the United States. We are still left with the challenge of steering these powerful, emotive social forces toward productive, world-building projects and away from narrowing projects of resentment and violence.

Notes

Introduction

1. Cited in Nguyễn Phan Quang, *Thêm một số tư liệu về hoạt động của Nguyễn Ái Quốc thời gian ở Pháp 1917–1923* [*More documents about Nguyễn Ai Quoc's activities during his time in France 1917–1923*] (TP. Hồ Chí Minh: Nhà xuất bản Thành Phố Hồ Chí Minh, 1988), 177–181. Translations from Vietnamese are mine unless otherwise noted.
2. Ibid.
3. Quoted in William Duiker, *Ho Chi Minh: A Life* (New York: Hyperion, 2000), 68.
4. Francis Fukuyama, *Identity: The Demand for Dignity and the Politics of Resentment* (New York: Farrar, Straus & Giroux, 2018), xiii.
5. Oliver Sensen, "Human Dignity in Historical Perspective: The Contemporary and Traditional Paradigms," *European Journal of Political Theory* 10, no. 1 (2011): 71–91, at 73.
6. Axel Honneth, *Reification: A New Look at an Old Idea* (New York: Oxford University Press, 2008), 40–44; Charles Taylor, "The Politics of Recognition," in *Multiculturalism: Examining the Politics of Recognition*, ed. Amy Gutmann (Princeton, NJ: Princeton University Press, 1992), 25–73, at 26.
7. Hannah Arendt, *On Violence* (New York: Harcourt Brace Jovanovich, 1970), 44. Emphasis mine.
8. This book joins the growing literature on how anticolonial movements challenge or reveal the limits of liberal discourses of rights and recognition. See Samuel Moyn's chapter, "Why Anticolonialism Wasn't a Human Rights Movement," in his *The Last Utopia: Human Rights in History* (Cambridge, MA: Harvard University Press, 2010), and Glen Sean Coulthard, *Red Skin, White Masks: Rejecting the Colonial Politics of Recognition* (Minneapolis: University of Minnesota Press, 2014).
9. Phan Chu Trinh, *Phan Châu Trinh and His Political Writings*, ed. and trans. Vinh Sinh (Ithaca, NY: Cornell Southeast Asia Program, 2009), 139.
10. Hồ Chí Minh, *Hồ Chí Minh Toàn Tập xuất bản lần thứ ba* [*The Complete Works of Ho Chí Minh*, third edition], Vol. 3, (Hà Nội: NxB Chính Trị Quốc Gia, 2011), 230.
11. Phan Bội Châu, "A Letter from Abroad Written in Blood (1907)," in *Sources of Vietnamese tradition*, eds. George Dutton, Jayne Werner, and John K. Whitmore (New York: Columbia University Press, 2012), 357.
12. Trinh, *Political Writings*, 107.
13. Phạm Quỳnh, *Nam Phong tạp chí*, "Malaise Moral," no. 106. All translations from French are mine unless otherwise noted.
14. Quoted in Duiker, *Ho Chi Minh*, 125.
15. Nguyễn Mạnh Tường, *Un Excommunié: Hanoi 1954–1991: Procès d'un Intellectuelle* (Paris: Quê Mẹ, 1992), 202.
16. Jean-Paul Sartre, *Being and Nothingness* (New York: Washington Square Press, 2021), 358.
17. Some exceptions are essays that engage the political thought of Hồ Chí Minh. See the third chapter of Margaret Kohn and Keally McBride's book, *Political Theories of Decolonization: Postcolonialism and the Problem of Foundations* (New York: Oxford University Press, 2011), 55–76; Quỳnh N. Phạm and María José Méndez, "Decolonial Designs: José Martí, Hồ Chí Minh, and Global Entanglements," *Alternatives: Global, Local, Political* 40, no. 2 (2015): 156–173; Bui Ngoc Son, "Anticolonial Constitutionalism: The Case of Hồ Chí Minh," *Japanese Journal of Political Science* 19, no. 2 (2018): 197–221.
18. A few notable books that cover the colonial period are David G. Marr, *Vietnamese Tradition on Trial, 1920–1945* (Berkeley: University of California Press, 1981) and *Vietnamese Anticolonialism, 1885–1925* (Berkeley: University of California Press, 1971); Hue Tam Ho Tai, *Radicalism and the Roots of the Vietnamese Revolution* (Cambridge, MA: Harvard University Press, 1992); Peter Zinoman, *The Colonial Bastille: A History of Imprisonment in*

Vietnam, 1862–1940 (Berkeley: University of California Press, 2001) and *Vietnamese Colonial Republican: The Political Vision of Vu Trong Phung* (Berkeley: University of California Press, 2014); Christopher Goscha, *Vietnam: A New History* (New York: Basic Books, 2016); William Duiker, *Hồ Chí Minh: A Life* (New York: Hyperion, 2000), Mark Atwood Lawrence, *The Vietnam War: A Concise International History* (New York: Oxford University Press, 2008); Keith W. Taylor, *A History of the Vietnamese* (Cambridge: Cambridge University Press, 2013); Tuong Vu, *Vietnam's Communist Revolution: The Powers and Limits of Ideology* (Cambridge: Cambridge University Press, 2017); Martina Thuchnhi Nguyễn, *On Our Own Strength: The Self-Reliant Literary Groups and Cosmopolitan Nationalism in Late Colonial Vietnam* (Honolulu: University of Hawai'i Press, 2021).
19. For a study on women intellectuals in Vietnam, see Bùi Trân Phượng, "Việt Nam 1918–1945, genre et modernité. Émergence de nouvelles perceptions et experimentations" (PhD thesis, University Lyon II, 2008). There has also been increased scholarly interest in the political thought of South Vietnamese anti-Communist thinkers who have been traditionally neglected in work on Vietnamese modern history. See Nu-Anh Tran and Tuong Vu, eds., *Building a Republican Nation in Vietnam, 1920–1963* (Honolulu: University of Hawai'i Press, 2022); Nu-Anh Tran, *Disunion: Anticommunism Nationalism and the Making of Republican Vietnam* (Honolulu: University of Hawai'i Press, 2022).
20. Most notable is Trần Văn Giàu's three-volume *Sự phát triển của tư tưởng ở Việt Nam từ thế kỷ XIX đến cách mạng tháng tám 1945* [The development of ideology in Vietnam from the nineteenth century to the August 1945 revolution] (TP. Hồ Chí Minh: NXB Tổng Hợp, 2019 [1973]).) Giàu was a Communist Party leader, and his books represent a distinct Communist interpretation.
21. Susan McWilliams, *Traveling back: Toward a Global Political Theory* (New York: Oxford University Press, 2014), 9.
22. Ibid., 12–13.
23. Farah Godrej, *Cosmopolitan Political Thought: Method, Practice, Discipline Theory* (New York: Oxford University Press, 2011), 17–18.
24. Martina Thuchnhi Nguyễn's detailed study, *On Our Own Strength: The Self-Reliant Literary Groups and Cosmopolitan Nationalism in Late Colonial Vietnam* (Honolulu: University of Hawai'i Press, 2021) provides a historical view of intellectual, artistic, and fashion trends in Vietnam during which thinkers freely borrowed from diverse cultural traditions.
25. Andrew March, "What Is Comparative Political Theory?," *Review of Politics* 71, no. 4 (2009): 531–565.

Chapter 1

1. Stephen M. Walt, "The Most Powerful Force in the World," *Foreign Policy,* July 15, 2011. https://foreignpolicy.com/2011/07/15/the-most-powerful-force-in-the-world
2. Liah Greenfeld, *Nationalism: Five Roads to Modernity* (Cambridge, MA: Harvard University Press, 1992), 7.
3. Farid Abdel-Nour, "National Responsibility," *Political Theory* 31, no. 5 (2003): 693–719, at 700.
4. Greenfeld, *Nationalism*, 7.
5. Ibid., 490, 487.
6. Anthony D. Smith, *National Identity* (Reno: University of Nevada Press, 1993), 176.
7. Abdel-Nour asks us to imagine a person who views the achievements of her compatriot not with pride but with mere approval and admiration, "without gaining for herself from them a sense of added authority, or added standing in the world," analogous to how a Chinese or Indian individual might admire a work by Shakespeare or Leonardo Da Vinci. "But about such a person we must ask whether she still has a national identity"; Abdel-Nour, "National Responsibility," 713.
8. See Emma Dresler-Hawke and James H. Liu, "Collective Shame and the Positioning of German National Identity," *Psicología Política* 32 (2006): 131–153; James Goodman, "Refugee Solidarity: Between National Shame and Global Outrage," in *Theorizing Emotions: Sociological Explorations and Applications*, ed. Debra Hopkins et al. (Frankfurt, Germany: Campus Verlag, 2009): 269–290; and Emile Therein, "The National Shame of Aboriginal Incarceration," *Globe and Mail*, July 2011, at http://www.theglobeandmail.com.
9. See David Miller, *National Responsibility and Global Justice* (Oxford, UK: Oxford University Press, 2007); and Larry May and Stacey Hoffman, eds., *Collective Responsibility: Five Decades*

of Debate in Theoretical and Applied Ethics (Lanham, MD: Rowman & Littlefield Publishers, 1992).
10. May and Hoffman, *Collective Responsibility*, 1–8.
11. Lawrie Balfour, "Reparations after Identity Politics," *Political Theory* 33 (2005): 786–811.
12. Thomas Pogge, "Cosmopolitanism and Sovereignty," *Ethics* 103, no. 1 (1992): 48–75.
13. Miller, *National Responsibility and Global Justice*, 164.
14. Antonio Y. Vázquez-Arroyo, "Critical Theory, Colonialism, and the Historicity of Thought," *Constellations* 25, no. 1 (2018): 54–70, 60.
15. Ibid.
16. See Burke Hendrix and Deborah Baumgold, eds., *Colonial Exchanges: Political Theory and the Agency of the Colonized* (Manchester, UK: Manchester University Press, 2017); Bill Ashcroft, Gareth Griffiths, and Helen Tiffin, *The Empire Writes Back* (New York: Routledge, 1989).
17. See Robert J. C. Young, *Postcolonialism: An Historical Introduction* (Oxford, UK: Blackwell Publishing Ltd., 2001); Ania Loomba, *Colonialism/Postcolonialism* (New York: Routledge, 2005); and Charles W. Mills, *The Racial Contract* (New York: Cornell University Press, 1997).
18. E. J. R. David and Sumie Okazaki, "Colonial Mentality: A Review and Recommendation for Filipino American Psychology," *Cultural Diversity and Ethnic Minority Psychology* 12, no. 1 (2006): 1–16, at 2.
19. Young, *Postcolonialism*, 6.
20. Cynthia Robinson-Moore, "Beauty Standards Reflect Eurocentric Paradigms—So What? Skin Color, Identity, and Black Female Beauty," *Journal of Race and Policy* 4, no. 1 (2008): 66–85. See also Albert Memmi, *The Colonizer and the Colonized* (Boston: Beacon, 1965); Paulo Freire, *The Pedagogy of the Oppressed* (New York: Continuum, 1970); and David and Okazaki, "Colonial Mentality."
21. Gayatri Spivak, "Can the Subaltern Speak?" reprinted in Marxist *Interpretations of Culture*, ed. Cary Nelson and Lawrence Grossberg (Basingstoke, UK: Macmillan Education, 1988 [1985]), 271–313; Leela Gandhi, *Postcolonial Theory: A Critical Introduction* (Sydney, Australia: Allen & Unwin, 1998).
22. Edward W. Said, *Culture and Imperialism* (New York: Alfred Knopf, 1993), 66–67.
23. Ibid., 89.
24. Edward W. Said, *Orientalism* (New York: Pantheon Books, 1978).
25. Ibid., 65.
26. Frantz Fanon, *Black Skin, White Masks*, trans. Richard Philcox (New York: Grove Press, 2008), 2.
27. Ngũgĩ Wa Thiong'o, *Decolonising the Mind: The Politics of Language in African Literature* (London: East African Educational Publishers, 1986), 3.
28. Jean Paule Sartre, trans. S. W. Allen, *Black Orpheus* (Paris: Présence Africaine, 1976), 20.
29. Ibid., 31.
30. Marie-Paule Ha, "On Sartre's Critique of Assimilation," *Journal of Romance Studies* 6 (2006): 49–60, 53.
31. Loomba, *Colonialism/Postcolonialism*, 78
32. Edward Said, *The World, the Text, and the Critic* (Cambridge, MA: Harvard University Press, 1983), 12.
33. Leela Gandhi, *Postcolonial Theory: A Critical Introduction* (Sydney, Australia: Allen & Unwin, 1998), 144.
34. Loomba, *Colonialism/Postcolonialism*, 60.
35. Gayatri Spivak, "Can the Subaltern Speak?" reprinted in Marxist *Interpretations of Culture*, ed. Cary Nelson and Lawrence Grossberg (Basingstoke, UK: Macmillan Education, 1988 [1985]), 271–313.
36. Megan Vaughan, "Colonial Discourse Theory and African History, or Has Postmodernism Passed Us By?," *Social Dynamics* 20 (1994): 1–23, at 3.
37. Ibid.
38. Ashis Nandy, *Intimate Enemy* (Oxford, UK: Oxford University Press, 1989), xii.
39. Homi Bhabha, "Of Mimicry and Man: The Ambivalence of Colonial Discourse," *October* 28 (1984): 125–133.
40. Ibid., 129.
41. Homi Bhabha, "Signs Taken for Wonders: Questions of Ambivalence and Authority under a Tree outside Delhi, May 1817," *Critical Inquiry* 12 (1985): 144–165.

42. Nick Bromell, "Democratic indignation: Black American Thought and the Politics of Dignity," *Political Theory* 41, no. 2 (February 2013): 285–311, at 285.
43. For a detailed account, see Pierre Brocheux and Daniel Hémery, *Indochina: An Ambiguous Colonization, 1858–1954*, trans. Ly Lan Dill-Klein, Eric Jennings, Nora Taylor, and Noémi Tousignant (Berkeley: University of California Press, 2009).
44. Truong Buu Lam, *Colonialism Experienced: Vietnamese Writings on Colonialism, 1900–1931* (Ann Arbor: University of Michigan Press, 2000), 46. Truong is citing from articles in the periodical *Tiếng Dân* (1927, 1928, 1929, 1930).
45. Sophie Wahnich, *In Defense of the Terror: Liberty or Death in the French Revolution* (New York: Verso, 2012), 19. I thank Kevin Duong for bringing this to my attention.
46. Ibid., 22.
47. Lam, *Colonialism Experienced*, 46.
48. Ibid., 47.
49. Ibid., 55.
50. Ibid., 60.
51. Hồ Chí Minh, *Hồ Chí Minh Toàn Tập xuất bản lần thứ ba* [*Hồ Chí Minh's Complete Works*, third edition], Vol. 2, 68.
52. "Nobel Lecture Delivered by Kofi Annan," United Nations, accessed May 3, 2020, December 2001. Retrieved at: https://www.un.org/sg/en/content/sg/speeches/2001-12-10/nobel-lecture-delivered-kofi-annan
53. For "enlightened patriotism," see Steven B. Smith, *Reclaiming Patriotism in an Age of Extremes* (New Haven, CT: Yale University Press, 2021), 143. For "liberal nationalism," see Yael Tamir, *Why Nationalism* (Princeton, NJ: Princeton University Press, 2019) and *Liberal Nationalism* (Princeton, NJ: Princeton University Press, 1995).
54. Rosen argues "that we ought, in my opinion, to resist any attempt by the state to extend the duty of being dignified beyond the realm of private tact and good taste. It seems plausible enough to say that the 'dignity of the human person' should be protected by the power of the state if we understand by the dignity of the human person their inner transcendental kernel—whatever it is about us that founds our claim to be of intrinsic value. But the case is far more dubious when that means giving the state the power to enforce the duty of being respectful to oneself and others—perhaps even of being respectful toward that abstract entity, the state itself. (Article 161 of the Ukraine penal code, for example, provides for imprisonment for up to two years for the 'humiliation of national honour and dignity.') We are coming close—frighteningly close—to those laws against lèse-majesté that tyrants have traditionally used to defend themselves." Michael Rosen, *Dignity: Its History and Meaning* (Cambridge, MA: Harvard University Press, 2012), 73.
55. Lam, *Colonialism Experienced*, 43.
56. Bromell, "Democratic Indignation," 287.

Chapter 2

1. Phan Bội Châu, *Overturned Chariot: The Autobiography of Phan Bội Châu*, trans. Vinh Sinh and Nicholas Wickenden (Honolulu: University of Hawai'i Press, 1999), 49.
2. For the most up-to-date work in English on Phan Bội Châu's political life and ideas, see Matthew A. Berry, "Confucian Terrorism: Phan Bội Châu and the Imagining of Modern Vietnam" (PhD dissertation, University of California, Berkeley, 2019).
3. Phan Bội Châu, "A Letter from Abroad Written in Blood (1907)," in *Sources of Vietnamese Tradition*, eds. George Dutton, Jayne Werner, and John K. Whitmore (New York: Columbia University Press, 2012), 357.
4. Phan Bội Châu, *Phan Bội Châu Toàn Tập*, ed., Chương Thâu [*The Complete Works of Phan Bội Châu*] (Huế: NxB Thuận Hóa, 1990), Vol. 2, 316.
5. This biography is adapted from William Duiker, "Phan Boi Chau: Asian Revolutionary in a Changing World," *Journal of Asian Studies* 31, no. 1 (1971): 77–88.
6. Goscha, *Vietnam*, 63.
7. Taylor, *History of the Vietnamese*, 447.
8. Phan Bội Châu, *Overturned Chariot*, 59.
9. Tai, *Radicalism*, 17.
10. Goscha, *Vietnam*, 93.

11. Ibid., 98.
12. Ibid., 95.
13. Quoted in Pankaj Mishra, *From the Ruins of Empire: The Revolt Against the West and the Remaking of Asia* (New York: Farrar, Straus & Giroux, 2012), 4.
14. For a more detailed discussion of Asian reactions to Japanese victory in the Russo-Japanese War, see ibid., 1–11.
15. Phan Bội Châu, *Overturned Chariot*, 136.
16. Ibid., 111.
17. Quoted in Vinh Sinh, Introduction to *Overturned Chariot*, 12.
18. Phan Bội Châu, *Overturned Chariot*, 90.
19. Phan Bội Châu, *Toàn Tập*, Vol. 2, 216.
20. Ibid., 204.
21. Samuel Popkin, "Review: Colonialism and the Ideological Origins of the Vietnamese Revolution," *Journal of Asian Studies* 44. no. 2 (February 1985): 349–357, 349.
22. Phan Bội Châu, "Tân Việt Nam" [A New Vietnam] (1907), accessed March 1, 2023 https://www.chungta.com/nd/tu-lieu-tra-cuu/tan-viet-nam-phan-boi-chau.html
23. Goscha, *Vietnam*, 15.
24. Cosmopolitan nationalism in Vietnam, particularly as expressed by literary groups, has been explored in Martina Thuchnhi Nguyễn's detailed study, *On Our Own Strength: The Self-Reliant Literary Groups and Cosmopolitan Nationalism in Late Colonial Vietnam* (Honolulu: University of Hawai'i Press, 2021).
25. Thi Hong Ha Hoang, "How the Vietnamese Cult of Heroes Promotes Nationalism in Politics," *The Conversation*, June 26, 2017, https://theconversation.com/how-the-vietnamese-cult-of-heroes-promotes-nationalism-in-politics-73144
26. Ranjoo Seodu Herr, "In Defense of Nonliberal Nationalism," *Political Theory* 34, no. 3 (2006): 304–327, at 313.
27. Goscha, *Vietnam*, 32–33.
28. Phan Bội Châu, "Letter from Abroad Written in Blood," 357.
29. Ibid., 357–358.
30. Ibid., 358.
31. Phan Bội Châu, "Tân Việt Nam."
32. Pierre Brocheux and Daniel Hémery, *Indochina: An Ambiguous Colonization, 1858–1954*, trans. Ly Lan Dill-Klein, Eric Jennings, Nora Taylor, and Noémi Tousignant (Berkeley: University of California Press, 2009), 127.
33. Truong Buu Lam, *Colonialism Experienced: Vietnamese Writings on Colonialism, 1900–1931* (Ann Arbor: University of Michigan Press, 2000), 141–156, at 42.
34. Ibid., 43.
35. Tran Tu Binh, *The Red Earth: A Vietnamese Memoir of Life on a Colonial Rubber Plantation*, trans. John Spragens, Jr., ed. David Marr (Athens: Ohio University Press, 1984), 32.
36. Ibid., 35. Bình's grim descriptions are confirmed in confidential reports that colonial administrators forwarded to Paris and that are now available for study in the Archives Nationales de France (Section Outre-Mer). For example, David Marr notes in his introduction to Binh's memoir, "the minister of colonies is told that 17 percent of Phu Rieng workers died in 1927, probably a conservative figure, since the plantation supervisory staff had reason to cover up some losses."
37. Lawrence, *The Vietnam War*, 13.
38. Lam, *Colonialism Experienced*, 39.
39. Ibid., 58.
40. Phan Bội Châu, *Đời Cách Mạng Phan Bội Châu*, trans. (from Classical Chinese to Vietnamese quốc ngữ) Đào Trinh Nhất [The Revolutionary Career of Phan Boi Chau] (Hà Nội: Nippon-Bunka-Kaikan, 1945), 33.
41. Phan Bội Châu, "Ái quốc" [Patriot] (1910), May 2, 2023, https://www.thivien.net/Phan-B%E1%BB%99i-Ch%C3%A2u/%C3%81i-qu%E1%BB%91c/poem-xTTlHcqLe1mLqb5z0nMc4Q
42. Phan Bội Châu, *Việt Nam Vong Quốc Sử*, translated from Classical Chinese to Vietnamese quốc ngữ by Nguyễn Quang To (NxB Tao Đàn, 1969), 45.
43. Phan Bội Châu, "Tân Việt Nam" [A New Vietnam].
44. Goscha, *Vietnam*, 101.

45. For more on Phan Chu Trinh and Phan Bội Châu's travels to Japan, see Marr, *Vietnamese Anticolonialism,* 128 and Trinh, *Political Writings,* xiv.
46. Quoted in Phan Bội Châu, *Overturned Chariot,* 108.
47. Phan Bội Châu, *Overturned Chariot,* 105.
48. Ibid., 109.
49. Trinh, *Political Writings,* 75.
50. Ibid.
51. Marr, *Vietnamese Anticolonialism,* 169.
52. Ibid., 166.
53. Ibid.
54. Lam, *Colonialism Experienced,* 141–156.
55. Alan Macfarlane, *The Making of the Modern World: Visions from the West and East* (New York: Palgrave, 2002), 148.
56. Edward W. Said, *Orientalism* (New York: Pantheon Books, 1978).
57. Marr, *Vietnamese Anticolonialism,* 166.
58. Vũ Văn Sạch, Vũ Thị Minh Hương, and Philippe Papin, eds., *Văn thơ Đông Kinh Nghĩa Thục (Prose et poésies du Đông Kinh Nghĩa Thục)* [Prose and Poetry of the Tonkin Free School] (Hà Nội: Nhà xb Văn Hoá, 1997), 28.
59. Trinh, *Political Writings,* 21.
60. Ibid.; my translation.
61. Marr, *Vietnamese Anticolonialism,* 166.
62. Thomas Eriksen and Finn Nielsen, *A History of Anthropology* (London: Pluto Press, 2001), 37.
63. Quoted in Masaya Shiraishi, "Phan Bội Châu Phan Bội Châu and Japan," *South East Asian Studies* 13, no. 3 (December 1975): 427–440, 431.
64. Marr, *Vietnamese Anticolonialism,* 176.
65. Ibid., 167.
66. Marr, *Tradition,* 146.
67. Marr, *Vietnamese Anticolonialism,* 169.
68. Quoted in John D. Phan, "Rival Nationalisms and the Rebranding of Language in Early 20th Century Tonkin," *International Institute for Asian Studies,* Spring 2018, https://www.iias.asia/the-newsletter/article/rival-nationalisms-rebranding-language-early-20th-century-tonkin
69. Phan Văn Trường, *Việc giáo-dục học-vấn trong dân-tộc Annam* [Educational Efforts among the Annamite People] (Saigon: NXB Xưa Nay, 1925).
70. Marr, *Vietnamese Anticolonialism,* 182; Goscha, *Vietnam,* 108.
71. Duiker, *Ho Chi Minh,* 83.
72. Ibid., 85.
73. Vinh Sinh, Introduction to *Overturned Chariot,* 21.
74. Phan Bội Châu, "The Trial Testimony of Phan Bội Châu (1925)," in *The Vietnam War: A Documentary Reader,* ed. Edward Miller (Oxford: Wiley, 2016), 6.

Chapter 3

1. Trinh, *Political Writings,* 116.
2. Michael Puett and Christine Gross-Loh, *The Path: What Chinese Philosophers Can Teach Us about the Good Life* (New York: Simon & Schuster, 2017), 21.
3. Seung-hwan Lee, "Liberal Rights or/and Confucian Virtues?," *Philosophy East and West* 46, no. 3 (1996): 367–379; Tu Wei-ming, "Confucianism and Liberalism," *Dao* 2, no. 1 (2002): 1–20.
4. Eske J. Møllgaard, "Political Confucianism and the Politics of Confucian Studies," *Dao* 14, no. 3 (2015): 391–402, at 394.
5. Chenyang Li, "The Confucian Concept of Jen and the Feminist Ethics of Care: A Comparative Study," *Hypatia* 9, no. 1 (Winter 1994): 70–89, at 71.
6. Daniel Bell, David Brown, Kanishka Jayasuriya, and David Martin Jones, *Towards Illiberal Democracy in Pacific Asia* (London: Macmillan, 1995), 17.
7. Sungmoon Kim, *Confucian Democracy in East Asia: Theory and Practice* (New York: Cambridge University Press, 2014), 10.
8. Ibid., 4. For arguments in the same vein, see Sor-hoon Tan, *Confucian Democracy: A Deweyan Reconstruction* (Albany: State University of New York Press, 2003), 2; David L. Hall and Roger T.

Ames, "A Pragmatist Understanding of Confucian Democracy," in *Confucianism for the Modern World*, ed. Daniel Bell and Hahm Chaibong (New York: Cambridge University Press, 2003), 127.
9. Bikhu Parekh, "The Cultural Particularity of Liberal Democracy," *Political Studies* 40, no. 1 (1992): 160–175, at 161.
10. Trinh, *Political Writings*, 126.
11. This argument about creative misunderstanding is supported by hermeneutic thinkers such as Margaret Leslie. See her article, "In Defense of Anachronism," *Political Studies* 18, no. 4 (1970), 433–447.
12. Phan Chu Trinh, *Political Writings*, 13.
13. Ibid., 16.
14. This biography is adapted from Phan Chu Trinh, *Phan Châu Trinh and His Political Writings*, ed. and trans. Vinh Sinh (Ithaca, NY: Cornell Southeast Asia Program, 2009), 1–56.
15. Daniel A. Bell, *Beyond Liberal Democracy: Political Thinking for an East Asian Context* (Princeton, NJ: Princeton University Press, 2009), 166.
16. Joseph Chan, *Confucian Perfectionism: A Political Philosophy for Modern Times* (Princeton, NJ: Princeton University Press, 2014).
17. Stephen Angle, *Contemporary Confucian Political Philosophy* (Cambridge: Polity, 2012), 18.
18. Brooke A. Ackerly, "Is Liberalism the Only Way Toward Democracy? Confucianism and Democracy," *Political Theory* 33, no. 4 (2005): 547–576, 552.
19. Sor-hoon Tan, *Confucian Democracy*, 15.
20. Kim, *Confucian Democracy in East Asia*, 10.
21. Shaun O'Dwyer, "Democracy and Confucian Values," *Philosophy East and West* 53, no. 1 (2003): 39–63, 51.
22. Hall and Ames, "A Pragmatist Understanding of Confucian Democracy," 132.
23. George Dutton, "革命, Cách Mạng, Révolution: The Early History of 'Revolution' in Việt Nam," *Journal of Southeast Asian Studies* 46, no. 1 (2015): 4–31, at 18.
24. See Phan Châu Trinh, *Phan Châu Trinh Toàn Tập* [The complete works of Phan Châu Trinh], ed. Chương Thâu, Dương Trung Quốc, and Lê Thị Kinh (Đà Nẵng: Nxb Đà Nẵng, 2005).
25. Trinh, *Political Writings*, 112.
26. Ibid., 103.
27. Ibid., 105.
28. Ibid., 104.
29. Ibid., 105.
30. Feminist scholars have criticized these and other aspects of Confucianism as promoting the idea of men's superiority to women. See Chenyang Li, ed., *The Sage and the Second Sex: Confucianism, Ethics, and Gender* (Peru, IL: Open Court, 2000).
31. Phan Châu Trinh, *Phan Châu Trinh Toàn Tập, Tập III* [The complete works of Phan Châu Trinh, Volume Three], ed. Chương Thâu, Dương Trung Quốc, and Lê Thị Kinh (Đà Nẵng: Nxb Đà Nẵng, 2005), 245. Vinh Sinh's translation excludes this passage in the original.
32. Trinh, *Political Writings*, 113.
33. David Marr, "Concepts of 'Individual' and 'Self' in Twentieth-Century Vietnam," *Modern Asian Studies* 34, no. 4 (2000): 769–796, at 773.
34. Sinh translates *thiên hạ* as "empire," though the term means "all under heaven" or "world," probably because for the Chinese at the time, the knowable world was their empire.
35. Trinh is speaking of Chinese and Vietnamese rulers, the latter being influenced by Chinese rule over the Vietnamese (111 BC to AD 938).
36. Trinh, *Political Writings*, 131.
37. Ibid., 132.
38. Ibid.
39. Ibid., 129.
40. Ibid., 131.
41. Ibid., 130.
42. Ibid.
43. Ibid., 137.
44. Ibid., 136.
45. Ibid., 124.
46. Ibid., 134.
47. Trinh, *Toàn Tập*, 245.

48. Trinh, *Political Writings*, 107.
49. Ibid., 105.
50. Ibid., 109.
51. Ibid., 110.
52. Ibid., 131.
53. Ibid., 106.
54. Trinh, *Toàn Tập*, 250.
55. Trinh, *Political Writings*, 106.
56. Ibid., 107.
57. Ibid., 113–114.
58. Ibid., 126.
59. Ibid., 99.
60. Ibid., 114.
61. David G. Marr, "Concepts of 'Individual' and 'Self' in Twentieth-Century Vietnam," *Modern Asian Studies* 34, no. 4 (2000): 769–796, at 769.
62. Trinh, *Political Writings*, 122.
63. Ibid., 107.
64. Ibid., 122.
65. Ibid., 115.
66. Ibid., 107.
67. Ibid., 21.
68. Ibid.
69. Ibid., 137–138.
70. Ibid., 138–139.
71. Ibid., 139.
72. Trinh, *Toàn Tập*, 247.
73. Trinh, *Political Writings*, 134.
74. Ibid., 135.
75. Ibid., 117–118. Mencius did in fact say that cruel rulers should be removed. See Justin Tiwald, "A Right of Rebellion in the Mengzi?," *Dao* 7, no. 3 (2008): 269–282. At the same time, Yuri Pines's claim that Mencius "did not present any alternative to the hereditary principle of rule" supports Trinh's. See Yuri Pines, *Envisioning Eternal Empire: Chinese Political Thought of the Warring States Period* (Honolulu: University of Hawai'i Press, 2009), 76.
76. Trinh, *Political Writings*, 105.
77. Ibid., 116.
78. Ibid.
79. Ibid., 115.
80. Leigh Jenco, "Histories of Thought and Comparative Political Theory: The Curious Thesis of 'Chinese Origins of Western Knowledge,' 1860–1895," *Political Theory* 42, no. 6 (2014): 658–681, at 661.
81. Ibid., 659.
82. Ibid., 662.
83. Leigh Jenco, *Changing Referents: Learning across Space and Time in China and the West* (Oxford: Oxford University Press, 2015), 4.
84. Jenco, "Histories of Thought," 660.
85. For more on Trinh's funeral, see Marr, *Vietnamese Anticolonialism*, 273, and Goscha, *Vietnam*, 134.
86. Bui Ngoc Son, "The Introduction of Modern Constitutionalism in East Asian Confucian Context: The Case of Vietnam in the Early Twentieth Century," *National Taiwan University Law Review* 7 (2012): 423–463, 456.
87. Ibid., 72.
88. Quoted in Trinh, *Political Writings*, 39.

Chapter 4

1. "L'Idéal de la Jeunesse Annamite" [Ideals of Annamite Youth] reprinted in the newspaper *La Cloche Fêlée* (Saigon), January 7, 1924. Annam under French colonialism refers to the central region of Vietnam (with Tonkin in the north and Cochinchina in the south). In the West, however, "Annam" and "Annamese" were used to refer to Vietnam and the Vietnamese as a whole.
2. Ibid.

3. Ibid.
4. Tai, *Radicalism*, 5.
5. Quoted in Vũ Trung Kiên, "Người trí thức dấn thân" [Committed Intellectuals], Đồng Nai Online, accessed June 13, 2021, https://baodongnai.com.vn/chinhtri/201808/ky-niem-75-nam-ngay-mat-chi-si-yeu-nuoc-nguyen-an-ninh-14-8-1943-14-8-2018-nguoi-tri-thuc-dan-than-2906571/; For more of Trần Văn Giàu's views on Ninh, see *Sự phát triển của tư tưởng ở Việt Nam từ thế kỷ XIX đến cách mạng tháng tám 1945: Tập 2* [The development of thought in Vietnam from the nineteenth century to the August 1945 revolution] (Hà Nội: Nhà xuất bản Khoa học xã hội, 1974), 454–468.
6. Tai, *Radicalism*, 3.
7. Leslie, "In Defense of Anachronism," 433.
8. Richard Rorty, *Achieving Our Country: Leftist Thought in Twentieth Century America* (Cambridge, MA: Harvard University Press, 1998), 3.
9. Ibid., 7.
10. Scholarship on national shame focuses primarily on countries such as Germany, the United States, Japan, and Israel. See Emma Dresler-Hawke and James H. Liu, "Collective Shame and the Positioning of German National Identity," *Psicología Política* 32 (2006): 131–153; and Larry May and Stacey Hoffman, eds., *Collective Responsibility: Five Decades of Debate in Theoretical and Applied Ethics* (Lanham, MD: Rowman & Littlefield Publishers, 1992).
11. Benny Morris, "The New Historiography: Israel Confronts Its Past," in his *Making Israel* (Ann Arbor: University of Michigan Press, 2007), 11–28.
12. James Goodman, "Refugee Solidarity: Between National Shame and Global Outrage," in *Theorizing Emotions: Sociological Explorations and Applications*, ed. Debra Hopkins et al. (Frankfurt, Germany: Campus Verlag, 2009), 269–290; and Emile Therein, "The National Shame of Aboriginal Incarceration," *Globe and Mail*, July 2011, http://www.theglobeandmail.com.
13. Pyong Gap Min, "Korean 'Comfort Women': The Intersection of Colonial Power, Gender, and Class," *Gender and Society* 17 (2003): 938–957.
14. Glenn Pettigrove and Nigel Parsons, "Shame: A Case Study of Collective Emotion," *Social Theory and Practice* 38 (2012): 504–530.
15. An exception is Howard Wiarda who suggests that national inferiority complexes help explain why some "peripheral" countries, through a desire to "wreak revenge on those 'superior' nations that earlier treated other countries with considerable disdain," have adopted Marxism-Leninism; see Howard Wiarda, "Political Culture and the Attraction of Marxism-Leninism: National Inferiority Complexes as an Explanatory Factor," *World Affairs* 151 (1988): 143–149, at 148.
16. Roberto Schwarz, writing in the context of Brazil, argues that the occasional superiority of a Latin American artist over their European model does not indicate the cultural parity of their respective spheres, though it might relativize the idea of "originality." Even so, while the idea of relativism might make Latin Americans feel better when it lets them know they "are not metaphysically predestined to suffer the inferiority of imitation, since in fact the Europeans imitate as well (hence the relativization of originality)," the fact remains that "innovation is not distributed equally over the planet, and that if the causes of that inequality are not metaphysical, they are perhaps something else." The "something else" that Schwarz has in mind is found in an "international space that is polarized by hegemony, inequality, and alienation—a space where we find the historical and collective hardships of underdevelopment." Roberto Schwarz, trans. R. Kelly Washbourne and Neil Larsen, "National Adequation and Critical Originality," *Cultural Critique* 49 (2001): 18–42, at 20.
17. Abdel-Nour, "National Responsibility," 698.
18. Léon Werth, *Cochinchine* (Paris: Rieder, 1926), 35.
19. This biography is adapted from Hue Tam Ho Tai, *Radicalism and the Roots of the Vietnamese Revolution* (Cambridge, MA: Harvard University Press, 1992), 74–88, 133, 140, 189, 190.
20. Samuel Huntington, *Clash of Civilizations and the Remaking of World Order* (New York: Simon & Schuster, 1996), 51.
21. Marr, *Vietnamese Anticolonialism*, 129.
22. Trinh, *Political Writings*, 116.
23. Mark Philip Bradley, *Imagining Vietnam and America: The Making of Postcolonial Vietnam, 1919–1950* (Chapel Hill: University of North Carolina Press, 2000), 31.
24. Tai, *Radicalism*, 2.
25. Ibid., 1.
26. Ibid., 4.

27. Ibid., 3.
28. Goscha, *Vietnam*, 133.
29. For a history of *La Cloche Fêlée*, see Tai, *Radicalism*, 125–131.
30. Ninh, *La Cloche Fêlée*, May 19, 1924.
31. For works on Nguyễn An Ninh, see Tai, *Radicalism*; Judith Henchy, "Performing Modernity in the Writings of Nguyễn An Ninh and Phan Van Hum" (PhD Dissertation, University of Washington, 2003); Pierre Brocheux, "Une histoire croisée: l'immigration politique indochinoise en France (1911–1945)," *Hommes et Migrations* 1253 (2005): 26–33; Ngo Van, *Vietnam, 1920–1945: Révolution et Contre-révolution sous la domination coloniale* (Paris: Nautilus, 2000), 28–45; Phương Lan Bùi Thế Mỹ, ed., *Nguyễn An Ninh, Nhà cách mạng* (Sàigòn: Tủ sách sưu khảo, 1970).
32. Ninh, "France in Indochina," in *La Cloche Fêlée*, November 30 and December 3, 1925; trans. Truong Buu Lam, in *Colonialism Experienced: Vietnamese Writings on Colonialism, 1900–1931* (Ann Arbor: University of Michigan Press, 2000), 190–207, 195.
33. Ibid., 196.
34. Ibid., 191.
35. Ninh, *La Cloche Fêlée*, January 7, 1924.
36. Lam, *Colonialism Experienced*, 191,
37. Ibid., 203.
38. Ninh, *La Cloche Fêlée*, January 28, 1924.
39. Ninh, *La Cloche Fêlée*, December 10, 1923; translation in Tai, *Radicalism*, 72.
40. Ninh, *La Cloche Fêlée*, January 7, 1924.
41. For an illuminating discussion on Zhuangzi's skepticism, see Philip J. Ivanhoe, "Zhuangzi on Skepticism, Skill, and the Ineffable *Dao*," *Journal of the American Academy of Religion* 61, no. 4 (1993): 639–654.
42. Ninh, *La Cloche Fêlée*, January 7, 1924.
43. Ninh, *La Cloche Fêlée*, December 24, 1924.
44. Ibid., January 7, 1924.
45. Ibid.
46. Ibid.
47. I thank Yen Vu for this observation and discussion. Ninh's emphasis on written texts as "culture" also bears resemblance to the Chinese literati view of culture. In Chinese, the first character in the word "culture" (文化) literally means "literature or writing."
48. Ninh, *La Cloche Fêlée*, January 7, 1924.
49. Ibid.
50. Ibid.
51. Farah Godrej, "Gandhi, Foucault, and the Politics of Self-Care," *Theory & Event* 20 (2017): 894–922.
52. Ninh, *La Cloche Fêlée*, January 7, 1924.
53. Quoted in Tai, *Radicalism*, 79.
54. Ninh, *La Cloche Fêlée*, January 14, 1924.
55. Ninh was attracted to an "anarchism heavily tinged with Nietzschean individualism"; see Tai, *Radicalism*, 73. David Marr shows that Ninh's *La Cloche Fêlée* devotes considerable attention to Nietzsche's writings; see Marr, *Vietnamese Tradition*, 161–162.
56. Tai, *Radicalism*, 80.
57. Ninh, *La Cloche Fêlée*, January 7, 1924.
58. Mahatma Gandhi, "I Owe Much," in *The Gandhi Reader: A Sourcebook of His Life and Writings*, ed. Homer Jack (New York: Grove Press, 1994), 233.
59. Ninh, *La Cloche Fêlée*, January 7, 1924.
60. Ninh, *La Cloche Fêlée*, December 10, 1923.
61. Bernard Williams, *Shame and Necessity* (Berkeley: University of California Press, 1993), 55.
62. Abdel-Nour, "National Responsibility," 699.
63. Ninh, *La Cloche Fêlée*, December 24, 1923.
64. For a critique of Bernard Williams's emphasis on causality and individual answerability for being only "vaguely concerned with sociological realities and contexts," see Antonio Y. Vázquez-Arroyo, *Political Responsibility: Responding to Predicaments of Power* (New York: Columbia University Press, 2016), 134.
65. Trần Văn Giàu, *Sự phát triển của tư tưởng ở Việt Nam*, 457.
66. Ninh, *La Cloche Fêlée*, December 10, 1923.

67. Tai, *Radicalism*, 289, footnote 73.
68. Goscha, *Vietnam*, 133.
69. Ngô Văn, *Au Pays de la Cloche Fêlée: Tribulations d'un Cochinchinois à l'Époque Coloniale* (Paris: l'Insomniaque, 2000), 60.
70. Ninh, *La Cloche Fêlée,* January 7, 1924.

Chapter 5

1. Phạm Quỳnh, *Thượng Chi Văn Tập* (Hà Nội: NXB Hội Nhà Văn, 2018).
2. Lam, *Colonialism Experienced*, 292.
3. Quoted in Tai, *Radicalism,* 249.
4. Ibid.
5. Ibid., 309, 249.
6. Marr, *Tradition,* 150.
7. Ibid., 155.
8. Ibid.
9. Gerard Sasges, "'Indigenous Representation Is Hostile to All Monopolies': Phạm Quỳnh and the End of the Alcohol Monopoly in Colonial Vietnam," *Journal of Vietnamese Studies,* 5, no. 1 (2010): 1–36, 2.
10. Phạm Quỳnh, *Thượng Chi Văn Tập,* inside flap.
11. Ibid., 5.
12. Marr, *Tradition,* 156.
13. "Phạm Quỳnh và bản án tử hình đối với ông" [Phạm Quỳnh and his Death Sentence], *Hội khoa học lịch sử Việt Nam: Tạp chí Xưa và Nay,* accessed June 10, 2021. https://xuanay.vn/pham-Quỳnh-va-ban-tu-hinh-doi-voi-ong/
14. Tai, *Radicalism,* 48.
15. Sarah Womack, "Colonialism and the Collaborationist Agenda: Phạm Quỳnh, Print Culture, and the Politics of Persuasion in Colonial Vietnam" (PhD dissertation, University of Michigan, 2003), 85.
16. Sasges, "Indigenous Representation," 22.
17. Yen Vu, "Phạm Quỳnh, Borrowed Language, and the Ambivalences of Colonial Discourse," *Journal of Southeast Asian Studies* 51, no. 1 (July 2020): 114–131.
18. Goscha, *Vietnam,* 113.
19. Ibid.
20. Albert Sarraut, *La Mise en Valeur des Colonies Françaises* (Paris: Payot, 1923), 19.
21. Lea Ypi, "What's Wrong with Colonialism," *Philosophy & Public Affairs* 41, no. 2 (2013): 158–191.
22. Quoted in Goscha, *Vietnam,* 126.
23. Ibid., 128.
24. Ibid., 116.
25. Marr, *Tradition,* 213.
26. Ibid., 151.
27. Quoted in Marr, *Tradition,* 152.
28. Sasges, "Indigenous Representation," 11.
29. Quoted in ibid., 30, note 46.
30. Tai, *Radicalism,* 163.
31. Ibid.
32. This biography is adapted from Sasges, "Indigenous Representation," at 10–12.
33. Phạm Quỳnh, *Nam Phong tạp chí,* no. 106, at 53.
34. Ibid., 54.
35. Ibid., 53.
36. Pham Quỳnh, *Nam Phong tạp chí,* no. 68, at 93.
37. Ibid., 94.
38. Pham Quỳnh, "Orient et Occident," in *Essais franco-annamites (1929–1932)* (Hue: Editions Bui Huy Tính, 1937), 81.
39. Ibid., 82.
40. Ibid., 79.

41. Ibid., 80.
42. Ibid., 82.
43. Ibid., 80.
44. Pham Quỳnh, "Les Saturnales de l'Intelligence," in *Essais franco-annamites (1929–1932)* (Hue: Editions Bui Huy Tính, 1937), 249.
45. Shirin S. Deylami, "In the Face of the Machine: *Westoxification*, Cultural Globalization, and the Making of an Alternative Global Modernity," *Polity* 43, no. 2 (2011): 242–263.
46. Ibid., 246.
47. Pham Quỳnh, "Orient et Occident," in *Essais franco-annamites (1929–1932)* (Hue: Editions Bui Huy Tính, 1937), 83.
48. Pham Quỳnh, *Nam Phong tạp chí*, no. 2, 92.
49. Phạm Quỳnh, *Essais*, 390.
50. Ibid., 191.
51. Tai, *Radicalism*, 51.
52. Phạm Quỳnh, *Nam Phong tạp chí*, no. 2, 89–92.
53. Ibid., 120–122.
54. Phạm Quỳnh, *Essais*, "Confucius et Confucianism," 118.
55. Chenyang Li writes, "In Plato justice is the highest moral ideal, which is achieved only when the other three virtues are duly practiced. But this ideal is missing in Confucius" (Chenyang Li, "The Confucian Concept of Jen and the Feminist Ethics of Care," *Hypatia* 9, no. 1 (1994), 70–89, at 74).
56. Phạm Quỳnh, *Essais*, "Confucius et Confucianism," 122.
57. Phạm Quỳnh, *Essais*, "Le Philosophe Mencius," 128–129.
58. Phạm Quỳnh, *Nouveaux essais franco-annamites* (Hue: Editions Bui Huy Tinh, 1938), 481.
59. Pham Quỳnh, "Politique," in *Essais franco-annamites (1929–1932)* (Hue: Editions Bui Huy Tính, 1937), 345.
60. Ibid., 346.
61. Phạm Quỳnh, *Vers une Constitution* (Hanoi: Imprimerie Tonkinoise, 1930), 26.
62. Quoted in Thi Ngoan Pham, *Introduction au Nam Phong 1917–1934* (1973), 252.
63. Phạm Quỳnh, *Nouveaux Essais Franco Annamites* (Hue: Editions Bui Huy Tin, 1938), 447.
64. For more on Quỳnh and language, see John D. Phan, "Rival nationalisms and the rebranding of language in early 20th century Tonkin," *International Institute for Asian Studies: The Newsletter*, 79. Spring 2018, https://www.iias.asia/the-newsletter/article/rival-nationalisms-rebranding-language-early-20th-century-tonkin
65. Marr, *Vietnamese Tradition on Trial*, 157.
66. Phạm Quỳnh, *Nam Phong tạp chí*, no. 30, 480.
67. Truong Buu Lam, "Review of 'The Tale of Kieu: A Bilingual Edition of Truyen Kieu. By Nguyễn Du. Translated and Annotated by Huynh Sanh Thong, with a historical essay by Alexander B. Woodside (New Haven, CT: Yale University Press, 1983)," *Journal of Asian Studies* 44, no. 3 (1985): 666–667, at 666.
68. Phạm Quỳnh, *Nam Phong tạp chí*, no. 30, 491.
69. Ibid., no. 86, 93.
70. Ibid., no. 86, 91.
71. Ibid., no. 86, 92.
72. Ibid., no. 94.
73. Amilcar Cabral, "Identity and Dignity in the National Liberation Struggle," *Africa Today* 19, no. 4 (Autumn 1972): 39–47, at 47.
74. Phạm Quỳnh, *Nam Phong tạp chí*, no. 86, 96.
75. Phạm Quỳnh, "Politique d'égards," in *Essais franco-annamites (1929–1932)* (Hue: Editions Bui Huy Tính, 1937), 349.
76. Ibid., 350–358.
77. Similar to Quỳnh, Lea Ypi argues that if "with the passage of time, the position of the historically wronged group changes such that the subsequent substantive principles of political association genuinely track its will and the effects of path dependence disappear, we can say that injustice has been superseded" (Lea Ypi, "What's Wrong with Colonialism," 180).
78. Phạm Quỳnh, "La Mission de la France," in *Essais franco-annamites (1929–1932)* (Hue: Editions Bui Huy Tính, 1937), 496.
79. Ibid., 497.
80. Ibid.

81. Phạm Quỳnh, "Politique d'égards," in *Essais franco-annamites (1929-1932)* (Hue: Editions Bui Huy Tính, 1937), 351.
82. Ibid.
83. Albert Sarraut, *La Mise en Valeur des Colonies Françaises* (Paris: Payot, 1923), 19.
84. Phạm Quỳnh, "Le Problème Orient-Occident," in *Essais franco-annamites (1929–1932)* (Hue: Editions Bui Huy Tính, 1937), 89. Quỳnh was not alone in having this vision of Eastern and Western unity. Niels Bohr, the leading physicist developing quantum theory, visited China in 1937, and "was one of the first to see the close similarities between the revolutionary new model of nature that was being forged and the ancient philosophies of the East, and his interpretation of quantum theory had the consequence of allowing the re-introduction of consciousness into the scientific understanding of nature. Following a visit to China he became especially interested in Taoist philosophy, and it is interesting to note that on being knighted by the Danish government he chose for his coat of arms the Chinese Taoist yin/yang figure of interlocking circles which he felt symbolised his most important idea, namely the principle of complementarity." J.J. Clarke, *Oriental Enlightenment: the Encounter Between Asian and Western Thought* (New York: Routledge, 1997), 167–168.
85. J. J. Clarke, *Oriental Enlightenment: the Encounter Between Asian and Western Thought* (New York: Routledge, 1997).
86. Ibid., 5.
87. Phạm Quỳnh, "Orient et Occident," in *Essais franco-annamites (1929–1932)* (Hue: Editions Bui Huy Tính, 1937), 83.
88. Phạm Quỳnh, "Le Problème Orient-Occident," in *Essais franco-annamites (1929–1932)* (Hue: Editions Bui Huy Tính, 1937), 93–94.
89. Chenyang Li, "Community without Harmony? A Confucian Critique of Michael Sandel," in *Encountering China: Michael Sandel and Chinese Philosophy*, eds. Michael Sandel and Paul D'Ambrosio (Cambridge, MA: Harvard University Press, 2018), 8.
90. Martina Thuchnhi Nguyễn, *On Our Own Strength: The Self-Reliant Literary Groups and Cosmopolitan Nationalism in Late Colonial Vietnam* (Honolulu: University of Hawai'i Press, 2021), 208.
91. Tai, *Radicalism*, 250.
92. Phan, "Rival Nationalisms."

Chapter 6

1. Hồ Chí Minh, *Hồ Chí Minh Toàn Tập xuất bản lần thứ ba* [*Hồ Chí Minh's Complete Works*, third edition], Vol. 1 (Hà Nội: NxB Chính Trị Quốc Gia, 2011), 4.
2. Trinh, *Political Writings*, 107.
3. Ibid., 116.
4. Tuan Hoang, "From Reeducation Camps to Little Saigons: Historicizing Vietnamese Diasporic Anticommunism," *Journal of Vietnamese Studies* 11, no. 2 (2016): 43–95, at 68.
5. Nu-Anh Tran, "How Democratic Should Vietnam Be?: The Constitutional Transition of 1955–1956 and the Debate on Democracy," in Nu-Anh Tran and Tuong Vu (eds.), *Building a Republican Nation in Vietnam, 1920–1963* (Honolulu: University of Hawai'i Press, 2023).
6. Sophie Quinn-Judge, *Hồ Chí Minh: The Missing Years 1919–1941* (Berkeley: University of California Press, 2002), 2. For other detailed discussions of Hồ Chí Minh's activities, see William Duiker, *Hồ Chí Minh: A Life* (New York: Hyperion, 2000); Pierre Brocheux, *Hồ Chí Minh: A Biography*, trans. Claire Duiker (Cambridge: Cambridge University Press, 2007); and Tuong Vu, *Vietnam's Communist Revolution: The Powers and Limits of Ideology* (Cambridge: Cambridge University Press, 2017), 31–61.
7. Olga Dror, "Establishing Hồ Chí Minh's Cult: Vietnamese Traditions and Their Transformations," *Journal of Asian Studies* 75, no. 2 (2016): 433–466.
8. Hồ Chí Minh, *Toàn Tập*, Vol. 4, 1.
9. This biography is adapted from Sophie Quinn-Judge, "Ho Chi Minh," in *A Dictionary of 20th-Century Communism,* eds. Silvio Pons and Robert Service (Princeton, NJ: Princeton University Press, 2012), 386–389; and Duiker, *Hồ Chí Minh: A Life*. See also Pierre Brocheux, *Hồ Chí Minh: du révolutionnaire à l'icône* (Paris: Editions Payot and Rivages, 2003); Jean Lacouture, *Hồ Chi Minh: A Political Biography* (Paris: Editions du Seuil, 1967); Quinn-Judge, *Hồ Chí Minh*.

10. Hồ Chí Minh, *Hồ Chí Minh on Revolution: Selected Writings, 1920–66*, ed. Bernard Fall (New York: Signet Books, 1967), vi.
11. Hồ Chí Minh, *Toàn Tập*, Vol. 1, 114.
12. Ibid., Vol. 2, 69–70.
13. Ibid., Vol. 1, 115.
14. Ibid., Vol. 1, 112–113.
15. Ibid., Vol. 1, 103–104.
16. Ibid., Vol. 1, 112.
17. Vittorio Bufacchi, "Colonialism, Injustice, and Arbitrariness," *Journal of Social Philosophy* 48, no. 2 (2017): 197–211.
18. Frank Lovett, *A General Theory of Domination and Justice* (Oxford: Oxford University Press, 2010), 96.
19. Philip Pettit, *Republicanism* (Oxford: Oxford University Press, 1997), 52.
20. Hồ Chí Minh, *Toàn Tập*, Vol. 3, 229.
21. Ibid., Vol. 1, 159.
22. Quỳnh N. Phạm and María José Méndez. "Decolonial Designs: José Martí, Hồ Chí Minh, and Global Entanglements." *Alternatives* 40, no. 2 (2015): 156–173, 161.
23. Hồ Chí Minh, *Toàn Tập*, Vol. 1, 136.
24. Ibid., Vol. 2, 74.
25. Phạm and Méndez, "Decolonial Designs," 161–162.
26. Hồ Chí Minh, *Toàn Tập*, Vol. 2, 124.
27. Ibid., Vol. 2, 60.
28. Ibid., Vol. 2, 68.
29. Ibid., Vol. 1, 330.
30. Ibid., 333.
31. Quoted in Duiker, *Ho Chi Minh*, 47.
32. Ibid., 50.
33. Hồ Chí Minh, *Toàn Tập*, Vol. 1, 81.
34. Ibid., Vol. 1, 35.
35. Ibid., Vol. 1, 423.
36. Ibid., Vol. 2, 42.
37. Quoted in Duiker, *Ho Chi Minh*, 125.
38. For a review of work that argues that Confucianism plays a prominent role in Hồ's political thought, see Bui Ngoc Son, "The Confucian Foundations of Hồ Chi Minh's Vision of Government," *Journal of Oriental Studies* 46, no. 1 (2013): 35–59.
39. Hồ Chí Minh, *Toàn Tập*, Vol. 5, 74.
40. Ibid., Vol. 9, 382.
41. See Arjun Subrahmanyan, "Education, Propaganda, and the People: Democratic Paternalism in 1930s Siam," *Modern Asian Studies* 49, no. 4 (2015): 1122–1142; John D. Holm, "Botswana: A Paternalistic Democracy," *World Affairs* 150, no. 1 (1987): 21–30.
42. Hồ Chí Minh, *Toàn Tập*, Vol. 8, 353.
43. Ibid., Vol. 11, 92.
44. Ibid., Vol. 7, 361.
45. Ibid., Vol. 7, 40.
46. Ibid., Vol. 10, 453.
47. Ibid., Vol. 11, 600–612.
48. Ibid., Vol. 5, 235.
49. Ibid., Vol. 5, 291–292.
50. Bui Ngoc Son, "The Confucian Foundations of Hồ Chi Minh's Vision of Government," *Journal of Oriental Studies,* 46 (1) 2013: 35–59, 51. Lisheng Cheng also argues that despite a long list of virtues that one may draw out from the Analects of Confucius, they can be subsumed under three cardinal virtues: benevolence, wisdom, and courage. "Courage in The Analects: A Genealogical Survey of the Confucian virtue of courage," *Frontiers of Philosophy in China* 5, no. 1 (2010): 1–30, at 2. Indeed, these three virtues appear to capture the five that Bui Ngoc Son mentions.
51. Quoted in Li Xiangjun, "An Explanation of the Confucian Idea of Difference," *Frontiers of Philosophy in China* 2, no. 4 (2007): 488–502, at 490.
52. Bui Ngoc Son, "The Confucian Foundations of Hồ Chi Minh's Vision of Government," 52.
53. Hồ Chí Minh, *Toàn Tập*, Vol. 9, 38.
54. Karl Marx and Friedrich Engels, *Marx and Engels Collected Works*, Vol. 5 (London: Lawrence & Wishart, 2010), 247.

55. Hồ Chí Minh, *Toàn Tập,* Vol. 2, 563.
56. Ibid., Vol. 7, 39.
57. Ibid., Vol. 6, 16.
58. Ibid., Vol. 15, 547.
59. Ibid., Vol. 6, 459.
60. Ibid., Vol. 11, 606.
61. Ibid., Vol. 4, 6.
62. Ibid., Vol. 8, 229.
63. Ibid., Vol. 12, 676.
64. Ibid., Vol. 4, 51.
65. Ibid., Vol. 11, 358.
66. Ibid., Vol. 12, 373.
67. Brocheux, *Hồ Chi Minh: du révolutionnaire*, 28.
68. Hồ Chí Minh, *Toàn Tập,* Vol. 15, 293.
69. Ibid., Vol. 11, 358.
70. Ibid., *Toàn Tập,* Vol. 5, 75.
71. Ibid., Vol. 8, 263.
72. Vladimir Lenin, *The State and Revolution* (1918), accessed March 2, 2022, https://www.marxists.org/archive/lenin/works/1917/staterev/ch05.htm
73. Hồ Chí Minh, *Toàn Tập,* Vol. 10, 466.
74. Ibid., Vol. 13, 454.
75. Ibid., Vol. 6, 457.
76. Ibid., Vol. 4, 7.
77. Ibid., Vol. 4, 7.
78. Ibid., Vol. 4, 166.
79. Ibid., Vol. 12, 375.
80. Ibid., Vol. 12, 376.
81. Ibid., Vol. 5, 233.
82. Ibid., Vol. 15, 325–326.
83. See Hannah Arendt, *On Revolution* (New York: Viking Press, 1963); Reinhart Koselleck, "Historical Criteria of the Modern Concept of Revolution," in *R. Koselleck, Futures Past: On the Semantics of Historical Time* (New York: Columbia University Press, 2004 [1969]): 43–71.
84. Susan Opotow, "Moral Exclusion and Injustice: An Introduction." *Journal of Social Issues* 46, no. 1 (1990): 1–20, at 1.
85. Charles W. Mills, "Racial Liberalism." *PMLA* 123, no. 5 (2008): 1380–1397, at 1386.
86. Aimé Cesaire, *Discourse on Colonialism* (New York: Monthly Review Press, 2000), 42.
87. Frantz Fanon, *The Wretched of the Earth,* trans. Constance Farrington (New York: Grove Press, 1963), 41.
88. Christopher Lee, *Frantz Fanon: Toward a Revolutionary Humanism* (Athens, Ohio: Ohio University Press, 2015), 151.
89. Samera Esmeir, "On making dehumanization possible," *PMLA* 121, no. 5 (2006): 1544–1551, at 1544.
90. Ibid., 1545.
91. Rianna Oelofsen, "De-and Rehumanization in the Wake of Atrocities," *South African Journal of Philosophy* 28, no. 2 (2009): 178–188, at 184.
92. Karina Schumann and Gregory Walton, "Rehumanizing the Self after Victimization: The Roles of Forgiveness versus Revenge," *Journal of Personality and Social Psychology* 122, no. 3 (2021): 469–492.

Chapter 7

1. Nguyễn Mạnh Tường, *Un Excommunié: Hanoi 1954–1991: Procès d'un Intellectuelle* (Paris: Quê Mẹ, 1992), 235.
2. Ibid.
3. Václav Havel, "The Power of the Powerless" (1978), accessed March 2, 2021, https://hac.bard.edu/amor-mundi/the-power-of-the-powerless-vaclav-havel-2011-12-23
4. Tường, *Excommunié,* 216.
5. Hoang Van Chi's preface to Nguyễn Mạnh Tường's October 30, 1956 speech, "Concerning Mistakes Committed in Land Reform," reprinted in *The Human Cost of Vietnam: a compendium prepared for the subcommittee to investigate the administration of the internal security act and*

other internal security laws of the committee on the judiciary United States Senate (Washington, D.C.: U.S. Government Printing Office, 1972), 26.
6. Tường, *Excommunié*, 328.
7. For a detailed account of the land reforms, see Alex-Thai D. Vo, "Nguyễn Thị Năm and the Land Reform in North Vietnam, 1953," *Journal of Vietnamese Studies* 10, no. 1 (2015): 1–62; Alec Holcombe, *Mass Mobilization in the Democratic Republic of Vietnam 1945–1960* (Honolulu: University of Hawai'i Press), 119–199.
8. Ibid., xxiii.
9. Nguyễn Mạnh Tường's "Concerning Mistakes Committed in Land Reform," speech reprinted in *The Human Cost of Vietnam: a compendium prepared for the subcommittee to investigate the administration of the internal security act and other internal security laws of the committee on the judiciary United States Senate* (Washington D.C.: U.S. Government Printing Office, 1972), 26.
10. Ibid.
11. Tường, *Excommunié*, 220.
12. Ibid., 154.
13. Ibid., 317.
14. Tường's liberal ethos would fit well with other twentieth-century figures such as Max Weber, Raymond Aron, Albert Camus, Reinhold Niebuhr, and Isaiah Berlin whose liberal ethos Joshua L. Cherniss explores in *Liberalism in Dark Times: The Liberal Ethos in the Twentieth Century* (Princeton, NJ: Princeton University Press, 2021).
15. Tường, *Excommunié*, 350.
16. Ibid., 251–260.
17. Ibid., 325–326.
18. Michel de Montaigne, *The Complete Essays of Montaigne*, trans. D. Frame (Stanford, CA: Stanford University Press, 1965), 331. All quotations of Montaigne will be from this English translation of the *Essais*.
19. Tường, *Excommunié*, 96–97.
20. Václav Havel, "The Power of the Powerless" (1978) https://hac.bard.edu/amor-mundi/the-power-of-the-powerless-vaclav-havel-2011-12-23
21. Tường, *Excommunié*, 27.
22. Ibid., 197.
23. Ibid., 188.
24. Ibid., 311.
25. Montaigne, *Essays*, 792.
26. Ibid., 111. Montaigne continues: "For if [the student] embraces Xenophon's and Plato's opinions by his own reasoning, they will no longer be theirs, they will be his. He who follows another follows nothing. He finds nothing; indeed he seeks nothing. 'We are not under a king; let each one claim his own freedom.' [Seneca]."
27. Tường, *Excommunié*, 44.
28. Ibid., 80.
29. Ibid., 311.
30. Montaigne, *Essays*, 112. Montaigne writes, "The gain from our study is to become better and wiser by it." And that "…mixing with men is wonderfully useful, and visiting foreign countries… to bring back knowledge of the characters and ways of those nations, and to rub and polish our brains by contact with those of others."
31. Alan Levine, *Sensual Philosophy: Toleration, Skepticism, and Montaigne's Politics of the Self* (Lanham, MD: Lexington Books, 2001), 28.
32. Ibid., 121.
33. Tường, *Excommunié*, 99.
34. Tường, "Concerning Mistakes," 30.
35. Montaigne, *Essays*, 368.
36. Tường, "Concerning Mistakes," 30.
37. Tường, *Excommunié*, 186.
38. Ibid., 343–344. Emphasis in the original.
39. Tường, "Concerning Mistakes," 30.
40. Ibid., 31.

41. "Tây cho Đông kỹ thuật, quan niệm về nhân quyền, về cái chừng mực và đa dạng của con người, về phương pháp suy tư và về một quan điểm đời sống." Quoted in "Phần XVII: Nguyễn Mạnh Tường (1909–1997) — Bài 1: Giai đoạn trước 1954." Radio France Internationale. July 15, 2011, accessed January 8, 2020, https://www.rfi.fr/vi/viet-nam/20110715-phan-xvii-nguyen-manh-tuong-1909-1997
42. Tường, *Excommunié*, 28.
43. Ibid., 29.
44. Ibid.
45. Ibid., 30.
46. Tường, "Concerning Mistakes," 32.
47. Ibid., 32.
48. Tường, *Excommunié*, 83.
49. Ibid., 142.
50. Montaigne, *Essays*, 414.
51. Tường, *Excommunié*, 119.
52. Ibid., 120.
53. Hồ Chí Minh, *Toàn Tập*, Vol. 2, 99.
54. Tường, *Excommunié*, 85.
55. Ibid., 224.
56. Ibid., 224–225.
57. Montaigne, *Essays*, 313.
58. Tường, *Excommunié*, 225.
59. Ibid., 162.
60. Montaigne, *Essays*, 392.
61. Tường, *Excommunié*, 162.
62. Ibid., 185.
63. Ibid., 185–186.
64. Ibid, 312–313.
65. Tường, "Concerning Mistakes," 29.
66. Tường, *Excommunié*, 44.
67. Ibid., 44.
68. Ibid., 100.
69. Montaigne, *Essays*, 177.
70. Tường, *Excommunié*, 102.
71. Ibid., 103.
72. Ibid., 298.
73. Ibid., 202.
74. Ibid., 84.
75. Ibid., 261.
76. Ibid.
77. Ibid., 263.
78. Ibid., 161.
79. Ibid., 298.
80. Montaigne, *Essays*, 499. For all of Tường's quotations of Montaigne in this passage, I use Donald Frame's translation.
81. Montaigne, *Essays*, 629.
82. Ibid., 117.
83. Ibid., 799.
84. Ibid., 800.
85. Ibid.
86. Ibid., 774.
87. Ibid.
88. Tường, *Excommunié*, 312–313.
89. Peter Zinoman, "Nhân Văn–Giai Phẩm and Vietnamese "Reform Communism" in the 1950s," *Journal of Cold War Studies* 13, no. 1 (2011): 60–100, at 73.
90. Vu, *Vietnam's Communist Revolution*, 253–254.
91. Tường, *Excommunié*, 11.

Conclusion

1. Christian Appy, *Patriots: The Vietnam War Remembered from All Sides* (New York: Viking, 2003), xviii.
2. See Huy Đức, *Bên Thắng Cuộc* [The Winning Side], (OsinBook, 2012).
3. Sophie Quinn-Judge, *Hồ Chí Minh: The Missing Years 1919–1941* (Berkeley: University of California Press, 2002), 75.
4. Phan Bội Châu, *Overturned Chariot: The Autobiography of Phan Bội Châu*, trans. Vinh Sinh and Nicholas Wickenden (Honolulu: University of Hawai'i Press, 1999), 43.
5. Phan Chu Trinh, *Phan Châu Trinh and His Political Writings*, ed. and trans. Vinh Sinh (Ithaca, NY: Cornell Southeast Asia Program, 2009), 36.
6. Ibid., 37.
7. Lê Trung, "Phan Châu Trinh: Ngọn cờ dân chủ mạnh mẽ nhất, tiêu biểu cho trào lưu canh tân đất nước." ["Phan Chu Trinh: The strongest flag of democracy, representing the country's reform movement"], *Tuổi Trẻ*, accessed May 7, 2023, https://tuoitre.vn/phan-chau-trinh-ngon-co-dan-chu-manh-me-nhat-tieu-bieu-cho-trao-luu-canh-tan-dat-nuoc-20220909105401047.htm
8. Ngo Van, *In the Crossfire: Adventures of a Vietnamese Revolutionary*, trans. Hélène Fleury, Hilary Horrocks, Ken Knabb, and Naomi Sager (Edinburgh: AK Press, 2010), 240.
9. Da Anh, "Nguyễn An Ninh- A Patriotic Lawyer," *Vietnam Law & Legal Forum*, October 29, 2012, http://vietnamlawmagazine.vn/Nguyễn-an-ninh-a-patriotic-lawyer-4662.html
10. Ninh, *La Cloche Fêlée*, January 7, 1924.
11. "Chuyện ít được biết tới về quan hệ giữa Nguyễn Ái Quốc với học giả Phạm Quỳnh: Một mối thân tình" [A little known story about the relationship between Nguyen Ai Quo and Pham Quynh: an close relationship], Báo Đại Đoàn Kết, accessed January 4, 2023, http://daidoanket.vn/chuyen-it-duoc-biet-toi-ve-quan-he-giua-nguyen-ai-quoc-voi-hoc-gia-pham-quynh-mot-moi-than-tinh-368816.html
12. Cù Huy Hà Vũ, "Chủ tịch Hồ Chí Minh biết được về số phận học giả Phạm Quỳnh trong hoàn cảnh nào?" [Under what circumstances did Ho Chi Minh know about the fate of the scholar Pham Quynh?], BBC, accessed January 4, 2023, https://www.bbc.com/vietnamese/articles/c2q4002kzpgo
13. Jean-Jacques Rousseau, *Basic Political Writings of Jean Jacques Rousseau*, trans. Donald Cress (Indianapolis, IN: Hackett Publishing, 1987), 164.
14. Ibid., 162.
15. Ibid., 163.
16. Ibid.
17. Christopher Kelly, "'To Persuade without Convincing': The Language of Rousseau's Legislator," *American Journal of Political Science* 31, no. 2 (1987): 321–335.
18. Olga Dror, "Establishing Hồ Chí Minh's Cult: Vietnamese Traditions and Their Transformations," *The Journal of Asian Studies* 75, no. 2 (2016): 433–466, 434.
19. "Tổng Bí thư Nguyễn Phú Trọng phân tích sâu sắc Tư tưởng, Đạo đức và Phong cách Hồ Chí Minh" [General Secretary Nguyen Phu Trong's in-depth analysis of Hồ Chí Minh's Thought, Ethics, and Method], Kinh Tế Và Dự Báo, accessed March 1, 2023, https://kinhtevadubao.vn/tong-bi-thu-nguyen-phu-trong-phan-tich-sau-sac-tu-tuong-dao-duc-va-phong-cach-ho-chi-minh-17503.html
20. *Đảng Cộng Sản Việt Nam: Văn Kiện Đại hội đại biểu toàn quốc lần thứ XI* [Vietnamese Communist Party: Documents of the 11th National Congress] (Hà Nội: NxB Chính Trị Quốc Gia, 2011), 88.
21. Dror, "Establishing Hồ Chí Minh's Cult," 434.
22. Angélica Maria Bernal, *Beyond Origins: Rethinking Founding in a Time of Constitutional Democracy* (New York: Oxford University Press, 2017), 11.
23. For more on conflict between Vietnamese Trotskyists and Stalinists, see Ngô Văn, *Au pays de la Cloche Fêlée. Tribulations d'un Cochinchinois à l'époque colonial* (Paris: L'Insomniaque, 2013).
24. "Kỷ niệm 100 năm ngày sinh Giáo sư Nguyễn Mạnh Tường" [Celebrating the 100th birthday of Professor Nguyen Manh Tuong], Công an nhân dân, accessed July 5, 2023, https://cand.com.vn/van-hoa/Ky-niem-100-nam-ngay-sinh-Giao-su-Nguyen-Manh-Tuong-i87590/

25. Phạm Khải, "Giáo sư Nguyễn Mạnh Tường (1909–1997)," accessed July 5, 2023, https://hnue.edu.vn/70namhnue/cacthehenhagiao/p/giao-su-nguyen-manh-tuong-1909---1997-8889
26. Marr, *Vietnamese Tradition on Trial*, 2.
27. See the end of "Ho Chi Minh Visits Village, North Vietnam during War 1960s | Kinolibrary," Youtube video, https://youtu.be/IExod2C3z-0
28. Originally called "the March of the Students" (La Marche des Étudiants), the "Call of the Youth" (Tiếng gọi Thanh niên) was slightly modified and renamed "Call of the Citizen" (Tiếng Gọi Công Dân) and made the anthem of the State of Vietnam and then the anthem of South Vietnam (Republic of Vietnam).
29. A Google search and image search of this quote will show many examples of its use.
30. "Ce n'est pas parce que l'Indochinois a découvert une culture propre qu'il s'est révolté. C'est parce que « tout simplement » il lui devenait, à plus d'un titre, impossible de respirer." Frantz Fanon, *Peau noire masques blancs* (Paris: Éditions du Seuil, 1952), 183.
31. Isaiah Berlin, "Nationalism: Past Neglect and Present Power," in *Against the Current: Essays in the History of Ideas*, ed. Henry Hardy (Princeton, NJ: Princeton University Press, 2013), 441.
32. Adom Getachew, *Worldmaking after Empire: The Rise and Fall of Self-Determination* (Princeton, NJ: Princeton University Press, 2019).
33. Hồ Chí Minh, *Toàn Tập*, Vol. 7, 445.
34. Desmond Jagmohan, "Between Race and Nation: Marcus Garvey and the Politics of Self-Determination," *Political Theory* 48, no. 3 (2020): 271–302, 284.
35. Amilcar Cabral, "Identity and Dignity in the National Liberation Struggle," *Africa Today* 19, no. 4 (Autumn 1972): 39–47.
36. Frantz Fanon, *Black Skin White Mask*, Trans. Charles Lam Markmann (New York: Grove Press, 1967), 155.
37. Malcolm X, "Make It Plain: transcript," PBS, accessed June 2, 2022, https://www.pbs.org/wgbh/americanexperience/films/malcolmx/#transcript
38. The seventeenth-century Dutch philosopher Baruch Spinoza had the same idea, suggesting that one has exactly as much right as one has power. See Baruch Spinoza, *Theological-Political Treatise*. Ed. Jonathan Israel. Trans. Michael Silverthorne and Jonathan Israel (Cambridge: Cambridge University Press, 2007), 195.
39. Fanon, *The Wretched of the Earth*, 171–172.
40. Ibid., 153.
41. Ibid., 171.

Index

For the benefit of digital users, indexed terms that span two pages (e.g., 52–53) may, on occasion, appear on only one of those pages.

Tables are indicated by an italic *t* following the page number.

Abdel-Nour, Farid, 15–16
accommodationist elites, 88, 100–1
Ackerly, Brooke, 58–59
Adorno, Theodor, 112
Ames, Roger, 59–60
anarchism, 88, 92, 95–96, 100
Angle, Stephen, 57–58
Annan, Kofi, 27
anticolonialism
    of Phan Bội Châu, 31, 37–38, 52
    of Phan Chu Trinh, 89–90, 99–100
    See also colonialism
anti-Communism, 2, 102, 109–10, 133–34, 135, 163, 182, 186–87
anti-intellectualism, 160–61, 167
Arendt, Hannah, 3
Asia–Pacific War (1937–1945), 84
Association for the Intellectual and Moral Formation of the Annamites (Hội Khai Trí Tiến Đức), 109–10
August Revolution (1945), 2, 103, 150
autocracy, 63, 165–66

Beau, Paul, 60–61
Being and Nothingness (Sartre), 6
Bell, Daniel, 54
Bhabha, Homi, 23–24
Black Lives Matters movement, 188–89
Black Skin, White Masks (Fanon), 21
Bonaparte, Louis-Napoleon, 33
Bonaparte, Napoleon, 33
Bromell, Nick, 24, 27–28
Burke, Edmund, 113–14

Cabral, Amilcar, 121, 191
Cần Vương ("Save the King") movement, 34, 37
Cao Tu, 116
capitalism, 14, 99, 132–33, 140–45, 150–51, 152, 158, 163, 171–72, 173, 177–78
Cesaire, Aimé, 156

Chan, Joseph, 57–58
Charter of the UN, 2–3
Chauvin, Derek, 24–25
Chenyang Li, 54, 125
China and Phan Bội Châu, 38
Cognacq, Maurice, 88
collective dignity, 27, 121, 192–93
collective indignation, 25–26, 43
colonialism
    defined, 25–26
    Hồ Chí Minh and, 132, 136–37, 138–39, 142–45, 156
    mentality of, 18–21
    national indignation and, 24
    Phạm Quỳnh and, 106, 122
    See also anticolonialism
comfort women, 84
Communist Party of Vietnam, 2, 102, 135–36, 159–60, 162, 173
Confucian democracy, 58
Confucianism
    democracy and, 57–59, 71
    Five Relationships of Confucianism, 62, 65–66
    Hồ Chí Minh, 131–32, 147–52
    Nguyễn An Ninh, 13, 82–83, 86–87, 91–92, 101
    Phạm Quỳnh (1892–1945), 105, 107, 108–10, 111–12, 114–19, 124–27
    Phan Bội Châu, 31, 34, 35
    Phan Chu Trinh and, 12–13, 56–61, 115–16
    Progressive Confucianism, 57–58
Coomaraswamy, Ananda, 94–95

Declaration of the Rights of Man and of the Citizen, 25–26, 90–91
dehumanization, 14, 126–27, 132–34, 136, 155
democracy
    Confucianism and, 57–59, 71

democracy (cont.)
  Hồ Chí Minh paternalistic democracy, 133, 145, 146, 154, 158
  liberal democracy, 12–13, 54–56, 59–60, 75–76, 154
  Nguyễn An Ninh and, 81, 87, 89–90
  Nguyễn Mạnh Tường and, 169
  Phạm Quỳnh and, 105, 115–18
  Phan Chu Trinh and, 57–59, 71–75
Democratic Republic of Vietnam (DRV), 150, 154
despotism, 63, 90–91, 118–19
Dewey, John, 59–60
Dialectic of Enlightenment (Horkheimer, Adorno), 112
Đông Du (Go East) movement, 32
Đông Dương tạp chí (Indochina Review), 108–9
Đông Kinh Nghĩa Thục. *See* Tonkin Free School (Đông Kinh Nghĩa Thục)
Dror, Olga, 186
Du Bois, W. E. B., 6–7, 36, 39

Empiricus, Sextus, 167
enlightened patriotism, 27
epistemic violence, 19
Esmeir, Samera, 156–57
European prestige, 89
exploitation, 4–5, 18, 25, 33, 39–40, 41, 45–46, 89–90, 106–7, 117, 123, 132, 140–43, 146–50, 152, 163, 188–89, 192–93

false consciousness, 7, 18–19, 22, 99
Fanon, Frantz, 21, 188–89, 191, 192
First Indochina War (1945–1954), 2, 136–37, 180
Five Relationships of Confucianism, 62, 65–66
Floyd, George, 24–25, 188–89
freedom of expression, 68, 107–8, 162, 171–72, 175–76
freedom of opinion, 174–75
freedom of speech, 142, 158, 171–72, 178–79, 180
freedom of thought, 14, 47, 90–91, 160–61, 175–76, 179–80
French Revolution, 9–10, 25–26, 136, 156

Gandhi, Mohandas, 36
Garnier, Francis, 33–34
Gaulle, Charles de, 136
gharbzadegi (westoxification), 112–13
global justice, 16–17
Greenfield, Liah, 15–16
Groupe des Patriotes Annamites, 2, 86

Ha, Marie Paule, 22
Hall, David, 59–60
Hàm Nghi, 34–35
Herr, Ranjoo Seodu, 39–40
Hoang, Tuan, 133–34
Hobbes, Thomas, 115
Hồ Chí Minh (1890–1969)
  arbitrary violence by, 136
  brief biography, 134
  colonialism and, 132, 136–37, 138–39, 142–45, 156
  Confucianism under, 131–32, 147–52
  dehumanization and, 14, 126–27, 132–34, 136, 155
  democracy and, 133, 145–54, 158
  introduction to, 1–3, 4–11, 13–14, 131–34
  liberalism and, 132
  morality and, 131–33, 145, 147–49, 157
  national dignity and, 131–32, 144–45
  national indignation and, 26
  national shame and, 131–32, 144–45
  Nguyễn Mạnh Tường and, 162
  paternalistic democracy of, 133, 145, 146, 154, 158
  Phan Chu Trinh and, 131–32
  rehumanization and, 14, 132–34, 144–55
  summary of, 185
Horkheimer, Max, 112
Hue Tam Ho Tai, 95–96, 100, 102, 104
humaneness, 61–63, 147–49
humanization. *See* dehumanization; rehumanization
human rights, 3, 16–17, 25–26, 27, 90–91, 171–72, 191–92
Huntington, Samuel, 124
hybridity, 10–11, 23–24

imperialism, 19–20, 33–34, 40, 47, 99, 105, 111–12, 113–14, 123, 125–26, 142, 146, 152
individual dignity, 27, 160, 180
individualism, 12–13, 58–59, 68, 69–70, 75, 92, 95–96, 112–14, 149
internalized inferiority, 18–19, 22–23
internalized oppression, 18–19

Japan and Phan Bội Châu, 36
Jim Crow era, 27–28

Kemal, Mustafa, 36
Khải Định, 60–61

Lao Tzu, 92, 99
Lea Ypi, 106–7

Leninism, 13, 49, 77–78, 100, 148–49, 150, 167–68, 177, 180, 186
Liang Qichao, 37, 60–61
liberal democracy, 12–13, 54–56, 59–60, 75–76, 154
liberalism
   Hồ Chí Minh and, 132
   Nguyễn An Ninh and, 81
   Nguyễn Mạnh Tường and, 162, 176–77
   Phạm Quỳnh and, 105, 112–13, 115–16
   Phan Bội Châu and, 47
   Phan Chu Trinh and, 53–56, 68, 75, 131–32
   political agency and, 17–18
liberal nationalism, 27
Loomba, Ania, 22–23

Macaulay, Thomas Babington, 22–23, 120
Macfarlane, Alan, 46–47
Mạc Phi, 103–4
Malcolm X, 191
marginalization, 22–23, 39–40, 75–76
Marr, David, 45–46, 69–70, 102–4, 108–9, 187–88
Marty, Louis, 107–8
Marxism, 13, 18–19, 49, 77–78, 100, 133, 148–49, 150, 166–68, 175–76, 177, 180, 186, 188
Mazzini, Giuseppe, 87
mechanical civilization, 112–13, 124–25
Mencius, 63–64, 65–66, 73–75, 115–17, 131–32
Miller, David, 16–17
Mills, Charles, 156
mimicry, 23–24, 89, 104, 176
monarchy, 12–13, 31, 35, 45, 51–52, 53, 55–56, 60–61, 63–69, 72–74, 78, 116–17, 131–32, 153, 183
morality
   Hồ Chí Minh and, 131–33, 145, 147–49, 157
   Nguyễn An Ninh and, 83, 91, 92
   Phạm Quỳnh and, 105, 115–16
   Phan Chu Trinh and, 53–54, 55–56, 61–62
   revolutionary morality, 147–49, 157
"Moral Malaise" (Phạm Quỳnh), 110
mutual enhancement, 59

Nam Phong (The Southern Wind) journal, 13, 107–9, 118–19
national dignity
   Hồ Chí Minh and, 131–32, 144–45
   national indignation and, 25–27
   national shame and, 23–24
   Nguyễn Mạnh Tường and, 159–61, 175–76, 180
   Phạm Quỳnh and, 105–6
   Phan Bội Châu and, 31, 37–38, 43–44
   Phan Chu Trinh and, 54, 55, 57, 61, 72, 77–78
national identity
   national shame and, 15
   Nguyễn An Ninh and, 83–85, 87–88, 97–98
   Phạm Quỳnh and, 118
   Phan Bội Châu and, 39–40, 45–46
national indignation
   colonialism and, 24
   Hồ Chí Minh and, 26
   national dignity and, 25–27
   Phan Bội Châu and, 41
national pride, 15, 40, 53, 83–84, 85, 89, 119, 188, 190
national responsibility, 15, 16–17, 22–23, 40, 43–44, 84–85, 97–98, 99
national shame
   defined, 6
   Hồ Chí Minh and, 131–32, 144–45
   introduction to, 5–6
   as motivation, 94
   national dignity and, 23–24
   national identity and, 15
   Nguyễn An Ninh and, 91–94
   Nguyễn Mạnh Tường and, 167–75
   Phan Chu Trinh and, 78
Native Americans, 16, 84, 140
Nazi Holocaust, 16
Nehru, Jawaharlal, 36
Ngũgĩ Wa Thiong'o, 21
Nguyễn, Martina, 126–27
Nguyễn An Ninh (1900-1943)
   brief biography, 85
   Confucianism under, 13, 82–83, 86–87, 91–92, 101
   democracy and, 81, 87, 89–90
   introduction to, 4–11, 13, 22–23, 81–85
   liberalism and, 81
   morality and, 83, 91, 92
   national dignity and, 81, 84, 101
   national identity and, 83–85, 87–88, 97–98
   national shame and, 91–94
   Phạm Quỳnh and, 94–95
   Phan Bội Châu and, 86
   quốc ngữ script under, 96–98
   radicalism of, 87
   summary of, 184
Nguyễn Du, 119–21

Nguyễn Mạnh Tường (1909–1997)
  anti-intellectualism of, 160–61, 167
  brief biography, 161
  conformity and, 175
  democracy and, 169
  excommunication of, 164
  Hồ Chí Minh and, 162
  introduction to, 4–11, 13–14, 159–61
  land reform fallout, 163
  liberalism and, 162, 176–77
  logomachy and, 173
  national dignity and, 159–61, 175–76, 180
  national shame and, 167–75
  summary of, 187
Nietzsche, Friedrich, 88

O'Dwyer, Shaun, 59–60
oppression, 3–7, 11, 14, 18–19, 27, 39–40, 73–74, 88, 93–94, 132, 136, 139–40, 143–44, 147, 150, 152, 156–57, 171–72, 177, 180–81, 184, 185, 188–92
orientalism, 125–26
Orientalism (Said), 19–20, 23

Paris Peace Conference, 2, 135, 142
paternalistic democracy, 133, 145, 146, 154, 158
peaceful coexistence, 166–67
Phạm Quỳnh (1892–1945)
  brief biography, 108
  colonialism and, 106, 122
  Confucianism under, 105, 107, 108–10, 111–12, 114–19, 124–27
  democracy and, 105, 115–18
  introduction to, 4–11, 13, 102–6
  liberalism and, 115–16
  moral disorientation among youth, 110
  morality and, 105, 115–16
  national dignity and, 105–6
  national identity and, 13, 118
  Nguyễn An Ninh and, 94–95
  quốc ngữ script under, 50, 107–8, 118–19, 126–27
  summary of, 184
Phan, John, 126–27
Phan Bội Châu (1867–1940)
  anticolonialism of, 31, 37–38, 52
  brief biography of, 32
  Cần Vương ("Save the King") movement, 34
  Chinese colonizers and, 38
  Đông Du (Go East) movement, 32
  French conquest and, 33, 41
  introduction to, 4–12, 13, 31
  Japanese relations, 36, 60–61

  liberalism and, 47
  national dignity and, 31, 37–38, 43–44
  national identity and, 39–40, 45–46
  national indignation and, 41
  Nguyễn An Ninh and, 86
  Phan Chu Trinh and, 44, 51, 56–57, 78
  quốc ngữ script under, 50
  summary of, 182
  Tonkin Free School and, 11–12, 32, 45, 51, 56–57, 87, 106
  Vietnamese Enlightenment and, 11–12, 45
Phan Chu Trinh (1872–1926)
  anticolonialism of, 89–90, 99–100
  autocracy and, 63
  brief biography, 56
  Confucianism under, 12–13, 56–61, 115–16
  democracy and, 57–59, 71–75
  ethics and, 62, 65
  Hồ Chí Minh and, 131–32
  introduction to, 1–11, 12–13, 53–56
  liberalism and, 53–56, 68, 75, 131–32
  morality and, 53–54, 55–56, 61–62
  mutual enhancement and, 59
  national dignity and, 54, 55, 57, 61, 72, 77–78
  national identity and, 12–13
  national same and, 78
  Phan Bội Châu and, 44, 51, 56–57, 78
  summary of, 183
  Tonkin Free School and, 11–12, 32, 45, 51, 56–57, 87, 106
  Western ethics, 65
Phan Đình Phùng (1847–1896), 34–35
policy of consideration, 105–6, 152
political theory, 2–3, 7–8, 10–13, 17, 55–56, 62–63, 144–45, 146
popular sovereignty, 11–12, 35
postcolonial theory, 7, 9, 11, 17–21
Progressive Confucianism, 57–58

quốc ngữ script, 50, 96–98, 107–8, 118–19, 126–27

racism, 22, 48–49, 133–34, 136–37, 139–42, 155–56, 192–93 *See also* dehumanization
Radhakrishnan, Sarvepalli, 124
radicalism of Nguyễn An Ninh, 87
rehumanization, 14, 132–34, 144–55
Renan, Ernest, 118–19
republicanism, 35, 51, 52
revolutionary morality, 147–49, 157
Rhodes, Alexandre de, 50

Rorty, Richard, 83–84
Rousseau, Jean-Jacques, 152–53

Said, Edward, 19–20, 23, 47, 125–26
Sarraut, Albert, 32, 106–7, 108–9
Sartre, Jean-Paul, 6, 22
Sasges, Gerard, 104
Second Indochina War (1955–1975), 2, 149, 180, 187–88
self-blame, 5–6
self-criticism, 5–7, 94, 149, 166–67
self-help, 5–6, 191
self-respect, 4–5, 14, 36, 81–82, 83–84, 101
self-sacrifice, 120–21
self-shame, 5–6, 19
self-strengthening, 48, 49, 126–27
self-worth, 4–5, 19, 82, 101
skepticism, 14, 92, 118–19, 167, 168–69, 173, 178–79
Smith, Anthony, 15–16
Social Darwinism, 11–12, 46, 48, 49, 63–64, 87–88
socialism, 51, 131, 135, 143, 145, 146–47, 154, 155, 157, 160–61, 162, 173–75, 180
Sor-hoon Tan, 59–60
Spivak, Gayatri, 23
Sungmoon Kim, 54, 59–60
Sun Yat Sen, 36

Tagore, Rabindranath, 13, 36, 86, 90, 96

Tale of Kiều (Nguyễn Du), 119–21
Tấn Bộ Dân Hội party, 109–10
thymos, 2
Tonkin Free School (Đông Kinh Nghĩa Thục), 11–12, 32, 45, 51, 56–57, 87, 106
Trần Hưng Đạo, 39–40
Trần Tử Bình, 41–42
Trần Văn Giàu, 82–83, 99
Truong Buu Lam, 42–43
Tự Đức, 33–34

US Declaration of Independence, 136

Vaughan, Megan, 23
Vázquez-Arroyo, Antonio, 17–18
Việt Minh, 102, 109–10, 126–27, 135–36, 150, 184–85, 188
Vietnamese Communist Party. *See* Communist Party of Vietnam
Vietnamese Enlightenment, 11–12, 45
Vietnam Modernization Society (*Việt Nam Duy tân Hội*), 36
Vietnam War. *See* Second Indochina War
Vũ Ngọc Phan, 109

Wahnich, Sophie, 25–26
Western ethics, 65

Zhuangzi, 92, 99